Rainbows in Cobwebs

Stories of Hope
In the Storms of Life

MARGARET HARDISTY

DR. VANCE HARDISTY

Rainbows In Cobwebs
Stories of Hope In the Storms of Life

Library of Congress Cataloging-in-Publication Data and Catalog Card Number Pending

ISBN 978-0-9824042-0-1

For further information contact:
Carodyn Publishers,
101 Gregory Lane, Suite 52,
Pleasant Hill, CA 94523

In Honor Of...

...our parents, grandparents and others who
introduced us to the glorious art of storytelling. By
recounting their experiences while lingering over
a meal, a campfire, photo albums and
memories suddenly recalled,
we gained a world of knowledge
and riches that can be found in no other way.
How you have blessed us! Thank you!!

Margaret & Vance

Before You Begin Reading

This has been an exciting group effort. First, the germ of an idea was planted long ago in Margaret's mind on a working vacation in Hawaii. You'll read about it in the first story, *Beauty & the Beast*. That led to writing *Rainbows in Cobwebs* but she did no more with it than to use the subject in some of her keynote talks to various groups.

The manuscript languished in her files until she and Vance Hardisty, her son, realized that here was a book that would make a powerful series. Vance came on board as co-author. George, Margaret's husband, and Julie, Vance's wife, gave their thumbs up. We decided, though, that instead of Margaret's voice being the only one, as in the original manuscript, we'd ask others to contribute. Why? Because everyone has had a stormy or trying situation in life (**a cobweb**). However, not everyone is able to see hope (**a rainbow**) that leads to victory.

Vance started on the technical end of it, as well as talking to some of his worldwide contacts and writing stories of his own. He also added the subtitle. All of us invited a few people to contribute. The response was enthusiastic and word spread. Accounts of experiences from people's lives began to pour in from throughout the United States as well as other countries and we soon had enough to fill the first volume and part of a second.

We now are a "family" of 65 writers, working together to offer glorious and lasting hope to those who need it. We trust that you'll enjoy reading it as much as we have enjoyed making it happen.

Our Deepest Gratitude

During the time we were formulating this book, family members encouraged, advised, read the stories that came in to give their approval – or not – were patient, prayed for us, put up with us, did without us, and remained, much to our delight, the same wonderful…George Hardisty, Margaret's husband; Elisa Manalisay, their daughter; Julie Hardisty, Vance's wife; Micayla, Colton and Tiara, their children; Barbara Gentner, Margaret's sister; and Brian and Vicky Burgess (nephew, niece, cousins). Several of them submitted cobweb/rainbow stories that you will enjoy as you read.

Friends, too, were more than supportive and some of them shared their hearts with you in this book: **Connie Fray, Samantha Moore, Connie Catalfio, Mark Gigliotti, Doug Bedinger** and **Michael Raymond.**

Then there are **others** whose influence has guided us: **Steve Harrison, Jack Canfield, Geoffrey Berwind** and **Mary Agnes Antonopoulos.** Steve and Mary Agnes contributed exciting stories.

No writer does it alone, for there are dozens who lend their expertise to any work, even when those individuals are unaware of doing so. And because there are so many, it is impossible to list them all here. Our heartfelt gratitude to them and all those mentioned above. You truly are Rainbows in any Cobwebs that come our way.

Contents

Note: The order of writers and their stories was not set up in its present form because of the superiority or status of one over another. Some of our writers are incredibly successful as the world would count success – CEO's, rags-to riches individuals, those who have earned prestigious awards and doctorates, builders of financial empires, and more. Others have lived rather obscure lives. But every experience they share in this volume is absolutely gripping and attention grabbing, each with the intent of helping you in your life.

Since these stories run the gamut from amusing to tragic, from educational to spiritual, we have attempted to space them so that you find a few of each type in each section. The sections reflect an aspect of our book title, not the content of the stories within the sections.

These are all true accounts…with happy or satisfying endings. They are ideal for your entire family to read together…seemingly a lost art. You will laugh, discuss, and cry together as you enjoy them. However, some speak of very heavy experiences and suffering, so we advise parents to read individual ones first to determine which are suitable for your younger children; although after viewing some of Hollywood's recent tales, we realize that ours are tame in comparison, so it's your call.

Rainbows In Cobwebs

Contents

I   Winds Offer Opportunity   **Page**

Beauty & the Beast — Margaret Hardisty — 3
Crushed — Vance Hardisty — 7
Wheelin' & Dealin' — Joe McNamee — 12
A Paramedic's Tale — Sam Bradley — 18
The Tent — Michael Farris — 25
Shakespeare, Hollywood & Me — Steve Harrison — 30
Abandonment, Abuse & Meteoric Success — Rick Pickering — 35

II   Sheltering Clouds

Katy – Part 1 — Barbara Greene Gentner — 45
Katy – Part 2 — Barbara Greene Gentner — 52
When Life Closes In — Mary A. Antonopoulos — 56
I Played for the Raiders — Art Thoms — 63
The True Bull of the Woods — Milt Thomas — 69
Man Overboard — Jerry Behymer — 76
Listen to Your Mother — Mark Gigliotti — 80

III   Refreshing Rain

Oh, No, I Killed a Man! — George Hardisty — 87
Calls in the Night — Leighton Ford — 90
Fire! — Trudy Creutzberg — 97
Mikie — Vicky Burgess — 100
I Am Not My Past — Valerie Jeannis — 105
Archie and Me — Don Hardisty — 111
Angels Spread a Cushion — Lynn Reid — 118

IV   Impressive Lightning & Thunder

Number Two — Hoyt Huggins — 125
You Know You Died, Don't You? — Eloise Carey — 130
Ice Storm — Emma Westerman — 133
Questions…Answer! — Andee Wise — 139
Warrior Cowboy — Shane Michael Taylor — 142

Drug Deal & the Snitch   Name Withheld _____ 146

Salt Princess   Keith Fleshman_____ 149

Who'll Catch You When You
Fall Off a Cliff?   Cydney O'Sullivan _____ 156

V   Storms Strengthen Resolve

Order to Appear   Kathy Young _____ 163

Orly   John Bentley _____ 165

September 11, 2001   Doug MacSwan_____ 172

Surprised by Hope   Sally MacSwan _____ 180

My American Guardian Angel   Diana Doroftei _____ 187

Tragic Loss – Amazing Victory   Cornell (Corkie) Haan __ 192

I Had to Lose Weight...or Die   Kevin O'Brien_____ 196

VI   Surprising Cobwebs

Go Mobile   Matt Holguin _____ 203

Redemption   Ginger Haan _____ 208

Remembering a Parent Who Can't   Walt Russell _____ 215

On Driving – Asian Style   Caitlin Halone _____ 219

Wheels in Action   Kyle Bryant_____ 223

Leaving My Love   Renée Roberge-Anderson _ 227

All Things Are Possible   Dara Feldman_____ 231

VII   Glorious Rainbows

Hollywood or Happiness   Karlee Holden_____ 237

Prepared for Battle   Nick Palumbo_____ 243

I Missed It? No Way!!   George Hardisty _____ 250

Rainbow – First & Last   Hyatt Moore _____ 254

The Myth of Perfection   Michele Clarke _____ 261

Disguised Blessing   Greg Asimakoupoulos __ 265

Opening Night   Constance Eve _____ 270

VIII Blue Skies

SAM Camp — Connie Segreto — 277
We Survived Communism — Lydia Popa — 285
Journey to Freedom — Julie Thuy — 293
Why? — Debbie Hardy — 297
Johanna's Place — Kevin Ring — 301
Through the Fire and Into Living — Terri LeVine — 308
Reagan at the Rexall — Kathy Young — 312

IX Healing Sunshine

The Last Coins — Risa Cranmer — 317
One Dark, Rainy Night — Kit Summers — 320
A Sensational Life — Sybil K — 326
Opa & Indonesia — Larry Wiens — 332
Better — Cindy Mendenhall — 336
Darkness Replaced — Daniel Hilson — 339
Journey of Faith — John Ridgway — 344

X Growth Springs Forth

Three Strands — Pauline Turner — 351
My Path to Peace — Siamack Yaghobi — 353
I Caught Myself on Fire — Barbara Greene Gentner — 359
Songs for a Broken Heart — Connie Cousins — 366
Paralyzed at Eighteen — Krishna Pendyala — 370
He Did What??!! — Vance Hardisty — 376
Chewing on Thistles — Margaret Hardisty — 381

Writers in Alphabetical Order

	Page		Page
Antonopoulos, Mary Agnes	56	Jeannis, Valerie	105
Asimakoupoulos, Greg	265	K. Sybil	326
Behymer, Jerry	76	LeVine, Terri	308
Bentley, John	165	MacSwan, Doug	172
Bradley, Sam	18	MacSwan, Sally	180
Bryant, Kyle	223	McNamee, Joe	12
Burgess, Vicky	100	Mendenhall, Cindy	336
Carey, Eloise	130	Moore, Hyatt	254
Clarke, Michele	261	(Name withheld)	146
Cousins, Connie	366	O'Brien, Kevin	196
Cranmer, Risa	317	O'Sullivan, Cydney	156
Creutzberg, Trudy	97	Palumbo, Nick	243
Doroftei, Diana	187	Pendyala, Krishna	370
Eve, Constance	270	Pickering, Rick	35
Farris, Michael	25	Popa, Lydia	285
Feldman, Dara	231	Reid, Lynn	118
Fleshman, Keith	149	Ridgway, John	344
Ford, Leighton	90	Ring, Kevin	301
Gentner, Barbara Greene	45, 52, 359	Roberge-Anderson, Renée	227
Gigliotti, Mark	80	Russell, Walt	215
Haan, Cornell (Corkie)	192	Segreto, Connie	277
Haan, Ginger	208	Summers, Kit	320
Halone, Caitlin	219	Taylor, Shane Michael	142
Hardisty, Don	111	Thomas, Milt	69
Hardisty, George	87, 250	Thoms, Art	63
Hardisty, Margaret	3, 381	Thuy, Julie	293
Hardisty, Vance	7, 376	Turner, Pauline	351
Hardy, Debbie	297	Westerman, Emma	133
Harrison, Steve	30	Wiens, Larry	332
Hilson, Daniel	339	Wise, Andee	139
Holden, Karlee	237	Yaghobi, Siamack	353
Holguin, Matt	203	Young, Kathy	163, 312
Huggins, Hoyt	125		

I

WINDS
Offer OPPORTUNITY

Winds can be...

Cold;
Unpleasant;
Mischievous and capricious;
A warning of dark things to come;
Destructive.

They also can...

Be pleasant;
Create fun;
Clear the air of pollutants;
Clean trees of debris;
Refresh;
Bring clouds and the promise of rain;
Inspire people to create.

When you receive hints that Winds are headed your way, face into them. They hold great opportunity to meet challenges and overcome them. In this volume, you will read of real life Winds of Opportunity that came into people's lives and how they faced into them with courage, just as you can.

Rainbows In Cobwebs

The spider takes hold with her hands and is in kings' palaces.

PROVERBS 30:28

Beauty and the Beast

If you shudder when you see a spider or when a cobweb becomes entangled in your hair, you may wonder why the Creator bothered. The little creatures reduce the insect population, provide nesting for hummingbirds, and become food for other critters, but really, like mosquitoes, are they that necessary?

I discovered the answer in part on a vacation to Hawaii. My family and I had gone there, weary and needing a rest, to enjoy balmy warm breezes and tropical delights. Instead, we came close to being washed out to sea by a storm of hurricane proportions. We bravely whistled while we worked to set out a dinner that reflected the culinary delights of the state we were visiting and belied the state we were in emotionally.

Huddling around the fireplace, we tried to think of funny things to say and stories to tell, but we barely could be heard over the roar of the wind. It was difficult to sleep that night wondering if we would find ourselves floating on the ocean at some juncture, rather than being anchored to the shore.

Startling Discovery

The following morning told the tale as I stepped onto the porch. We still were on land and the small house we were renting on the north shore of the Big Island hadn't moved. Nor was there damage as far as I could see. What's more, sunbeams were piercing the crisp break-of-day air.

A bit awed with the calm after the fury of the night, I sauntered into an unkempt garden; then stopped, for I had seen a flash of color to my left. Curious, I moved toward a stone walkway that was almost obliterated by foliage. Stretched across it was a web the size of a round kitchen table. It was an astonishing sight; for on every inch of this spider's silver patio the rain had left sparkling droplets of water, each of which cradled a miniature rainbow.

As I stood transfixed, wishing I had a camera, a barely discernible movement pulled my eyes to the right of the exquisite creation. The lady of the house had arrived. The size of a dime, she glided silkily over the splotches of color to the center and stretched full length to the front, back and sides. She was a pure bright yellow, as beautiful as she was deadly. The only spiders I'd seen were brown or black. Was she soaking in the warmth of the sun? Or preening to show me how lovely she was? Perhaps she was trying to compete with the glory of her decorated handiwork.

Fascinating Analogy

Regardless, the contrasts she represented fascinated me. She was beauty and beast. Life and death. Hope and cannibalism. Fear and fascination.

While studying the daffodil colored arachnid and her painted web, I realized that the ensnaring cobweb meant trouble for any insect if it flew into or crawled onto the sticky substance the lady had used for her weaving, for it would become her breakfast; but what if it landed on one of the water encased rainbows? Wouldn't it bounce off to freedom?

Yes, scientifically, I was all wet...but my thoughts sped across the sea to the mainland where there were individuals I was trying to help through their troubles: Mona, whose husband had died; Jack, a very angry divorced man; Mike and Sharon, whose son had just been consigned to prison. Couldn't they find rainbows of hope in their cobwebs of despair?

Always Hope

So, what has this to do with you and your life? Why cobwebs? Why rainbows?

The cobwebs are obvious. You run into a physical cobweb and it sticks itself to some part of you. In no way is the experience pleasant. Neither is trouble that comes into your life and refuses to leave.

The analogy of rainbows is obvious, as well, because rainbows shout, "Hope!" And hope leads to solutions and victory.

One time when we were in South Carolina, I came across a spider's web so large I had to look far above my head to see the top of it. Even though the situation spelled doom for the creature that was caught in it and buzzing its distress, a large beetle, there was hope for the critter. Me. I was the rainbow and victory at that moment for the beetle. My husband, George, after he quit feeling sorry for the spider that had done all the work to get a tasty lunch, helped me extricate the hapless prisoner with a long stick, set it free and it happily waddled off into the safety of the undergrowth.

Do you need hope? Freedom from the miseries that have encased you?

In this book, people from all walks of life, varied occupations and wildly different experiences have shared their hearts with you, relating the amusing or miserable cobwebs in which they have been entangled and how they clung to rainbows of hope and found victory. If they could do it, so can you. Some will have the cobwebs clinging to them for life – but even in those situations, they have burst through in triumph, as you will see. They have cared enough about you to reach out a helping hand to show you how.

And just in case that doesn't work, and you still are despondent, or you refuse to look beyond your problems, both Vance and I have inserted some other helps on our website www.RainbowsInCobwebs.com where you also can click on writers' pictures to hear them speak for themselves. Spiritual help is available on the site, as well.

We have found that bouncing off rainbows is a lot more satisfying and productive than struggling incessantly to be free of sticky, stubborn cobwebs of trouble that encase you in fear and dread.

Margaret Hardisty

*For **bio**, see information on book cover. For her **video** visit our websites: www.RainbowsInCobwebs.com and www.ThriveInMarriage.com.*

Margaret Hardisty

Above: Elisa (daughter) and Margaret

Left: With husband, George, at a dinner dance.

Rainbows In Cobwebs

Reach high, for stars lie hidden in your soul.
Dream deep, for every dream precedes the goal.

PAMELA VAULL STARR
(POET, ARTIST, WRITER 1909-1993)

Crushed

"Ummm, Dad? What was that?!!!"

The noise of a huge crash from the front of the house had violated the beauty of a lazy holiday morning. The family, apprehensive, watched as I pulled open the front window drapes. My son, close behind me, stared out the window at our driveway, trying to make sense of what we were seeing.

"Dad, is that the oak tree from next door?"

"It sure looks like it," I said, realizing how dumb that sounded. What else could it be? Oak trees didn't fall randomly from the sky.

"Dad, where are the cars?"

The Oak

The night before had been one of those incredible evenings that I really enjoyed. We were in that wonderful transition period between winter and spring. In Northern California, that meant that many of the trees were putting on their first batch of new green growth. Renewed life was forcing its way into our consciousness everywhere, if we were willing to look. The winter, though, not yet willing to give up its hold on the world, had stomped through our area, howling and blowing, bending and swaying trees, tearing new leaves from their nascent hold. But in the end, spring won out and the day dawned, crystal clear, full of hope, the skies cleared of their impurities.

The old oak tree next door was truly a marvel. Over 300 years old, it had stood as a landmark for those in horse drawn carriages, announcing for miles around the presence of water near its base. Our house, built in the late 1950's looked up into a few of its massive branches. That night, though, proved too much for the old giant. The combination of winds and the weight of the new spring leaves tore at the sinews holding those magnificent branches in place.

Lasting through the night, the new day dawned with no visible damage to the tree, but the death blow had been delivered. Inside, tendon after woody tendon continued to rip apart until the giant no longer could sustain its own weight. Letting go, the entire side of it that had been hanging over our yard and driveway, crashed to the earth.

"Sweetheart," my wife, Julie, said as she stood at my side, "where **are** our cars?"

"I think they are underneath."

Suddenly aware, we all raced out the door and stood in the front yard. Poking out from the mass of jumbled branches were our two vehicles. One of the main branches, weighing many tons, lay directly across the middle of each. Smashed was an understatement. The footstep of Godzilla couldn't have been more effective.

The Why's of the Matter

If there was an upside to this personal travesty it was that, a week later, I was able to use pictures to illustrate a presentation on seeing God at work in tough times. An arborist had told me that the tree had been weakened by a common practice 50 years ago. Men would cable large branches of trees to the center so they wouldn't break in winds such as the one we had just experienced. Over time they discovered that without allowing the tree to sustain minor damage in each successive windstorm, the tree increased the length and size of its branches without increasing its ability to maintain weight, relying instead on the cable. When, years later, the cable came loose, all it took was a strong windstorm and down came the whole tree.

Everybody listening to the presentation was fascinated. What an illustration! Truths were conveyed and learned. I went home, delighted that the time and frustration it would take to replace the cars would, at the least, have some positive effect on others.

In reality, though, that was the small payoff. God's graciousness and his ability to use nasty circumstances in our lives to turn them to good, didn't take form for another 18 months.

So here's the rest of the story.

Closing the Loop

Throughout the two years before the tree destroyed our cars, Julie and I had been going back and forth about adopting a little girl from China. Lots of pros and lots of cons. It was no easy decision. Our youngest was almost eight. We would be starting over. We'd already given all of our baby stuff away, and having started late with our own, we were not youngsters. But it was a lifelong desire of my wife's. We could radically impact the life of a young girl destined for…who knows what?

Our prayer was, "Lord, what would you have us do?" So, here's how God closed the loop for my wife and, eventually, me.

Both cars needed to be replaced. Not an easy task when our insurance was reluctant to pay anything but the minimum value. It was before the days of Craigslist, so we began to look in newspapers and let a few people know. A few days later a friend called to tell us that he had found a car, and though he'd like to get it himself, he knew our need. A quick phone call later and pictures were sent to us. They looked great. It was a vehicle that my wife had not dared to dream of having. We set up the appointment and were on our way.

Although we were looking forward to having a new car, my wife still was in turmoil about our much larger decision and our prayer continued to be, "Lord what do you want us to do? Do we adopt? Please, Lord, let us know clearly your leading."

The Surprise

Meeting us at his house, the owner of the car took us for a drive and we were sold. Now to sign the papers.

As we walked through the door, a little Chinese girl scampered past us to a back room. Julie caught her breath. The man who had shown us the car was Caucasian. Could God have arranged something here? Then the man's wife walked into the room. Ahhh, that explained things. She was Chinese.

Back to signing papers. Almost finished, Julie just couldn't let it go; and so, offhand, she mentioned our desire to adopt from China. Pens froze midair. Silence. Then smiles. Suddenly, they both were speaking at once. Their little girl, Katie, had been adopted from China. It was a wonderful idea, they said. Best thing they had ever done.

Clear Direction

As we drove away, much later than we had planned, there was no more doubt in my wife's mind. Our gracious heavenly Father, the one who spoke all the universe into being, loved her – us – so much that he was willing to arrange a fallen tree, a friend looking at newspaper ads and just the right car that would place us in another city to sit across the table from people we had never met, in order to assure us that our lives would never be the same; but we could go forward with confidence that this was his will.

That was 11 years ago. My older ones are in college. God's gift to us from China just finished a swim meet. Yes, I am older than most of the other parents. Yes, we have missed many a romantic dinner. Yes, it was expensive. But that little gift just ran across the lawn and grabbed me around the neck.

"Daddy, I love you so much," she exulted.

Thank you, God, for really big oak trees that fall on cars!

Vance Hardisty

My Family

For Vance's Bio and videos, see cover of this book and visit our Websites at: www.RainbowsInCobwebs.com & www.ThriveInMarriage.com.

That story that you've been thinking about writing may be just what others need to encourage them as you share a cobweb (challenge) that you have had, the rainbow (hope) that you saw in the midst of it and the victory that became yours because of the experience. Go to our website, www.RainbowsInCobwebs.com. We'll give you the guidelines for submission.

Rainbows In Cobwebs

All misfortune is but a stepping
stone to fortune.

HENRY DAVID THOREAU
(*AMERICAN AUTHOR 1817-1862*)

Wheelin' and Dealin'

As a child it verbally was beat into my head: *Don't ever consider going to college. You'll lose your common sense if you do.* As a result, I looked down on others who had an education but who didn't know how to fix stuff. That pride, even though it might have been misplaced, was what got me through some very difficult times.

A Culture of Survival

Fixing stuff was a continual lesson to learn in whatever house we happened to find ourselves in. I remember helping my father fix anything that went wrong in all those places we called home at the time, as well as the vehicles we drove. We didn't use replacement parts, though. We disassembled broken parts and repaired them. We always had a variety of junk hardware that we often acquired from other people's trash cans.

We had an oil heater just like the rest of the houses in an area, with the oil storage tank filler tube outside. However, we never could afford to have the oil truck stop at our house and fill up the tank. So that the neighbors never realized our situation, my dad would get a five gallon can of kerosene from somewhere. I was never allowed to go with him when he got the kerosene. Once he got it, though, it was a game to me, holding the flashlight while my dad poured the kerosene in the tank, all the while hiding the activity from the neighbors.

Poor? Oh, Yea

We were very poor. I remember my sister and I eating left over pizza several days old for breakfast. The pizza would be on the kitchen counter and hard as a rock (no microwaves at that time). I would scrape off cigarette butts and ashes to put a piece of pizza in my mouth. To soften it enough to chew, I first built up saliva in my mouth and let it soak.

Many times I took a bath in the same water that the rest of the family used first, with the soap scum floating on top. And you haven't lived until you are forced to use used toilet paper.

Yes, we were poor, but that's part of the fabric that made me who I am.

A Searing Memory

One day, when we were at the boardwalk in Seaside, NJ, and I was about eight years old, I was sitting on a bench. A little boy and his grandmother walked by. The boy had a balloon on a string that flew toward me. I jumped up and swatted at the balloon, which knocked it out of the boy's hand, and it floated away. My mother, who witnessed this, screamed at me and pointed out how poorly they were dressed, and that was probably their last dime that bought the balloon.

I felt horrible about what I had done, and will carry that guilt with me to my grave.

Life Change

That incident changed who I wanted to be. In junior high and high school I studied the martial arts. Without fear, I quickly became really good at it, fighting in knockout matches against 25-30 year old black belts and backing them down. In school I would protect the weak from the bullies.

But the balloon boy...the balloon boy, I could never rectify. So this turned into the driving force behind my success in life, specifically in the real estate investing business.

Young but Savvy

In telling about my very first real estate venture, I guess I should say, like Bill Cosby did one time in one of his comedy skits, "I started out life as a child."

For me the first real estate deal I remember being involved in was when I was six years old. That's not a misprint. I was six years old. So let me explain; that way you can stop snickering.

My mother was a realtor and my father worked construction. As a matter of fact, my grandparents on both sides of my family worked construction. When you sat at my family dinner table you talked about real estate and construction or you weren't worth listening to.

Out of desperation, my parents would create a real estate deal.

It Worked Like This

Since Mom and Dad rarely had any money, they would farm us out and we would be living separately as a family. My sister, Donna, would be staying in someone's house – maybe a family member or friend. My parents would be at a different person's house. I'd be in a third house of a family member or friend.

So Mom and Dad would look for creative ways to get the four of us living together again using practically no money. I remember the typical scenario worked like this: Donna and I would have to dress up in our best Sunday clothes so that we could make a good impression on the landlord who wanted to sell a piece of property he owned. Usually the property was in a ghetto (today it's referred to as a war zone) or a less than desirable neighborhood. Also, the property usually was destroyed, almost, by the previous tenant(s).

The landlord happily would negotiate a sales price with Mom. So she would lock in the purchase price which was an "as is" sum. Next, Dad would negotiate with the landlord about the rent. We wouldn't pay any. Rather, in exchange we would repair the house and pay for the material. Dad was an expert at finding material for just a few dollars that spruced up a house in a less than desirable neighborhood.

I remember one building supply company that used to go to estate sales, going-out-of- business sales and buy material that never sold, for next to nothing. Then Dad would get it for just a few cents above that. So with way less than a hundred dollars a month we could easily take a house in deplorable condition and make it really nice.

The Next Step

So up to this point we've locked in the purchase price for a house in "as is" condition. We've rented the house without paying rent. We have provided the material and we have to do the work. We'd start by cleaning one or two rooms. That job belonged to my sister and my mom.

We'd move into the two rooms. From there we would battle rats, roaches, and maybe even the neighborhood, while we fixed up the rest of the house. By battling the neighborhood I mean, well, mostly that was my problem. I remember getting suspended from first grade for beating up two third graders and a fifth grader. I realize that sounds crazy, but I was always the new kid in town and I had to fight…a lot.

So now we had the vermin taken care of and we were living together while we repaired the rest of the house. Once the repairs were finished, Mom would put the house up for sale.

More Wheelin' and Dealin'

Remember, my folks didn't own the house. But once Mom found a buyer, then she would schedule a back-to-back closing at an attorney's office, where she was buying in the morning with no money and selling in the afternoon (or just a few hours later) to the buyer. The attorney would do the closing because the funding was already there from the sale of the house in the afternoon. The attorney knew that was a safe deal because he or she could just nullify it if the deal fell apart in the afternoon, for whatever reason.

Six Years Old

As I said earlier, the first deal that I was involved in was when I was six years old. This one house had hardwood flooring running through-out and it squeaked really, really badly. So dad chalked a line everywhere there was a floor joist. I drove a 6d galvanized nail in each one of those boards to stop the squeaking.

I still remember the feeling in my right hand. My index finger, where it connected to my palm is where dad's hammer used to pinch my finger when I used it. It was a leather ring wrapped 16 ounce curved claw hammer. Some of the leather rings were missing which is why it pinched my finger all the time. Once I was finished nailing down that floor, then it was time for beautiful wall-to-wall shag carpeting to be installed.

My parents would make a lot of money from these types of deals, somewhere in the neighborhood of $6000 to $10,000.00 profit, good money in the 1960s. But, when they made $6000, in their minds they had $12,000 to blow.

Here's an example of what they would do when they made a decent amount off of one of those deals. At this particular time we lived in New Jersey because we had moved 19 times by the time I was 19 years old. They purchased a used moving truck, and we loaded it and our car with our belongings. Then we'd move to chase a dream. This time it was Florida.

There was no job, no family or friends. So we lived in a rundown style motel. Mom and Dad would leave every day in the car looking for work, driving sometimes a couple hundred miles away from the motel, spending every bit of the money they made chasing their newest dream. Somehow, at the last minute, they'd work a deal like I told you about and the whole cycle would start all over again.

Lesson Learned

Years later I learned to use my mind more, and started drifting away from physical labor and living on the edge. I joined the Army at 19 and became an officer 6 ½ years later; then retired at 39, with 20 years plus a couple of hours in three combat zones. Four, if you count a bad marriage. I've moved 47 times, living in six countries and seven states. Currently, I live near Savannah, Georgia, in the same 4500 square foot house that I built by myself in seven months turnkey, while I was finishing up my last year in the service.

I created several companies with my two favorite being Absolute Investment Group and Absolute Investment Training Company. Absolute Investment Group is the one in which I buy and sell real estate. AITC is the company in which I train people interested in real estate investing and building or marketing any business, product, or idea.

I've discovered a few things along the way. 1) Always expect life to happen when you're planning to do something else. 2) Protect and guide your children for they are the future. 3) And remember, no matter what obstacles are in front of you, those obstacles are helping to mold the fiber that constitutes you.

Joe McNamee

Author: Timeless Real Estate Investing

Joe McNamee is a retired Senior Army Warrant Officer. He is married to Victoria and has five children. He has attended 7 colleges and 12 military schools; and he is the only person on the planet with a Triple Master's Degree in Real Estate Investing.

He has negotiated nearly 3000 real estate deals and counting (residential, commercial, and industrial). Joe became a self-made millionaire at the age of 42, and multimillionaire by the age of 45.

His primary work experience includes but is not limited to: Construction as a builder and land developer, Real Estate Investor, Marketing, Drafting, Automotive Engineering, Management, Inventor/ Creator, Entrepreneur, Teacher of multiple subjects from Real Estate Investing, Martial Arts.

He is called by his students "America's most credible real estate investing Guru."

Rainbows In Cobwebs

Life shrinks or expands in proportion to one's courage.

ANAIS NIN
(AMERICAN AUTHOR – 1903-1977)

A Paramedic's Tale

When I became an Emergency Medical Technician (EMT), my career path was clear – I would devote my life to saving the lives of others. Yeah, right. Lofty goal, but my instructor failed to tell us that an EMT's job is moving people (mostly the elderly) from Point A to Point B, and dealing with a lot of psych patients. The latter were particularly unhappy about being transported against their will. I had to deal with everything from slanderous personal attacks to death threats. Oh, and did I mention all the sick people that threw up on my boots?

Upgrade?

I eventually landed an assignment in an area where we transported 911 calls for the fire department. I enjoyed the challenge and the excitement of responding to emergencies, but this also had a downside. I learned first-hand about people at their worst: domestic violence calls, child abuse cases, and what happens when a drunk takes out a family of five. It takes a toll. I didn't know what critical incident stress was, much less how to mitigate it. I also didn't understand the long-term effects of cumulative stress.

Gotta' Be Something Better

I decided things would improve if I changed the pace and upgraded my skills. I went to paramedic school. I graduated at the top of my class and felt newly inspired about my job.

Hitting the ground running with a busy 911 transport contract, life was good – for awhile. Unfortunately, only months later, the county took over the city fire department and we were out. There was another city with a similar transport contract, but they didn't allow women. Did I mention that discrimination was alive and well in the 80s? I went back to running transports and, occasionally, got to start an IV when the firefighter-paramedic felt sorry for me.

Then I learned about post traumatic stress disorder (PTSD). I became the poster child.

You see, my partner and I were standing in dispatch when we responded to a motorcycle accident on a busy four lane highway just a few miles away. No big deal. I'd run hundreds of them. What I wasn't prepared for was being told by the first responder firefighter that it was "Frank." It took several minutes for the reality to set in. Frank was one of our paramedics. He had just bought the motorcycle and failed to notice a car stopping to make a left turn.

The trauma center was right around the corner, but Frank didn't survive the trip. We didn't know how to react or what to expect, much less have any idea what to do for each other. So, one of the EMTs held a party that night.

Critical Incident Stress Management (CISM) existed, but we didn't have any local resources. I thought I did well through the next week making plans, attending the rosary, then the funeral. I thought it was finally over when they put Frank's casket in the ground.

Closure – Right? Wrong

Two years later I hit a "trigger" that brought it all back like a Viet Nam vet hearing fireworks and suddenly thinking he's back in a rice paddy in Da Nang. Post Traumatic Stress, you say? I was toast. So, what do you do when you're feeling burned out? Become a supervisor, of course. At least it gave me a chance to exercise a new skills set and do something different.

Being out of the field would be safer. Less stress. Or so I thought.

Now It's Me – Plus Others

Did I mention the major airline crash two miles away from my office that killed 265 people? A Cessna hit an Aeromexico jetliner on the flight path to LAX and both planes came down. It wiped out a residential area and took a direct hit on a home where 15 people were attending a birthday party.

This time, I saw post traumatic stress (PTS) from another vantage point. Employees started coming to me with their stories of nightmares, eating disorders, increased drinking, and reacting to triggers.

Trust me, I knew what it was. Ironically, official CISM people came out and debriefed the fire department personnel and city workers, but the private ambulance company employees were left to their own resources – none.

I was angry about that, and engaged in the task of finding private mental health resources for my people. I told myself if I ever had an opportunity to make sure something like this never happened again to private EMS people (Emergency Medical Services – pre-hospital care), I would grab it.

Enough Supervising

After a few years of supervising, I realized I wanted to be back in the field again – not just on an ambulance, but working one of those fire department transport contracts - the ones that didn't allow women. Maybe it was the challenge of breaking through the bigotry, maybe it's because I had the seniority and the *right* to that assignment. Maybe both. The fire department's excuse was that there were no sleeping accommodations for a woman.

So, I called them on it. I made an agreement with another paramedic. I would work the day half of the shift, and he would work the night half. He went to school during the day so it was perfect for him. I did all the work during the day, then he came on shift, studied for a while, then slept all night.

A year later I got my chance. My shift partner acquired a knee injury and was unlikely to come back to paramedic work. By then I had achieved credibility as a paramedic **and a woman**, and they decided creating sleeping quarters for me wasn't that tough to accomplish after all. It was a great gig for five years.

Slap in the Face

Then, a visibly chauvinist captain was promoted to battalion chief and decided his first order of business was to "get rid of the female." I didn't have one negative thing in my file. I got nothing but positive reports from my captains. In fact, I won the "EMS Person of the Year" award from the California Ambulance Association while I was working there. A contrived story was all the ambulance company needed to force a reassignment of me.

"Sorry to throw the baby out with the bathwater," said my Operations Chief, "but they're threatening to tear up the contract if we don't move you out. You can't complain, though. You still have a job."

"I can't complain??" I asked, staring at him in disbelief.

"You know, this isn't a good business for a woman to be in, anyway. Maybe you should go work for the Red Cross or something."

Seriously? If then was now, I would have had his job and the discrimination suit from hell against the city. I didn't pursue legal action because of the advocates I had on the department, mostly captains, who would have put their jobs on the line to defend my honor and the blatant inappropriateness of the decision. And…I still had a job. Uh huh.

It Finally Got To Me

That issue had all but destroyed my self-esteem. No place for a woman in a man's world. No support from the company I had invested so many years with, just more discrimination. I'd sacrificed so much to gain the trust of this department just to have one bigot wave his magic axe and make me go away. I was devastated. I couldn't see going back in the field as a paramedic who never got the chance to do any real patient care.

I considered quitting, but what else would I do? This was my life – my chosen career. I wasn't burned out on being a paramedic, really I wasn't, but I wouldn't be saving lives like I had wanted since the day I received my EMT certification 17 years prior. I wasn't sure about anything anymore.

Victory Just Ahead

I stayed. I took a position in training. It turned out to be a wise choice. As fate would have it (or possibly divine intervention) I came to work one day to the announcement that the owners had just sold the operation to the largest ambulance company in the country. Because I was in a training position, I was able to lateral to their version of the same – as a Clinical and Educational Coordinator. They had a position available in Northern California. Suddenly, the worst thing that had ever happened to me became a huge blessing. If I still had been working an ambulance, I would have become just another rank and file employee driving an ambulance with a different paint job.

I had a strong feeling right from the beginning that it was something I was supposed to do. My heart told me there was a reason - a purpose for engaging with this new company and moving to the other end of the state.

It was destined to be more than just a job. The fact that I was infused with this new energy and motivation was even more surprising given that, only weeks earlier, I had felt worthless, dispirited and indecisive.

Even though I felt like a country bumpkin in the big city, I caught onto the job and liked the people I worked with. It didn't take me long to realize that Alameda County (ALCO) had an unusually high call volume with a high number of intense, life-threatening calls. I could also see the toll it was taking on the employees, especially those that had worked the field for years.

They would come in my office to "visit," and soon I would be hearing a horror story of a call they had just run. I would automatically transition into a CISM mode. These people had a level of comfort with me, and I felt an obligation to them. I didn't want any of them to go where I'd been because there was no **real** intervention when they needed it.

My own experiences had taught me how to recognize a critical incident stress reaction. But mitigating it was another thing. I had no formal training and depended on what felt right.

I had a few allies. One of the operations supervisors was a firm believer in critical incident stress management and had been taking classes from the International Critical Incident Stress Foundation (ICISF), the people who had refined the field specific model of CISM. "Lisa" became my friend and my mentor. I started taking classes and soon became an official CISM peer counselor myself.

CISM Team

Unlike my predecessor company, this county had a professional resource for CISM. His name was "Joe." He was a paramedic getting a degree in psychology and was a trusted colleague. Paramedics and EMTs don't feel comfortable talking to anyone outside the business about things that bother them. They don't want to be seen as vulnerable. So, when ALCO employees had a critical incident, they would talk to Joe.

Initially, they would come to Lisa or me. There also were a few field employees that recognized the importance of CISM and functioned as ad hoc peer counselors. We bonded as a group and realized it was time to try to get the company to formalize a program. We painstakingly worked on a proposal. After a number of rejections, the company recognized the value in mitigating a stress reaction right after an event rather than paying for years of therapy after PTSD set in. There was also the issue of taking responsibility for mistakes made by an employee who was rendered dysfunctional by a stress reaction.

We finally had an official CISM team - and I had found my purpose.

Not only did the company buy into the program, but other counties in Northern California wanted it. We created a training program. Our small team went to other counties to discuss the program with their operations people, then trained their teams…hundreds of peer counselors. We were making a difference for thousands of EMTs, paramedics and dispatchers.

A few years later I moved to an adjacent county and refined their team. I eventually ran the program for all of Northern California. Within my county, I also became a resource for the county's fire departments. I've helped people work through child abuse cases, murder-suicide calls, horrible traffic collisions, and line of duty deaths.

It felt safe being on the helping side of the equation. I no longer craved action in the streets and putting myself in stressful situations. Those days were over…until September 11, 2001. Ground Zero was a cobweb of immense proportions. But that's another story.

Sam Bradley

Sam Bradley and Associates, EMS Training and QI Pittsburg, California

"Seasoned" Paramedic and educator, published freelance writer, photographer, and video producer. Training Officer for DMAT CA-6 and Secretary for the Coalition for Tactical Medicine.

Work in progress: Partners — Odyssey of the Phoenix; a trilogy following the lives and relationships of three Firefighter-paramedics.

Rainbows In Cobwebs

The Tent

A few weeks before my third birthday, my family moved from Arkansas to Washington State. There were four of us in the cab of a '49 Chevy pickup. All of our belongings – the largest of which was an old wringer-style washing machine – were in the back of the truck. Picture the Beverly Hillbillies and then upgrade by 10%.

We were moving because my father, who taught school, had learned that teachers in Washington State made $400 a month whereas teachers in Arkansas made only $200 a month. Moreover, it was a chance to escape from the local political corruption that touched the public schools in Arkansas.

My dad was hired the week of the 4th of July, 1954, to teach in the Kennewick public schools. But we had nothing to live on until school started in September. To keep us alive, the school district gave my dad a job as a janitor for the summer.

While he was doing his job, something else was happening in another area close by that was going to affect our lives – and those of millions of others. I would start hearing about the first part of that story when I was three – the other part many years later.

Opportunity

The first part of the story began to shape up soon after Dad started his work as janitor. The head custodian for the system soon discovered that my father was not a believer in Christ. When he was told that an evangelist was going to rent the auditorium for a week of revival meetings, he saw it as a perfect opportunity. He assigned my dad to be the janitor on duty during the services, with the hope that he would pay attention to the messages and respond to an invitation to go forward for prayer.

And that's what happened. My dad was struck to the core with the truths he heard and went forward one evening to pray to receive Jesus Christ as his Savior. His attitude toward God and the Bible changed so quickly and so definitely that he brought my mother to the services. Shortly thereafter she, too, responded to the Gospel (good news about God).

There's More to This Story

What I didn't know about my parents' conversion to Christianity didn't come to light until 2011. Kennewick High School started a high school Hall of Fame. And I was chosen as the representative from the decade of the 1960s to be inducted in the inaugural class. The induction ceremony was in the same auditorium where my dad had heard the evangelist fifty years earlier.

After the ceremony, I asked him to rehearse the story of his salvation, and here is what I learned that I didn't already know.

A tent evangelist had been traveling through that part of the Washington country. He and his staff would set up a large tent, invite people to come to services and hold a number of meetings where he would preach.

I'm sure they felt they had reason to believe it was a good idea, because five years before that, Billy Graham had set up circus tents in a Los Angeles parking lot for the same reason. Media giant, William Randolph Hearst, sent word to his newspaper editors to "Puff Graham." The newspapers printed stories and photos, and the evangelist became nationally known overnight. (Since then Billy Graham has preached to over two billion people in countries throughout the world.)

But the not-so-well-known evangelist in Washington, and his staff, was about to run into a big problem. They erected their tent without trouble; but then, much to their dismay, a powerful wind storm suddenly whipped up and destroyed it.

I can imagine the evangelist's thoughts: *Why is God allowing this to happen? Here I am doing His work and now my tent is destroyed. Why?*

He didn't stay in a funk for long, though. People were expecting a revival, and a revival they would have. Since the Kennewick school where my dad worked was nearby, the determined evangelist arranged to hire the auditorium for his week of revival meetings.

The simple truth is that my parents never would have gone to a tent meeting to listen to a preacher. And had my dad not been assigned to attend as a part of his job, they never would have gone to meetings at the auditorium, either.

That's Just the Beginning

My parents joined the church attended by the head custodian. Nearly sixty years later, they are still members of that same church. My two sisters and one brother are all Christians. My older sister is married to the Yakima area director of Child Evangelism Fellowship, a group that reaches children while their hearts are young and tender which saves them from a lot of grief in their teen years. Their oldest son is a worship pastor in active ministry in his church and his community on the Olympic Peninsula. My younger sister runs the Christian bookstore in our hometown.

And my work has been in several far-reaching Christian and secular ministries and activities – defending homeschoolers, starting a Christian college, founding a church as its first pastor, writing over fifteen books, and leading a great number of people to Christ.

One example of the incredible reach of our family's conversion comes from the book my wife wrote called *A Mom Just Like You.* In that book she talks about our decision to let God plan our family size. Vickie now receives mail from all over the world from parents who have decided to have more children because of what she has written.

The Power of a Destroyed Tent

There's probably no way that the evangelist who lost his tent ever heard what happened because of it:

- A blown-down tent has led to children being born to Christian families in Sweden and Japan.

- A blown-down tent has led to the foundation of a leading Christian college.

- A blown-down tent has led to a pro-life ministry on the Olympic Peninsula.

- A blown-down tent has led to children hearing the Gospel in the Yakima Valley (Washington).

- A blown-down tent led to the founding of a Christian orphanage in Romania.

And so much more.

When God tells us that all things work together for good for those who love Him, we tend to think that the good He promises is limited to the person who has suffered some trouble or inconvenience.

I have no idea what good came directly to the evangelist as a result of his tent being destroyed. But I have a pretty good idea of the absolutely wonderful things that happened to one family as a result of it.

No, It's Not All a Joy Ride

My family is now suffering with Lyme disease. As a result of our experiences, I asked the Governor of Virginia to appoint me to be the head of a task force on Lyme disease to fix some of the problems that politicians and bureaucrats have caused in the proper diagnosis and treatment for that disease.

We will not benefit directly – at least not a lot – from the work of this task force. But our hope is that a great number of others will be helped by my efforts. The tendency for self-centeredness would rob us of the grand scope of God's promise. He promises to use our troubles for good – and not just for us but for a whole host of people that can be blessed through our times of suffering and difficulties.

God does good on a very grand scale.

Michael Farris

Michael Farris is the chancellor and founding president of Patrick Henry College as well as Chairman and founding president of the Home School Legal Defense Association.

He also is a constitutional appellate litigator who has served as lead counsel in the United States Supreme Court, eight federal circuit courts, and the appellate courts of 13 states.

As a leader on Capitol Hill for over 30 years, he is widely known for his leadership on homeschooling, religious freedom, and the preservation of American sovereignty.

At Patrick Henry College, Dr. Farris teaches constitutional law, public international law, and coaches PHC's Moot Court team which has won six national championships.

A prolific author, Dr. Farris has been recognized with a number of awards including the Salvatori Prize for American Citizenship by the Heritage Foundation and as one of the "Top 100 Faces in Education for the 20th Century" by Education Week magazine.

Rainbows In Cobwebs

Be great in act, as you have been in thought.

WILLIAM SHAKESPEARE
ENGLISH DRAMATIST & POET (1564 - 1616)

Shakespeare, Hollywood & Me

Most of us have things we enjoy doing outside of work…hobbies, interests, activities. And we probably all have at least one thing we're passionate about that is of no interest to the rest of the world. Well, I'm passionate about William Shakespeare. Are you a die-hard Shakespeare fan? No, I didn't think so. Most people aren't.

The Burning Flame

It started for me in Mrs. Ortman's 10th grade English class. She showed us a video of Sir Derek Jacobi and other actors from the Royal Shakespeare Company in a production of *Hamlet*. It was the first time I had ever seen a Shakespearean play and one I'd never forget. I was so blown away by the power, the passion, the majestic language of Shakespeare that I devoured my copy of the play. I became an instant Shakespeare freak.

I learned Hamlet's speeches. I'd dress up in my bathrobe, look in the bathroom mirror and recite, "To be or not to be." When I was sick and tired of homework, I'd say, "How weary, stale, flat and unprofitable seem to me all the uses of this world! Fie on it, ah fie." I remember one day, after a girl I liked blew me off, that I walked home saying, "Frailty, thy name is woman."

Let's face it. I was a total geek in high school. Yet, I said to myself:

Someday…somehow, when I'm thirty, I'm going to play that role and say those lines on stage.

I'd like to tell you that immediately after graduation I went to acting school in London and became an actor. That never happened. Actually that was more of a fantasy than a deliberate goal. I became busy with other things. Still, the dream was buried somewhere deep in my heart, even though years went by and I had concluded that I would never play *Hamlet*.

The Flame Reappears

Yes, my dream was buried; but then, something astonishing happened. I heard about a small community theater that was going to do *Hamlet* the following year. I knew they would have open auditions and invite actors to try out for the parts. My heart responded. I leaped into action, determined to make up for my lack of experience by showing up at the auditions completely prepared. I memorized all the lines. An acting coach worked with me on every phrase. A voice coach taught me how to shout at people night after night without losing my voice. I worked…I studied…I practiced. Over and over again.

Audition day arrived. I showed up. I remembered what I had to do…and did it. And…

I GOT THE PART!!!

Smooth Sailing?

Problem of getting the part solved, right? Yes, but actually I was faced with two additional problems. One: I had to play the role and do it well. Two: How was I going to get people to come see the play? This theater group had never done Shakespeare before.

"Nobody's going to come to this," people were saying. "Who's going to pay $12 to sit for four hours in folding chairs in a musty church basement to hear a language they can't understand? And besides, Steve, with all due respect, who's going to want to see YOU play Hamlet?"

I took their comments seriously – so seriously that I spoke to the show's producers. "Look," I said, "even though you've never run a show longer than two weekends, you need to run this one for **three.** It's the greatest play in the English speaking language."

They were skeptical. "Tell you what," I said boldly, "if you don't think it will work, I'll do the marketing. I think we can have a full house every night."

"You're on," they said.

Uh Oh

I was elated – and then I realized that we were in deep trouble. For one thing, my promotional budget was zilch. I had no track record, no experience, no reason whatsoever for people to take me seriously. Furthermore, with all the work I had to do to get ready to play the part, what time did I have to spend marketing the show?

Then I remembered something I'm always telling my clients: *Publicity can solve almost any problem.*

Okaaaay. Publicity. That meant media. But why would the media be interested in me? As I said earlier I said to myself again: *I have no credentials, no track record, no real experience as an actor.* Well, actually that wasn't quite true. I had played the Frog Prince in *Alice in Wonderland.*

Still, it was worth a try. I decided on a publicity technique that I teach called, "The Personal Story Hook." I sent out a press release to newspapers around town. Essentially, it said this: "We all have dreams we've never pursued. Here's an interesting story about a guy who's pursuing his dream of playing Hamlet."

They loved it. They ran story after story about me. However, that didn't mean we'd sell out the show. I'd have to reach my target audience – the artsy people who loved Shakespeare. Where I live, those people read publications like the *Philadelphia Weekly.* Somehow I'd have to get written up in that newspaper. But how? That paper's response to amateurs was, "We write about **professional** actors and **professional** theater companies."

Next Idea

I had to consult myself again. I teach a technique called, "The Celebrity Advice Hook." So why not use it now? I hired a freelance assistant to write letters to famous actors and Hollywood celebrities who had performed in some kind of Shakespearean production during their careers. I asked them to give me one piece of advice; and also to send an autographed photo.

Would it work? A few weeks passed. And then…then I started getting photos, letters, and notes of encouragement from famous people: Dustin Hoffman, Al Pacino, Mel Gibson, Charlton Heston, Patrick Stewart, Denzel Washington and many more.

I jumped on it and wrote a letter to the *Philadelphia Weekly* that basically said: "Why don't you do a story about what all these famous actors told this guy who's going to play Hamlet?" **They ran the article.** And, very important: they put in our phone number for ordering tickets.

The phone rang. Then again. And again. "Hi," people would say, "I want to see Steve Harrison play Hamlet." Orders flooded the box office, nearly overwhelming the hapless lady who had volunteered for the job of taking them. I was famous before I even started!

The show opened; and the actor in me is happy to say that I received a standing ovation every night. Dream come true! But the marketer in me is even more happy to tell you that every night we performed to a FULL HOUSE!

Continuation and Denouement

It didn't end there. A cable company got wind of our success and shot a made-for-TV production of it. It aired in markets – not just in Philadelphia – but around the country.

A friend of mine, who had been skeptical about my doing this from the beginning, said, "Steve, you'll never believe this. I go down to this wedding in Atlanta, flip on the TV and there you are, doing, "To Be or Not to Be."

My story proves that anyone, regardless of having experience or no experience, despite having realized much or little success…can realize his or her dream.

Now, here are my questions for you. What's *your* dream? Which direction are you going to get *your* full house?

Steve Harrison

Steve Harrison's company, Bradley Communications Corp., has helped launch such bestsellers as Chicken Soup for the Soul and Rich Dad Poor Dad as well as many others.

His clients have gotten publicity in numerous media outlets. Examples: Oprah, Good Morning America, Today, Fox News, The View, Entrepreneur, and USA Today.

He and his brother Bill produce Radio-TV Interview Report (RTIR), the magazine producers read to find guests; and the National Publicity Summit plus other publications.

Steve has been happily married for 23 years to his wife, Laura. They live in suburban Philadelphia.

Both Margaret and Vance have attended conferences hosted by Steve & Bill at Bradley Communications. Outstanding experience. They give back far more than attendees pay for their services.

*Success usually comes to those who
are too busy to be looking for it*

HENRY DAVID THOREAU
(*AMERICAN AUTHOR 1817-1862*)

Abandonment * Abuse * Meteoric Success

The West Texas desert was where I was born to a mother I never knew. I am told that she was a teenager. She deserted me once – and then, again. After that, my father married a woman who was a child's worst nightmare.

Kids see Walt Disney's movies, such as Cinderella or Snow White and the Seven Dwarfs, and shudder at the wicked stepmothers in them. Yet, they know they are pretend, so they can tolerate them. But I couldn't pretend, because in real life, I actually had a wicked stepmother.

I was a young child, but I remember the times she purposely scalded my hands and feet with hot water. Nor do I forget the beatings with a belt buckle. After one such beating, the scabs on my back became part of the fabric of my shirt. In order to remove my clothes, a woman I called "grandmother" had to soak me in the bathtub to loosen the scabs so the fabric could be peeled away.

By the time I was five, I was less afraid of the rattlesnake slithering next to me on the front porch, than I was of going into the house where I would be beaten again. The woman truly was evil. When my sister, Sheila, who was one year older than I, began first grade, she was afraid to be away at school, knowing that her brother would be treated cruelly again at home.

A Welcome Change

My father finally left the woman who took her constant rage out on me, and took us to Texas to live with our maternal grandmother. He wanted to relocate to California, and children didn't fit into the picture.

"No one wants to take care of these kids," our grandmother said. "They need to be put in an orphanage."

My father's parents came to our rescue. Our dad signed over legal custody of us and Grandmother and Grandfather Pickering took us home with them. I remember looking out their front window and waving goodbye as our father drove away to go to California.

Although it was sad to be left behind, these grandparents loved us. Grandmother had never learned to read or write. Perhaps it was because of her illiteracy and a secret yearning in her heart, that she made education a high priority for me. I was taken to church every Sunday where I learned to read stories in the Bible. Grandmother also made certain that I participated in Cub Scouts and sports.

Another New Life Begins

A few years later, our father remarried and made arrangements for Sheila and me to visit him for a few summers in Oakland, California. It was pleasant for the most part, and when it came time for us to leave, my dad surprised us with a question.

"How would you like to live permanently with me here in Oakland?" he asked. "Rick? Sheila?" It was incredible. My dad wanted us! Besides, I liked this stepmother and she seemed to like me.

"Uh…yea," I said. "I'd like that."

"You'll have to get permission from your grandparents, of course, since they're your legal guardians. Sheila, what about you?"

"I appreciate the offer," she said, "but I have my friends and everything in Texas. And Grandma and Grandpa. I'd like to go back."

So Sheila returned to Texas, but I stayed in Oakland. I was motivated. Among other things, I joined the Boy Scouts and completed elementary school. Soon after that, Dad moved us to Pittsburg, a city that was inland from Oakland.

Not Easy

I was a "latchkey kid," because my parents had to work. In order to keep busy, I became more active in sports and joined Boy Scouts Troop 89. I also joined a local church, by myself.

Although my parents worked hard, they had little financial stability. One time, when our hot water heater broke, I had to shower at my high school for almost a month before they could afford to buy a new one.

School was a problem for me, too. Many teachers and coaches made it clear that to them I was a lost child because of what I had gone through in the past. "I'm sorry, Son," I was told, "but with a background like yours, you aren't going to succeed in life. You might as well know the truth." Yet other adults, like my Scoutmaster, Bill Sullenberger, were drawn to me, perhaps out of pity for what I'd experienced. Their encouragement was what I needed.

Interestingly enough, though, I didn't feel disadvantaged, because in my mind, what my life had been had become my sense of what a normal childhood was like. It would be awhile before I discovered otherwise.

Defying the Odds

Probably because I didn't consider my life a disaster and kept a positive outlook, I worked hard in school; and, contrary to the gloomy predictions of failure from teachers and coaches, I excelled. My peers accepted me as one of their own and elected me as Student Body President. All of this spurred me on so that I earned letters in six separate sports, and received numerous leadership awards and local scholarships.

Scouting still was of great interest to me and I became an Eagle Scout, earned Crossed Palms and spent five summers working on staff at Wolfeboro. At my Eagle Scout award ceremony, my Scoutmaster announced to the entire audience that my accomplishment was even more amazing, because I had no support or participation from my family.

I also worked at several jobs during high school – newspaper delivery boy, dishwasher at a Chinese restaurant and church janitor, for example – so I could help with family expenses.

Every experience I went through increased my confidence and gave me the assurance I needed to forge ahead in life.

College Bound

I couldn't afford to attend a major college, so I completed a year at a local community college while I worked full time selling sporting goods at JC Penney's. By my Sophomore year, I was able to obtain student loans and transfer to Biola University in La Mirada, California.

So that I could keep costs down and finish Biola in three years, I carried 18 to 21 units most semesters. I played on the college soccer team, too, and was able to pick up a few extra meals during the season that way. I also coached intramural sports and my teams often bought me dinner after their games.

Still, money was tight. The only way I could get home for holidays was to share rides with kind friends like Vance Hardisty, whose family also lived in the Bay Area.

I was chosen to be a Resident Assistant in my dorm during my Junior and Senior years at Biola, and that position covered a portion of my housing costs. One of the students I was responsible for in my dorm became a United States Senator – John Thune.

Given my outdoor expertise, Biola also hired me as a part-time assistant instructor in backpacking, rock climbing and wilderness survival. Then, during my senior year of college, the Chairman of the Recreation Administration and Camping Department at Biola, Robert Frembling, hired me to help start the Genesis Account Christian Outdoor Education company.

A Dream Come True

As you've seen, there was little time for socializing; but in my senior year, I met Dawn. She was a Christian Education major at Biola, and served as a successful Junior High Youth Pastor at a large church in the area. I fell deeply in love; and it wasn't long before I asked her to be my wife. But there were those who were worried.

"Do you know what you're getting into, Dawn?" our premarital Counselor asked. "Rick's abusive childhood and family experiences are huge red flags." He asked that question several times over the course of our sessions. Dawn, whose background was that of a very godly and stable family, would smile and say, "God has made him a wonderful Christian man in spite of his past."

Our Family

As of this writing, Dawn and I have been happily married for 30 years; and together, we have built a strong family and successful careers. Our three sons, Chris, Nick and Josh, each became Eagle Scouts, California Boys State delegates, athletes and scholars. Dawn recently was selected as "Teacher of the Year" at her high school, where she also serves as a Department Head. I became a Deacon and Elder in our local Church, and served on the Board for the Western United States of our denomination.

Meteoric Success

My education continued. I obtained a Masters Degree in Public Administration from the University of Southern California where I received the Dean's Award, the Outstanding Master's Student Award, and held a 4.0 GPA.

That led to a first career in City Management in Southern California, working for the Cities of Cerritos, Manhattan Beach, Torrance and Costa Mesa.

My second career has been in non-profit management and government. As CEO, I took the Alameda County Fairgrounds from the edge of bankruptcy in 1999 to becoming the "Most Award Winning Fair in America." In 2009, with a 22% annual growth rate, my organization was recognized as the "Fastest Growing Fair in North America," out of more than 3,000 Fairs. One business unit of the 268 acre Fairgrounds became a $100,000,000 a year business entity, so that contributed to my being recognized by a national trade publication as "One of the Most Creative CEO's in America."

I've also been recognized as an international expert in my industry and have spoken abroad to government leaders and to graduate students at major universities.

In 2010, the prestigious Distinguished Eagle Scout Award was awarded to me. This national award is presented to only 1 in every 2,000 Eagle Scouts who have distinguished themselves in their careers and communities for at least 25 years. This award places me in the company of US Senators, accomplished scientists, university presidents, and captains of industry.

I Try to Give Back

Although my young life was filled with cobwebs of abandonment, physical abuse and haunting pain, I am beyond grateful for the way my teenage and adult life has gone. My past is a daily reminder that I've been called to help others who are less fortunate, so I try to express that thanks, not only in my worship but by helping others tangibly.

In that capacity, I actively connect non-profit organizations and ministries around the world, mentoring and partnering for the purpose of feeding starving children, drilling water wells so villages can have clean water, working with orphanages, etc.

Each year Dawn shares part of my life's story with her high school students. She points out that no matter what their past has been, they have choices to make about their present and their future. They can choose to make excuses, or like her husband, they can choose to embrace God's healing power, enabling them to have an abundant life.

It's my hope that you will use this story to encourage others who have lost hope. Most people don't have a horrible childhood as I did; but some do. And too many people have a defeatist attitude because things aren't the way they'd like them to be.

Not to be trite, but if I could do it, so can you if you are determined and keep your thinking right. Nothing…bad parents…lack of money…

messed up circumstances…nothing should keep you from working for a better life.

I know that God was with me as an abused child, and in many ways shielded me from further harm. He continues to heal the wounds of my childhood.

Rick Pickering

Rick is now CEO of the California Exposition and State Fair.

As the largest State in the Nation, this State Fairgrounds is considered to be in the Top 25 Fairs in North America.

Rick's family

A note from Vance:

Although I used to ride home from college for holidays with Rick, I lost track of him. And then I discovered him again years later. I was blown away when I learned of his childhood and the success he's had, despite the pain he suffered. He, like other writers in this book, is a stellar example of how the human spirit can triumph over great odds.

On our website, www.RainbowsInCobwebs.com, you'll find ways to …

* Enrich your life;
* Be victorious, despite discouraging situations;
* Banish cobwebs that seem too sticky to handle;
* Access eye opening, encouraging, practical steps you can take to have a superior marriage.

You'll also find there:

* Stories your children will love;
* Spiritual guidance…

And much more. Visit us as soon as you drink in all the wisdom found in the stories in this book.

II

Sheltering

Clouds

Clouds can...

Bring worries of a storm approaching;
Darken a day;
Be oppressive.

Clouds also can:

Bring hope that needed rain is on its way;
Give a different perspective to a day;
Provide entertainment by forming images in the sky;
Be a shelter from too much sun and heat;
Reflect glorious color from a setting sun;
Inspire people to create art, writing, cinema.

Clouds of discouragement can threaten anyone's day. Ignore the dark ones or deal with them quickly and positively.

*A dog is the only thing on earth that
loves you more than he loves himself.*

JOSH BILLINGS
(*AMERICAN HUMORIST 1818-1885*)

Katy

Part 1

We were running a band of sheep and knew we needed at least six good working dogs trained and ready to go. Where we live in Oregon, there are many top cattle dogs all in service, but to find trained Border Collie sheep dogs became a big problem. I contacted the Sheep Growers Association and was given the name of a breeder in the East.

I made the call. Some guy answered. "Yo," he said.

"Uh…hi," I said. "We are looking for a trained sheep dog. A Border Collie if you have any available."

"Are we talkin' a farm flock or what?"

"Well, we have about one thousand sheep, not counting the lambs. We'll summer them in the mountains, lambing them at the home farm during the winter."

"Gotcha," he answered. "I have a dog that should do the job. You'll need to pay up front, including air freight. I'll send along her registration papers, some whistles and instructions for hand and voice commands. Remember, once you get the dog, it's yours, not returnable. That's the way it works in this business, just in case you are new at this. Do we have a deal?"

"Uh…yes. You bet," I answered, getting into his swing of things.

1st Cobweb

Ten days later my husband, Bob, and I picked up Betty at the Portland Airport. She was a beautiful black with some white markings.

When we got home, we studied the commands and practiced using the whistles. As soon as Bob felt he was a pro at this, he took her out to the pasture and gave her the command to round the sheep and bring them to him which was: **"Way to Me!"** She took off, herding them right to Bob in the corral.

We were elated! "Good dog," we gushed. And then as I was closing the gate, I saw it.

"Bob, look. Blood! There's blood on the gate...and the ground."

We walked through the sheep, looking for injuries. Bloody back legs! Bob was shaking his head as I started out the gate to call the guy back east, hoping he could advise us. Just then our neighbor drove up.

"Need any help?" he asked.

"Don't know," Bob said. "Something is wrong with a lot of the sheep."

The neighbor caught a ewe, and as Bob held her, examined her back legs. "I think that dog works cattle instead of sheep," he said. "You don't want her. She'll do them more harm than good. I'll help you doctor them before the flies get in those wounds." He stood with his hand wrapped around his chin. "Tell you what," he said. "I need a good cow dog. I'll buy her from you at the same price you paid."

We made the deal. He got an excellent cow dog...but we still needed a sheep dog.

2nd Cobweb

We finally saw an ad in the paper from a guy who was training sheep dogs. We called him.

"Yep. Got just what you want," he said.

We left the next day and traveled three hundred miles to see what he had. As I got out of the pickup, I crossed my fingers. *I hope this is the one,* I breathed to myself.

The man demonstrated a dog named Annie. He sent her out to

round up five ewes in a fairly large pasture. She followed his commands perfectly.

"She isn't registered," he said, "but I'll file for her papers and mail them to you." Trusting and naïve? That was us. We made the deal and took her home.

She just worked great…at first. We were delighted…until…until we moved the sheep to another area a couple of miles away. The reason we moved them was, it was a large meadow with plenty of feed; and until we could get into the mountains, we needed the extra feed. In one way it wasn't ideal, though. Even though the meadow was sitting high over the river, we had to haul water in. Still, it was a small price to pay to get the grass.

We were busy getting the water troughs set when we heard Annie barking. We whirled around, wondering. A coyote?

What we saw made my heart sink. Annie was running the sheep across the meadow.

Bob took out after her yelling the command to lie down. She didn't pay attention. Before he finally got through to her, one hundred head of good ewes tumbled over the cliff to their death.

We gave Annie away.

3rd Cobweb

"Gee, we are really having good luck with these dogs," Bob and I said to each other sarcastically. What to do? We couldn't go to the mountains without dogs, not with the amount of sheep we had. Even though we'd lost the hundred, we still had 900 left.

We kept searching and finally found a male Border Collie. Not trained, not registered, not even named – just a male Border Collie. But he was good looking. We named him Bud and took him to a trainer to get him ready.

Bud was smart, friendly and he seemed to like the sheep, so we figured that maybe we had found one good dog to start with. The trainer said to give him a month to train him and then he'd deliver him; so we paid him, shook hands and went home.

Three days later, we got a call from the trainer.

"Don't have very good news," he said. "The dog was doing just great so I turned him loose to herd a few sheep and he just suddenly took off. We haven't seen him since. We lost him, I'm afraid."

We were pretty upset by now, so we went to the guy's home and said he could either pay us back for the dog or give us another one.

A Cripple?

He had one dog left that no one wanted because she had an old hip injury.

"She don't have no problem with it, though," he assured us. "She's a purebred but I never filed the papers because of that injury. She's trained, so you can take her or not. Up to you. Her name is Katy."

I looked at Bob. He looked at me. Our looks said: *Here we go again, but what can we do? Might as well try her and see what happens this time.* We took her home.

Our Rainbow of Hope

We had a leash on Katy as we headed for the high meadow. She got excited when she saw all those sheep. Then she whined. Bob looked at me, sucked in his breath and took the leash off. She didn't move. Instead, she stood there looking at Bob.

He gave the command: **Way to Me.** She was off like a shot, circled and bunched all 900 of the sheep and brought them to Bob at a walk. Then she waited. My stomach was churning. I was afraid to hope too much.

Victory!!

We started out of the meadow. I watched in amazement as Katy walked the sheep home, put them in the corrals and held them there until we got the gates closed.

"Oh, my gosh!" we shouted. **"Oh my. Looks like we have a winner at last!"**

I marveled again and thought back to how we had gotten into this business. The sheep were ours only because our daughter, Barbara Ann, started with a few as a 4-H project when she was a teenager. We knew nothing about sheep at the time. These were Suffolk sheep (the ones with black faces) and they produced good meat. Huge critters, their backs were as high as my waist. After Barbara Ann left home to become a nurse, we inherited her project.

We were delighted and dismayed as the flock grew – and grew – and grew. Later, we would start buying Ramboullet sheep. If we thought the Suffolk were big, now we knew what big was. The Ramboullet were white, their backs as high as our chests (that's right) and their wool so fine it was wonderful for clothing, blankets and more. Ramboullet, as you might guess, needed lots of room – so they did excellently in the mountains.

A good sheep dog was a necessity and it never failed to amaze me at how cleverly and efficiently they worked.

Replacements

We needed to replace the hundred ewes we had lost over the cliff before we moved to the mountains, so the next day we took Katy and headed for a rancher's place. He had about three bands of sheep (when you have a thousand sheep, that's a "band"- not a flock). He told us he had too many and needed to sell down.

We watched as he worked Katy. She helped bring the sheep in, run them through the chute and separate them. We picked out three hundred head.

"I never saw anything like that dog," the rancher declared. "I'll meet any price you ask if you'll sell her to me."

We just laughed. No one was going to get near our Katy.

Preparing for the Mountains

Once we had the new sheep home, we worked them, checked their feet, ran them through footbaths, and looked for any problems. Then we separated out the Suffolk and any old Ramboullet ewes and took them to auction. The mountains would have been too hard on them.

We then ordered the trucks needed to transport the sheep we had purchased, plus the ones that were at home. We loaded them all up and headed for the high hills and meadows.

We needed more dogs, but for now, it was just Bob, Me, Katy and a massive guard dog, Ralph, that we had rented from the government. Ralph didn't work sheep. He was trained only to run big predators away from wherever we were.

That meant we all worked triple time, herding, moving sheep to new areas about every week or so, depending on the feed, hoping that Ralph could keep the predators at bay.

Katy's Distress

We had leashed Katy this one night because her hip was bothering her to the point that she was using only three legs; and she was exhausted. If we hadn't leashed her, she'd keep working.

It was just before daybreak when she woke us up scratching on the trailer door, whining. We both jumped up, dressed and stepped out, hoping she was all right. Bob took the leash off and away she went, racing toward the bed ground. We raced after her.

"Bob," I screamed. A coyote was moving the sheep toward the timber, working them back and forth exactly like Katy would do. Coyotes are very cunning; and we could hear more of them in the timber waiting to make the kill.

Katy tangled with that coyote. Bob shot the gun in the air. The predator took off.

Katy started rounding up the sheep. It was a close one. If it hadn't been for Katy, we would have had a great loss. Needless to say, we never leashed her again.

Our beloved dog started resting more each day. Her hip seemed to really bother her and she used just three legs more and more. We tried to keep the sheep from roaming too far from camp so she could get more rest. Each morning she would be waiting by Lady, the horse, for Bob to mount and start toward the band.

Surprise!

One morning Katy wasn't there when Bob went outside. He couldn't wait for her. The sheep were on the move and he had to stay with them.

I went outside, wondering why Katy would go ahead of Bob. Then I heard a, "Yip" from under the trailer. Then, another, "Yip." I got down on my hands and knees and peered underneath.

"Katy," I called softly. She was there, all right. And with her were five little black and white puppies. "Oh, my gosh," I said.

She'd given birth to them during the night. No wonder she'd been so tired the last few days.

"Stay, Katy," I told her. Then I left to help Bob.

On the fourth day Katy went back to work. When the sheep were nooning (taking a nap, which they did every day, wherever they were), she would race back to camp, feed the pups, then head back to her work. Faithful dog. A true friend. Our Katy.

Barbara Greene Gentner

Before Barbara and Bob became sheep owners, Barbara was Head Office Manager for Gourmet Foods Inc. and Farm Chemicals in Pendleton, Oregon.

She has written a number of short stories based on personal experiences.

Bob, her husband, a former Navy man, had his own auto repair shop and drove ambulance, during which he saved numerous lives.

A dog owns nothing, yet is seldom dissatisfied.

IRISH PROVERB

Katy

Part 2
(Read Katy Part 1 for background)

Katy always kept her eye on Bob when they were working the sheep, waiting for any commands. If Bob gave the wrong hand signal or voice command, she just stood there looking at him until he got it right. One day he gave the same command three times but it was wrong. Katy finally gave up on it, went ahead and did her own thing, which was perfect. Guess she was teaching Bob a lesson.

Training the Pups

When the puppies were about eight weeks old, Katy started weaning them. She still returned to the trailer during the sheeps' nooning time (their daily nap) to check on her babies. They were to stay under the trailer in the depression she had dug. If they got out, she put them back in, growled, then went back to the sheep.

We started fixing puppy food and mixed dry milk with it to feed them four times a day. That kept them happy and their mother wasn't as stressed. There were four females and one male. The girls wanted to work and would copy everything Katy did after she allowed them to follow her around. The boy would find a shady spot, hide himself and sleep. That was his daily ritual and he had no interest in anything except sleeping and eating.

As the pups grew and learned from their mother, each one took a liking to a particular job she wanted to perform. Since Katy was so versatile, we would put one pup at a time with her; for instance, in the pens where the sheep were. If that was what that particular little dog wanted to do, she would stay and work. If not, she would leave and gravitate elsewhere.

Choices

It was fascinating to watch. One liked the chute, one preferred the unloading and loading of the sheep; one went for trailing; and all of them would work herding. Once their desires were established, whatever dog had chosen a particular task, we kept with Katy for her training. Katy actually trained her better than any trainer could. If the pup made a mistake or she lost her concentration, Katy whipped her by grabbing her by the back of the neck and shaking her. She never hurt any of them, but this breed of dog will do anything to please, so it didn't take much to hurt their feelings. Katy repeated the dogs' training until they knew their jobs completely. It was something you had to see to believe.

Girls and Boy

Border Collies are not very large. When the young dogs were ready to get down to business for real, they were about a foot tall at the shoulder, which meant they were about half grown in comparison to Katy, but they worked hard and long.

Except the male. He never did know what work was. *Heck, leave that chore to the girls,* I guess he thought. He wanted to sleep and dream.

The girls loved to come in at night, eat and then have us remove any ticks, burrs or cheat they might have picked up. We'd brush them good, praise them and hook them up for the night. These dogs aren't what you call real pets. They are working dogs. Seems like they are ready to work the day they are born. They love it and that is one way they use their excess energy. Otherwise they get themselves in trouble.

Frightening

Katy retired with us. We had wearied of sheepherding and we weren't about to let her go. It was an enormous lot of work and it certainly wasn't a way to get rich. Her pups now were full grown dogs that had been sold to cattle ranchers, who later mentioned that they worked better than any of their other dogs.

Yes, sheepherding was an up and down deal – cobwebs, rainbows and some victories. But cobwebs keep coming into a person's life, no matter what you're doing. One was when we visited my sister in California. They live in an area where everyone is situated on an acre, so no one pays much attention to what's going on around them.

One morning when Bob took Katy for her usual walk, she trotted on ahead. When he got up to where she had turned a corner, she wasn't there. He whistled. She didn't come.

The entire family hunted frantically for her. Evidently there was a rash of dog stealing in the county at that time. When we found that out, we felt sick. We made posters and tacked them to telephone poles through several neighborhoods, adding a photo of her:

Retired Couple's Beloved Dog Missing.
Reward if Returned.

A few days later, my sister got an anonymous and guarded phone call. "Your dog is in an animal shelter in Benicia." Benicia was a good 10 miles away on the other side of an expanse of water accessible by a large bridge.

As we drove there, our hearts were in our throats. What if it wasn't Katy? What if...

We drove up to the shelter, went inside, were shown into the cage areas and gasped. Tears began streaming down our faces. Katy! There was Katy.

We felt sure that she was there because she had been stolen. For one thing, with her bad hip and since she was completely unacquainted with city areas, she wouldn't have walked any distance at all. For another, a friendly or local person would have taken her to a closer shelter…unless the thief dropped her off when he/she got frightened, compassionate, felt threatened – whatever…and a kind person nearer Benicia picked her up. We'll never know.

The End of a Very Good Thing

Katy went to dog heaven at the ripe old age of twenty three, no doubt dreaming of her wonderful adventures. Maybe she's still herding sheep.

Barbara Greene Gentner

To see a picture and a bio of Barbara, read KATY, Part 1, the story that precedes this one.

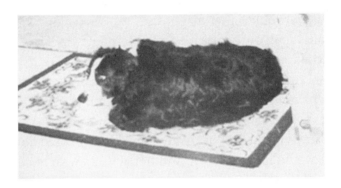

KATY

Do you have a true, unusual or moving animal story? We'll be happy to look at it. Submission information: wwwRainbowsInCobwebs.com.

Rainbows In Cobwebs

If I can stop one heart from breaking, I shall not live in vain.

EMILY DICKINSON
(AMERICAN POET – 1830-1886)

When Life Closes In

Theresa – we usually called her Terry – was sick for a long time. When the diagnosis was made, it left everyone reeling. I pulled the keyboard closer and carefully typed in what I thought that Billy, Terry's husband, had said on the phone between his sobs. Gliosblastoma Multiforme Grade 4. Survival rate? 1%. A few made it to 2%, which meant a possible two years of life after diagnosis.

The words spun out before me on the computer, as if in slow motion. My mind could read them, but could not comprehend. It was like the air had been sucked out of the room. I looked around. The furniture was still in the same place. The sun was still shining. Everything was the same – and yet it never was going to be the same.

Theresa was the best of us. And as quickly as I could do the math, I knew that I would have only 100 additional visits with her IF someone could get her into the 2%.

The horrible news came on Christmas Eve. My husband, Tommy, was Christmas shopping with our little daughter. As I rushed out the door to get to the hospital in Danbury, Connecticut, I called him. "Terry's diagnosis is bad. She has one, maybe two years to live. I'm on my way to see her."

Tender Moments

An hour later I walked into Terry's hospital room. She was surrounded by her siblings.

"Mary Agnes, you came?" her sister Susan asked sweetly, as they gathered around me with hugs and greetings of love and welcome.

"Of course. Of course I came," I said. "Our Theresa? Nothing could keep me away."

Theresa was laughing at us all. She looked fine, her beautiful smile and quiet way still intact, as it would be through every day that she would be there for all of us. Before I left that night, I would put my crucifix on her neck. "Here, T, this will keep you safe."

Remember?

We had been friends for a long time – ten years? Fifteen? It felt like a lifetime. I struggled in the car on the way home to calculate it, my mind racing through the million cups of coffee in a thousand diners spread across the thread of a friendship. Through sobriety and non-sobriety, through boyfriends and husbands and lovers and chaos and peace, through birthdays and holidays, we had cut an invisible path through every diner in New York State, leaving an invisible line of memories and love. She had read at my wedding, and that was a decade earlier.

Extension Granted

We did get the two years; and my not having a fear of death made my times with her invaluable. Her gifts to me would be obvious – and some so subtle and hidden that we would discover them only weeks after her death. It would be hard to believe that there was some design to it all – but even harder to deny it.

The last few days she ever spent "home" were at her sister Elaine's house in Mount Kisco in New York. I had told her family to please count on me to relieve them at some point – that I was more than a friend; I was family. So I was there one day when events took an ominous turn.

There was a lot of chaos before everyone would leave that day, and Terry and I would curl up and watch old movies until she dozed off. Her husband, Billy, was almost frantic by this point, rushing around, talking far too fast about where I would sleep and how I could help Terry move from one place to another since her body no longer responded to her own wishes.

I stopped trying to communicate with him since he was so agitated and just looked at Theresa. "I'm going to sleep in the next room, Terry," I said. "I'll be less than twenty feet away from you all night. If you need me, I'll hear you. Okay?" She seemed to relax then. As if she had permission to stop trying to hold it together.

Billy was still terribly upset, going on and on about a good night's sleep and finally, unable to handle it, he left. I smiled at Terry. She looked at me with a deep love. That was the last time we would really ever communicate with each other. She simply wasn't able to form words by the end of that weekend.

A Startling Truth

Theresa had dozed off watching *An Affair to Remember,* and I had stayed up to see the end, wondering if the protagonists ever would find one another again. I must have dozed at some point because I woke up to Terry calling me to help her to the commode.

I wrapped my arm around her, facing the same direction, in some bizarre synchronized ballet – the way her husband had explained I was to move her. I would help her, pivoting her weight from side to side. It was like we were under water – slow.

Something outside the glass doors caught my attention, and as we pivoted, moving slowly to the right, I turned my head to look out. An electric shock shot through my body. I held Terry tighter as everything seemed to go white for a moment, like I'd been hit by lightning.

Don't drop Theresa, whatever you do, I mentally told myself. *Just do not drop Theresa.*

Then I seemed to answer myself from some other place, in some other voice. *I think I'm hurt. I think I really hurt my arm.*

In some weird 20/20 hindsight...in my thoughts?...in my daydreams?...in actuality?...an angel slowly descended in that moment, wrapped me in winged arms and helped me with Terry. Then this angel leaned in close, and in a sort of breathy whisper said: *You broke your neck.*

I broke my neck? Yes, we would find out the truth, eleven weeks later, long after Theresa had left us, that in that moment of helping her, I had broken my neck. Somehow I had smashed, wide open, two of the cushiony gelatin disks that keep the vertebrae from hitting each other, and in the process, I had slammed the fluid that should be *inside* those disks, all over my cervical spinal column.

Hurts and Healings

So many memories about Terry ran through my mind about our friendship over the next eleven weeks. How beautiful she was always started them flowing. She was my one true friend. How would I live life *without that?* The movies and the parties that seemed to run together in a big string of happy pearls; from the dawn-to-midnight housewarming when my husband and I first moved into our big old house by the lake, to birthdays and Sundays, and Superbowls, and indoor picnics in the rain.

Tommy and I could always scrape up a hundred bucks and an excuse to have a house full of friends. Theresa never missed being there, laughing and listening intently to another person, nodding in compassion or humor. The next morning would find her curled on our couch reading – her blankets neatly folded at the bottom by her feet.

Terry's gift to Tommy

My husband's favorite gathering definitely was a birthday party, BBQ'ing under a big golf umbrella, smoking, and passing plates of burgers and sausage back into the house.

Eventually he ended up inside that day, frying a variety of things in an assortment of pans on the stove in our tiny kitchen, while the rain pounded the skylight overhead. The men filled the stairs from our kitchen to the apartment upstairs, an endless line of guys smoking cigars, drinking beer and eating fried stuff on forks just pulled from the pan.

Tommy is everybody's friend – you just can't resist his big gentle guy thing. He's probably 6'3", and he's very broad – kind of like one of those Russian dancing bears. And he has a big voice, deep and calm.

Friends would come and go in our lives. Some would move and then move back. Some would even move in and stay with us to heal when life was too rough. But Terry was a constant. She was the finest of all of us. She was funny, beautiful, petite and bigger than life, all at once. She had strawberry red short hair, and in the summer, her fair skin warmed to a golden tan. She had the art of conversation down to a science and would ask how you were, and then listen to you answer, for twelve hours if need be. Quite simply, knowing Theresa was like standing next to the most lovely tree in the forest.

I can see me, in my mind's eye, at that birthday party, rifling through the many junk drawers in my kitchen, one of which had given up the fight and collapsed backward into the cabinet. I was fruitlessly searching for birthday candles, panicked. Theresa's face lit up with something like, *Eureka, I've got it!* "A parade!" she said. "Let's make a parade! Just the girls." And she handed out long, tapered candles in holders and scented candles in jars or other containers to all those women, one by one.

Magically, as if on cue, we all lined up, lights off, and marched into the dining room – me carrying the cake like a drum majorette carries her baton – singing happy birthday to loyal, rock-solid Tommy, surrounded by all these friends. We built a human halo around Tom.

Tommy loved both me and Theresa. He was like a big brother to her. So while we know she couldn't have *known* what would happen after she died those eleven weeks later – it's hard not to tie an incredible event to that birthday party – a sort of last gift from her to Tommy – to us.

It happened like this.

Tommy

As my neck became more and more injured, my own body began to stop responding.

Even brushing my teeth become difficult. The mere act of making a fist became impossible. I finally wrote to my doctor, in perfect calmness amidst the agony, to say that I was running out of options.

And somehow, as the earth would spin and rotate, I moved through time. Days and nights passed and finally I sat in the car beside Tommy and noticed that *he was quiet*. I would notice this, and then forget it until much later. I was worrying about being incubated awake, which is how they would begin my surgery to remove the broken disks in my neck. I worried about my job. A million thoughts flowed by as we drove to Good Samaritan Hospital.

What I didn't know at the time was that, simultaneously, during every single moment that passed, unfolding for days and weeks and months while Theresa was diagnosed; after she was diagnosed; while she struggled; when my neck was broken while I helped her that night; and after she died…every moment, a blockage in Tommy's artery, just outside his heart, was growing. It began closing like a pursed mouth, allowing less and less blood into his heart.

It was later, during my surgery, that he would stop and think: *I don't feel well.* He would stand there in Good Samaritan hospital and miraculously *stop* being quite so quiet and say the words, "I don't feel well." Weeks and weeks of wanting to cut my arm off with a hacksaw after my neck was injured, weeks of sleeping on the couch for only a few moments at a time because of the pain, weeks of grieving over losing Theresa… every single second that freight train was headed toward Tommy.

And yet, he chose to stay with me.

So it was in *that* hospital with *that* doctor at *that* moment in time, that Tommy collapsed onto the hospital floor. He instantly was surrounded by nurses directed by *that* doctor who immediately started procedures that saved his life.

Inevitable Questions

So okay, You, the great I AM. The God of heaven. I don't understand this life. How we lose people. How we *don't* lose other people. But I think: *Am I right? That underneath it all, if we are present in the day and the moment, we are surrounded by the love of friends; but more deeply, much more deeply, by your love for us?*

It's hard to understand:

- that I would get hurt helping Theresa;
- that I would feel certain that an angel visited me in that moment;
- that I would be misdiagnosed for 77 days;
- and that the very day my husband's heart would stop, I would be IN the hospital that would save him – the only hospital within half an hour of that beautiful old house on the lake. If we had been HOME that day, quietly watching TV or reading the news, that freight train headed toward Tommy for so many, many days would have hit him – stopping his heart, ending his life.

In my mind's eye, an angel descends. She looks, not surprisingly, like Theresa. She holds a candle in one hand and takes Tommy's hand by the other. She gently leads him off the train tracks and whispers in his ear, *"Happy Birthday, Tommy."*

Mary Agnes Antonopoulos

Mary Agnes is a respected social media strategist with over 100 successful social branding and marketing campaigns for a variety of clients, including NY Times bestselling authors, such as: Jack Canfield, JJ Virgin, and Christine Comaford.

She also has added numerous Amazon bestsellers to her list of accomplishments for Libby Gill, Kelli Richards, and many others.

In addition, her clients include a long list of entrepreneurs and corporations, including AT&T, Midas and Panera Bread.

Hundreds of entrepreneurs have graduated from her 6-week course on social marketing. She speaks all over the country, teaching winning social media tactics and audience building techniques. In addition, she is a sought after ghostwriter, YouTube Coach and podcast producer.

Rainbows In Cobwebs

"Half this game is ninety percent mental."

Yogi Berra
(*American Major League*
Catcher, Outfielder, Manager)

I Played for the Raiders

When fans watch their favorite professional football team, they often form an emotional attachment to the team, a coach or a player. They read or learn about them in the media; but they seldom know what those individuals had to go through to reach the position they're in.

So it was with me. I was a defensive lineman with the Raiders for eight seasons, but it was amazing, even to me, how and why I got there.

Mentor & Father Figure

I was always a big kid, too heavy to play Pop Warner football, so I had to wait until high school. In the meantime, since I enjoyed sports and was built for them, I played basketball and baseball.

Finally, at High School in Bricktown, New Jersey, I was ready to play some football! My life at home had been difficult, because my father was an alcoholic. If any of you reading this grew up with an alcoholic parent, you know what that means – emotionally, physically and financially. If you're one of them, remember, you don't have to be dysfunctional because someone in your family is. You can go on to bigger and better things.

When I started playing on the high school varsity football team, Warren Wolf, my coach, became a welcomed mentor and father figure. If it had not been for him, I never would have gone to college. Our family couldn't afford to send me and when I graduated from high school I didn't have any significant offers to move on to a higher education.

Coach Wolf suggested that I attend a preparatory military school in Virginia. I wasn't too sure that was what I wanted, but I had to make that decision because it was the only avenue I had available.

The Right Thing to Do

I went to Hargrave Military Academy. While there, I grew another few inches, reached 6'5" in height and began to excel in my studies and in sports.

By the end of that year, I had offers to play for the New York Mets and the Philly's *baseball* teams. I also had *football* scholarship offers from colleges and universities like Brown University and Syracuse University.

It was a good situation to be in for an 18 year old. I had to decide whether or not to take the money now and play professional baseball or go to college and hope for a career in the NFL.

I finally decided that while the money in hand looked pretty good for a kid who had never had money, the choice for me had to be to reach for a goal in the future. I needed to earn a college education and, hopefully, play ball well enough in college to make a pro team someday.

College at Last

In 1965 I made it to Syracuse University. It was an overwhelming experience to know that I would be the first in my family to go to college. It turned out to be one of the most exciting times in my life up to that point. We had remarkable men attending there – like Big Jim Brown, Larry Csonka, Floyd Little – the list is long of the men from Syracuse who went on to play in the NFL. That was during the time I was there. You can read about each of them online.

1969 – A Crucial Year

It was time for the NFL draft. I really had no idea if I would be drafted or not; and if so, it would probably be in the later rounds. I decided to drive home to New Jersey. I had no way of hearing who was being drafted and I didn't have high hopes it would be me.

After a three hour drive, I could see a sign on my parents' garage.

Unusual. As I drove in, I read: "Congratulations! You are now an Oakland Raider!" Al Davis, the owner of the Raiders, had handpicked me in the first round as a defensive lineman! There's no describing how I felt at that moment.

I found out later that the other scouts thought Al Davis was crazy to take a lineman in the first round when they had so many other needs in order to field a great team. In those days, though, he seldom was wrong in his choices. He saw qualities in me that I didn't see in myself. He took a chance on me and I tried never to let him down. I always had a great relationship with Mr. Davis. He also was a Syracuse University alumnus, I might add.

California – Here I Come!!!

Get me out of this cold east coast winter and let the party begin! And party we did! All of a sudden I had money, businesses, women, cars, clothes, fame. The opportunity to play before 55,000 people every Sunday afternoon plus millions more on television was a heady experience. What could be better than this? I had reached the pinnacle of life! I had reached the glory land. Every man's dream.

Maybe because of the amazing progression of it all, I was nicknamed King Arthur. I still see some guys who call me "King" and it brings back a lot of good memories. A few stand out in my mind.

For example: In '72 I earned NFL Defensive Player of the Week honors for my performance in our game against the Houston Oilers. The game was at Houston. We went into the Astrodome and killed them. We won 34-0. Their quarterback, Dan Pastorini, was 3 of 21 for 31 yards with four interceptions. I had one of those picks. Otis Sistrunk had a pick off of a ball I deflected. They put the backup quarterback in and we picked him off, too.

The best part, though, and one that always gives me a chuckle, is that I still see Pastorini from time to time. "There goes that damn Art Thoms again," is all he ever says.

We had our good and bad times. On a Monday night game at Buffalo, we had two minutes left. The Bills were trying to run the clock out because they were up 14-13. Jim Braxton went right and fumbled the ball. I picked it up and rumbled into the end zone for a 29-yard touchdown fumble recovery. We went up 20-14. That was the good news. The bad news for us was: the Bills came back and won the game on a 13-yard touchdown pass to Ahmad Rashad.

I respected the other teams and their coaches, but I enjoyed playing the Cowboys most of all, I think. It sounds weird but I liked having to match wits with Coach Tom Landry. He had such creative offenses. It was a challenge to read and react to his schemes.

Super Bowl XI

Winning Super Bowl XI was great, but bittersweet for me. I had played for the team for seven years. When we made it to the Super Bowl, we were elated; but I had been severely injured, so I was on injured reserve for the big game. We won, and I got a super bowl ring that I treasure today, but man, I wanted to play.

In the 1970's there were a lot of drugs and drinking. I began to see my life style change and what I had become. It was blurred and confusing. I thought: *Who really cares about me? Are these my friends or do they just want access to a professional ball player?*

I began to doubt myself and my self worth. Even so, the longer one plays this game, the harder it is to leave it. The whole self worth issue becomes dependant on being that great ball player. There I was, alone in my thoughts, debating the reality of my life. Adding up the pro's and con's, though, I seemed to be doing well. I asked myself: *What more could I possibly want?*

I Was About to Find Out

In 1972, I met Darlene Drake. There was something really different about her than all the other women I had ever dated. She had a special quality that I was curious about. After having lunch with her a few times she revealed that she was a committed born again Christian.

As a boy, I had gone to church but I never really liked it, so as soon as I left home I stopped going. But there was something really special about the Drakes. Their faith was genuine. The more I was around them, the more I wanted to be like them.

I also liked Darlene. During that next year I began to go to church with her and her family. I figured I could spare an hour on Sunday morning. I had no idea that she was going to church, not just on Sunday mornings (Sunday School and church services) but Sunday evenings, and Wednesday Prayer Meetings! It was an eye opener, to say the least.

I had gone to impress her family but I began to want to know more. One day, I was sitting at the kitchen table with Darlene, her sister and mother. They told me what it meant to be "born again" which, I soon found out, meant to enter into a personal relationship with Jesus Christ. That's when I prayed so I could enter into that relationship.

Trouble!

To be honest with you, things got worse for me after I made that commitment. My teammates with the Oakland Raiders jokingly began to ask me to bless the hot tub after practice...or they would say that I could still be a Christian but didn't have to change who I was.

I began to experience an internal warfare. It was a struggle between wanting to live my own life as I saw fit versus doing what God wanted me to do. I did some things I'm not proud of...things that didn't make me happy or satisfied.

I thought: *These guys will be here today and gone tomorrow but Jesus Christ is never changing and will always be there.*

I began to straighten up and live my faith. It was not an easy decision. God continually had to work in my life to keep me on track. But from that turn-around I now have much more patience and I have love for people that I couldn't love before.

Darlene and I dated for five years and then married. She had a career in movies, television and commercials; and yet, she made the choice to walk away from her career to raise our children. Our faith has kept us together. There are always good and hard times in any marriage, but without a Christian spouse, I think it would be much harder.

Winding It Up

These days at golf tournaments and celebrity autograph sessions, I see a lot of guys I knew in football, such as Marv Hubbard and Ted Kwalick. I've played in Kenny Stabler's golf tournament in Mobile, Ala. and we remain good friends. And George Buehler married my wife's sister. I get to see quite a bit of him because we're family now.

I played for the Raiders from 1969-1977. Then one year with the Philadelphia Eagles. I was a free agent that year and wanted to come back to California.

In 1978, I had to own up to something every professional athlete must face sooner or later: retirement. For nine years I'd given my life to football. Looking back over the years, I can easily say it was a good career.

Art Thoms

Art has a sports and Hollywood memorabilia business that provides items for charities, schools, churches and any organization seeking to raise money and awareness.

He makes personal appearances and takes his Super Bowl Trophy and Super Bowl Ring to the events.

He and Darlene are leaders in their church (Calvary Baptist, Lafayette, CA) where Art mentors young men and counsels.

Hear more from this sports hero on his video: www.Rainbows in Cobwebs.com.

There comes a time when one must take a position that is neither safe, nor politic, nor popular, but he must take it because his conscience tells him it is right.

MARTIN LUTHER KING, JR.
(*CIVIL RIGHTS LEADER 1929-1968*)

The True Bull of the Woods

Perhaps differences in people and how they look at life might all come down to roots – them's that's got 'em … and them's that ain't. Good roots, that is.

Try as one might, it's hard to look further than those roots. Beyond our core foundation, our heritage, there is little more than the brief experiences of a few years, from birth to the current moment, from which any of us are able to draw and formulate who and what we are. And absent that heritage, the rest merely is wrapping – experience-based commentary that has little relevance.

It is vital that we, at least, glance over our shoulders at those who have come and gone before us. Some of those ancestors were Rocks of Gibraltar, while others resembled only sandstone worn down by unyielding life lessons and stresses of young truculent descendants.

My maternal grandfather, Joseph, was hewn from parents that were first-generation descendants of slaves. Their influence still resonates in me, as well as within all those whom I have touched and continue touching. The story I'm about to tell about Joseph and a Brahma bull, Billy, will demonstrate that.

Billy the Bull

Billy was large – an understatement – a Brahma bull in Southern Georgia. Though Billy was a dumb brute under the care and dubious control of men, he likely enjoyed more freedom than my grandfather and others during those days of Jim Crow. He grazed alone in a large pasture and would charge any intrusion that dared to come from outside the fence. Though pressing the scales in tonnage, Billy could close distances at speeds that belied his size.

Joseph

Although the bull held undisputed dominion over where so many feared and avoided him, Billy was destined to meet and tangle with an intrepid nemesis who was as much his own man as Billy dared to be his own bull. Billy and that nemesis were meant to face off and determine just who owned the pasture and who would come and go at whose pleasure and permission.

It happened one late summer afternoon when my grandfather and grandmother, Joseph and Harriett, decided to venture from their house to pick blackberries. There was just one problem – a major one. Like a lot of field hands' homes during that time, their house was located in the middle of the pasture where Billy reigned as king. That made their comings and goings outside the fence that stood between Billy's pasture and their house, a matter of life and death, should they misjudge the bull's whereabouts.

Having lived in the center of the pasture for years, Joseph and Harriet were quite aware of the bull's routines and could tell when he was a safe distance away – or not. But, on this particular and fated day, Billy would come to know that neither size nor speed mattered when push came to shove with regard to fortitude and resolve.

Presiding over the fortitude and resolve was the Honorable Joseph who claimed the ground on which he walked, swinging the cudgel of man pride hewn from self-awareness and years of knowing that only the best of his parents flowed through his veins.

Not to Worry

On this particular blackberry picking day, Billy was whiling away his time in a shady clump at the far end of his kingdom, a vantage point from where he could see and scent the entire unimpeded sweep of the terrain. His retreat from the pasture was because it was sweltering, a Southern Georgia testament to summer, when the thermometer slaved to harness the sun's impact.

So it was that Joseph and Harriet reached their berry patch unimpeded and spent a pleasant afternoon, anticipating the fine food preparation that would result from the largesse they were gathering.

It was approaching sundown when they finished gathering the berries and began walking home along the edge of the pasture, well away from where the bull had kept to himself all day, and where he was heard occasionally, snorting and stirring under the cover of the trees.

The Beast Stirs

Only a few yards from the house, Joseph sensed a shift in the wind which carried their human scent across the pasture. Billy sniffed the air and knew that he had intruders. The bull trotted from the shade, snorted and pawed the ground. Joseph and Harriet heard and saw him simultaneously. The bull appeared larger than normal.

They knew they were in trouble if they didn't make it to safety on the other side of the fence, for the beast now was in a full trot, coming straight toward them.

Joseph turned to Harriet and said, "Git over dat fence dere, gal. T'day, me or dat bull gon' go to hell 'fo duh sun go down."

Clearly, Joseph had come to the end of a rope that had been frayed by their continued retreat from Billy's reign, and it was time for one of them to be taught the most unforgettable and unforgiving lesson by the other. With a fighting weight of a mere fraction of Billy's mass, Joseph intuitively and viscerally knew that size would no longer determine the extent to which he would have Billy's brutish will imposed on him and his wife. Hell he welcomed, if it meant no longer being under the bull's cloven threat.

No sooner had Harriet settled on the other side of the fence, safe from Billy, than she became terrified of what might now happen as the Brahma thundered toward them, fearing that her husband had overstepped the bounds of good sense and let his half-breed virility pit him against more than a ton of raging muscle. After all, he was incredibly unmatched both in size and a primal instinct with the bull; but there was no backing down. Resolve had come to face down instinct, and only fate knew at the time which would rule; fate AND Joseph.

The bull raged toward Joseph and then – suddenly – came to a halt. Somehow he sensed that his quarry was not going to run. The beast tried to stare down the man while characteristically pawing the ground with his fore hooves and tossing the sun-bleached sand up and over his mighty shoulders.

All Nature Stands Still

The two, man and beast, sized up their next move. And it must have been one hellacious scene – very unlikely opponents about to duel for dominance against the backdrop of the setting sun. But there was nothing gentle or romantic about what was about to take place.

On the ground behind Joseph, next to the fence, lay an old, wild, cherry fence post. It had shed its outer layers, leaving only the solid and unbreakable core. Lightweight but durable, it would have made a wonderful Louisville Slugger; but at that moment, it became Joseph's battleaxe – the cudgel of his will – and the only hope standing between Billy, Joseph, and his certain annihilation.

Time … and Joseph's heart … stopped.

Moment of Reckoning

Billy charged!!

Joseph whirled toward the fence, which must have given Billy the impression that he was fleeing. But instead, the quick thinking man grabbed the cherry post and swung it with an arching Thor-like might at the bull.

The post connected with Billy's right eye, snapping and shattering with a loud crack against the quiet afternoon stillness. From the accounts related to us, the sound of the impact was enough to slaughter *three* bulls, two counties away.

Conquered King

The bull dropped to his knees, dazed by the blinding lightning bolt in the form of a slight man, five-feet, eight inches tall. Then, the beast crumpled and rolled in the sand with a loud snort. Once the deafening lack of consciousness abated, he scrambled onto staggering legs and trotted off to the safety of the tree-lined lair from where he had emerged minutes earlier. Shaking his head and snorting mucous all the way, he struggled to throw off the pain of the shattered eye socket and the new hegemony that had settled over the pasture.

The sun set behind the man. He and Harriet, who still was shaking, took their newly picked berries home, knowing that one of life's problems inexorably had been resolved. They no longer would have issues with… Billy the Bull…for the true bull of the pasture and the woods now…was Joseph.

Still the True Bull

Years later, my grandfather became very ill. So much so, that some said he was on his deathbed when there came a yell from outside the pasture fence.

"Joseph, the boss man wants you up at the house. They're selling Billy and need your help getting the bull up the chute and onto the truck."

Obligingly, the much respected half-breed climbed out of bed, got dressed and went to help. Once there, he picked up a very small stick that was lying on the ground next to the stall where Billy stood, defying any approach.

Frail from having been ill for some time, Joseph weakly climbed over the fence. Billy backed away, seemingly familiar with the man who had joined him in the stall.

"Git on dat truck, Billy," Joseph commanded, gesturing toward the chute with the stick, a stick that, no doubt, tacitly signified to the bull the return of an all-too-familiar bolt of misery.

Without hesitation, the bull turned and trotted up the chute. Evidently, going to whatever fate awaited him was, to Billy, a welcome relief, in contrast to facing his conqueror.

Carved Into My Heart

Time and time again, this was a story that was told to us as kids as part of our inculcation into knowing from which and whom we sprung. As a result, we grew up knowing the character passed on to us from my grandfather, a character that had the resolve to surmount any challenge.

As his grandson, I, too, am unwilling to turn and run from any ordeal that might cleave me apart from my will. To me nothing is more important and identifying as one's character and standing against mounting odds and disrespect.

Joseph and Harriet's story never changed, nor was its moral ever missed. We become nothing more or less than our resolve, and that resolve is hewn from our ability to resist yielding to our emotions, even when those emotions are in response to what sounds like the proverbial singing voice of the Fat Lady.

Like the man whose moral imperative emboldened him to face down a marauding Brahma Bull with only a toothpick of a weapon, I follow a compass fueled by moral courage, unfettered by fears of populace dissent.

If we are to persevere, there must be the willingness to stand on principle in the face of paralyzing dejection, despite the appearance of there being no other way out, over, under, or around sticky situations. Instead, we must man-up and go through our challenges versus continuously re-solving the same miscalculated dilemma, time and time…and time, again.

Milt Thomas

Milt Thomas is a former marketing communications executive and "ideation architect" with keen interest in predictive market analytics. He has produced numerous radio & television scripts, as well as strategic [business] communication pieces, and is holder of several patents. He is an executive business coach, public speaker, and blogger.

Having grown up in the Deep South, during the waning days of Jim Crow, as well as a time that was pre-King's movement for nonviolent social change, he brings a unique perspective to the socio-political DNA of America's black electorate and is extremely motivated by this book and its concept, recognizing its potential to trumpet the unsung "silent pejorative."

See this remarkable man's **video** on our website: www.RainbowsInCobwebs.com.

Your loved ones may or may not appear to be interested in details of events in your life – now, that is. We can assure you, however, that someday, someone related to you will be digging through boxes, checking out the family trunk and the internet, pouring through photos, and asking questions…all to discover information about you.

If you are around to tell them, fine. If not, you can leave a legacy and heritage by writing some of those events down.

If one of those events – or more – is published, all the better.

www.RainbowsInCobwebs.com

Do not anticipate trouble, or worry about what may never happen.
Keep in the sunlight.

BENJAMIN FRANKLIN
(*A FOUNDING FATHER OF THE UNITED STATES*)

Man Overboard!

I was born and raised in the small town of Cordova, population of about 1000 people, in a beautiful fishing area in pristine Prince William Sound in south central Alaska. No roads in or out; wooden buildings and sidewalks; telephone party lines; doors that never were locked; and you could count on a man's handshake to be as good as his word. It was an idealistic existence for a kid.

Even though I liked school, I had no ambitions of going beyond high school. Why would I? Most of us wanted to be connected to the fishing industry and my thoughts were: *Who wouldn't?* After all, we enjoyed beautiful scenery and wildlife most people never see. Furthermore, I could be my own boss, make good money and enjoy the fulfillment of a sense of adventure.

Such was my life from the time I was 15 when I began commercial fishing. I served under our captain, Les Maxwell; and with his crew of three, we fished for halibut, dungeness crab, and what was the most fun: wild Alaskan salmon.

Vietnam

My fishing was interrupted by the Vietnam war during which I was very proud to serve with the United States Marine Corps. I was in a grunt unit (infantry} and was involved in more action than I would have wished. But that's another story.

Upon completion of service I returned to Cordova and Les, my former captain, asked me to come on board the Icy Cape as a crew hand. It was my chance to get back into fishing and with one of the best captains in the area. I was excited.

We fished the summer and purse seined for salmon. We called it that because we would circle the fish with the boat, and men on a smaller skiff (jitney} held the net. As the boat circled the fish, the bottom of the net was drawn until it closed, like a purse string, and the fish were caught. The net was then gathered in, and all of the salmon were packed together in the bunt end.

We used a brailer, a super big scoop with a long handle and a net, to scoop the salmon from the net into the boat. The net was released by the worker at the end of the brailer and the salmon were released into the fish hold of the boat.

Catastrophe

It was the last day of fishing for the year and we were making the final set of the day. I was in the jitney and we were brailing fish into the boat. Several hundred pounds of fish were in the brailer when suddenly, the brailer handle slipped out of the handler's hands, swung through the air and...hit me in the head.

I was knocked to my knees. I experienced all of the symptoms of a severe concussion. Somehow I pulled myself to my feet and acted as if I wasn't hurt. After all, I was a macho ex-Marine and an Alaskan fisherman. I wasn't about to let on that I was injured, and badly so. My ears were ringing. Pain was coursing through my head. I waved off the other men's concern.

We finished the set and headed back to port. About six hours before we were to dock at Cordova I awakened from a night's sleep and, not feeling well, I swung my feet out of my bunk.

It was my thought that I would get some fresh air top side and, in the process, get the ropes ready for docking.

Tragedy in the Making

I bent over the side of the boat to grab the line. The next thing I remember was that I was in the ice cold water, holding on to the rope and being dragged by the boat. The rope was burning my hands. They were slipping. I couldn't hold on! I released my grip.

I watched in despair and a feeling of hopelessness as the boat left me behind. I screamed in hopes of someone hearing me, but the roar of the 671 diesel engine was too loud.

I didn't panic but you can bet I was very concerned. I treaded water until that moment came when I knew I was going to lose the battle, go under and drown. The boat was getting smaller as it distanced itself from me. Trying to swim to shore was wishful thinking. Land was miles away.

Even though I knew I couldn't make it, I decided to try. I began to swim. Then I stopped, looked up to the sky and said silently, "God, you can't let me die now. Not this way. I know I asked for your help once before in Vietnam and you answered. If you help me get through this, I will go to college and help other people. I will leave the work of fishing to others."

As I looked in the direction that the Icy Cape had taken, it appeared to be turning around. It was like in the movies of World War II where a destroyer is coming up fast on a submarine. Smoke was bellowing out of the Icy Cape and I could hear the 671 diesel was full throttle. It was heading for me!

How they even spotted me in that wide expanse of water is something I'll never know. I nearly was drowned when the crew pulled me into the jitney. There were words of encouragement from them; and I tried to mutter my thanks and gratitude.

Change of Direction

After we unloaded the fish at the cannery and docked, I looked at the captain. "Les," I said, "this is my last trip. I've had my time with fishing. It's time to move on."

Les looked at me and nodded his head. "Yes," he said. "I don't blame you, Jerry. I think I would quit, too, if that happened to me."

As Gary Cooper said in the movie *Sergeant York:* "The good Lord sure does work in mysterious ways."

Jerry Behymer

Dr. Behymer has practiced as a chiropractor for years in Lafayette, CA, since nearly drowning that day; and he has helped thousands of people, including members of the Hardisty family and our friends.

Not only that, but for awhile, at the request of one of his patients, a veterinarian, he adjusted the spines of dogs. That's right: Dogs. They were at the point of being "put down" because of intense pain they were having. He saved the lives of many before he went back to concentrating solely on people.

His wife, daughter, son-in-law and son have become chiropractors, as well.

He is known for his positive outlook as suggested in the Benjamin Franklin quote at the beginning of this story.

Hear more from this fantastic doctor on his video at www. RainbowsInCobwebs.com.

Rainbows In Cobwebs

Honor your father and mother…that you may live long on the earth.

THE BIBLE
(*EPHESIANS CHAPTER 6, VERSES 2 & 3*)

Listen to Your Mother

It was when I was driving to Folsom in California to visit with my Mom that, with no warning, the left side of my car started to shake violently. I quickly pulled over to the side of the freeway, got out and searched for the trouble. Flat tire. I called for roadside assistance. While I was waiting, I called my Mom to tell her I'd be delayed. I started to explain what had happened when she interrupted.

"Where are you?" she asked, tension lining her voice.

"Actually, I'm leaning against the trunk of my car and having a cigarette," I said.

"Get back in the car or you're going to get killed," she said urgently.

I laughed. "Mom, I'm on the side of the freeway. I have my hazard lights on and put the flares out, too. I'm fine."

"Get back in the car, now!"

"You're being dramatic, Mom."

"MARK GIGLIOTTI, YOU GET BACK IN THAT CAR."

The only time my mother would say my full name, when I was a kid, was when she was really serious. "All right. All right. I'm getting back in the car."

No sooner had I closed the door and put the phone to my ear to say, "Okay, I'm back in the car," then a large truck slammed into **the spot I had been in some 30 seconds before**.

The impact knocked me out. I dropped the phone. The crash automatically sent a signal for help. Voices came over the speaker in the car to ask me if I was all right. I couldn't respond.

A nurse who was getting off duty witnessed the accident and rushed to my aid. I came to as she was checking my vitals and making sure I didn't go into shock. After that, it was complete chaos around me. The paramedics and police arrived. My mother, who had heard the crash over the phone, was trying frantically to reach me.

I could barely stay awake. As they put me on the stretcher, I noticed everyone at the scene staring at me. One of the policemen said, "I've been an officer for a long time. You are one of the luckiest people I have ever seen. You shouldn't have survived that accident."

He was right. The car not only was totaled, but it was crumpled up like an accordion, stopping just a couple of inches short of my seat.

Excruciating

I was in more pain than I had ever been in my life. My Mom arrived as they were performing an MRI to assess my condition. The news was devastating. According to the scan, I had three vertebrae in my neck almost completely blown out and my discs were damaged as well. That certainly explained the severe pain I was experiencing. They controlled the pain that night with heavy medication and the doctor told me to consult with a surgeon.

I was grateful that I was alive but I had no idea what was about to transpire and how it would change my life forever.

Continuing Nightmare

Within six months after the accident, I had no feeling in my left arm but I still was experiencing the stabbing pain. It was constant at that point and I needed help to move around. The medication that once helped numb the pain, was no longer effective. I had been treated with more than 15 injections and every scan and procedure possible, with no improvement at all. The nerve damage was so severe that my neck literally was breaking down. The prognosis was grim and my only chance was to have surgery. My doctors cautioned me that there was no guarantee that an operation would be successful; and considering the complex nature of my condition; it might leave me in a condition that would be worse than before. The thought of that gave me chills.

I sought out the best surgeons I could find in California. Within six months I had seen eight. They virtually gave the same response. As the pain increased and continued to ravage my body, I would lose more and more hope. My last appointment was at Stanford and I lost **all** hope that day because I heard the same response. "You should find a good pain management doctor," the surgeon said. "I can't help you." It seemed as though time stood still for a moment.

That final prognosis echoed in my head for weeks. As my condition continued, I needed help to do anything, even getting out of bed. The accident and the pain that came from it, had taken everything from me. Even family and friends. It was very hard for them to see me in this condition; made even more difficult coupled with the heavy pain medication I was on. Some of them even thought that I was faking it.

I hadn't been able to work since that fateful day and my finances were exhausted. I was helpless. There were no more treatments possible. I felt like I had just received a death sentence. My only escape was to sleep, but even my dreams were about being in pain. I remember wondering why God would allow me to survive such a horrific accident only to be in severe pain 24 hours a day.

Broken in Every Way

I was angry, very angry; and I didn't feel as lucky as the officer said I was that night. I was broken spiritually, mentally and physically. I was ready to give up on life. In my estimation there was no reason to believe I would ever be healed. As the New Year was approaching, it was the first time that I wasn't looking ahead for what it would bring. I told my Mom that I was ready to give up.

"Nonsense," she said. "I won't listen to that. Just hold on."

One night as I was lying on my couch watching TV and crying from the pain, my Mom called. She told me she had found the surgeon who would fix me. She made me promise to look at his website. I did, and all of a sudden I had a bit of hope again. His credentials were more than impressive but what made me smile for the first time in a long time, was when I saw the subject of his doctorate: *How to repair severe trauma to the cervical spine.* I couldn't believe it when I read it. It seemed as if this man had been in training his whole life to help me.

The following morning I called to make an appointment. Besides getting all of my data to his office, I was told that he had a three month waiting list. I literally began to cry when I heard that. I couldn't imagine waiting that long. I asked the nurse if I sent the scans would it be possible for the doctor to take a look at them? She told me that would be no problem.

Surprisingly, his nurse called me three days later to tell me that the doctor wanted to see me. I asked her if that meant he could help me and she said that's what it meant. That hope and faith that I had lost so long ago felt like it was coming back. When I did meet this incredible doctor, I finally saw a light at the end of a very dark tunnel. He put me at ease and promised that he could fix me completely. The surgery date was set and I left his office crying tears of joy because I knew then that I was going to be normal again. The nightmare was almost over. My family and I quickly got ready for the surgery. It felt as if we were preparing for Christmas.

Surgery

On the day of the surgery my emotions were in turmoil. I was full of anxiety and worried. At the same time, I couldn't wait to wake up from the anesthesia. My doctor said he would be there when I did. He was. He told me that everything went perfectly and that now was the moment of truth. He asked me to lift my arm. I did. No pain. Then he asked me to lift my head. That was always the action that would cause the most pain and set off a chain reaction. Reluctantly, I did it. To my utter shock, there was absolutely no pain! I was so happy that I gave my amazing surgeon a high five.

That night, alone in my hospital room, I felt gratitude for every word of encouragement and every smile that I had received along the way. Of course, what I was most grateful for was the love my mother gave me and, yes, love conquers all. Thank God I listened to her both times. For the first time in almost 18 months I went to sleep smiling and woke up that way the next morning.

Mark Giolotti

Mark is an expert in consulting, business strategy and marketing while empowering his clients to meet their business objectives. He formed strategic executive-level relationships with companies that included Microsoft, HP, Intel, Cisco, EMC, and Sybase.

He has advised and consulted for many companies regarding all stages on raising capital, sales training, business planning and market positioning.

Mark also has been involved in politics for over 15 years. Among other things, he has been Campaign Manager for two Congressional campaigns.

*He has been a co-host on the radio program: **Patriot and Preacher Show**. You'll enjoy this delightful man's **video** on our website.*

III

Refreshing
Rain

Rain can...

Cause rivers to overflow or become dangerous;
Chill people and animals to the bone;
Find its way through ceilings;
Destroy fruit blossoms and other sources of food.

Rain also can...

Fill reservoirs and wells with needed water;
Freshen water supplies;
Provide mud puddles in which children can splash;
Fill lakes;
Give needed drinks for animals, plants and crops;
Cool down very hot days;
Relieve drought;
Bring out the noble and caring in people;
Inspire people to create art, writing, cinema;
Inspire people to accomplish great feats.

If you feel you are going to drown because of the emotional or circumstantial rain that is falling in your life, throw your head and shoulders back, breathe deeply and drink in the best it has to offer, rather than the worst.

Rainbows In Cobwebs

*"All the art of living lies in a fine
mingling of letting go and holding on."*

HENRY ELLIS (1721-1806);
2ND ROYAL GOVERNOR OF GEORGIA

Oh, No, I Killed a Man!

The first real look I had at the town of Tacoma, Washington, was from an iron barred window on the eighth floor of the Tacoma jail. I was a prisoner, clad only in my shirt and pants.   It all had happened so fast. My three debate team buddies and I, all 17 years of age, had graduated from Butte High School in Montana. Full of enthusiasm, a sense of adventure and a desire to make good money, as well as serve the war effort, we had decided to go out to the coast to get jobs in the war industry. We traveled in my Chevrolet that I had purchased from my mom.

We landed jobs in the lumber yard, but they wouldn't sign us on until we found a place to eat and sleep. Excited about our success, we began our search.

Dreadful Experience

In Butte, we didn't have blinking red lights that told us to stop and then go, so I barreled right through one and hit a truck broadside. Aghast, we huddled together as the police came and we were hustled into a police car.

As we drove away, I saw something that horrified me. The driver of the truck I had hit was lying on the road unconscious. His teeth were knocked out. I had killed him. I just knew it.

This was not a great day in my life.

Prisoner

I was ushered into a cell and I can hear the door clanging behind me, even yet. Another prisoner was there. Totally miserable, I didn't feel any better when the guy proposed a business deal. "I've got me some tools staked under the pier," he said. "I use them to get into houses that I burglarize. You can be my partner when we get out of here and we'll make a lot of dough." Things were going from bad to worse. I declined his offer.

Two very long hours passed – and then I heard the elevator rumble. The doors of my cell clanged open as two officers took me arm in arm down to the second floor where courts were in session. The big leather covered door to the courtroom swung open, and to my amazement, the judge sat behind his bench surrounded by my three buddies. All of them were laughing and seemed to be having a great time.

A Huge Turn Around

It turned out that the judge was an alumnus of the university all of us planned to go to in the fall or after the war, and he wanted us to join his fraternity.

The rainbows of hope kept coming. He gave my three friends letters of recommendation to the electrical union – and me a letter to the shipwright's carpenter union. He fined me $2.00 for violating the truck driver's right of way.

Still, I wondered. Was the man…?

"Oh, and by the way," the judge said, "he isn't dead. And those were his false teeth that got knocked out."

I was one very grateful 17 year old. I sought the man out, he assured me that he wasn't hurt, and I arranged to pay for damages to his truck.

We all got jobs in the Kaiser shipyards at double the salary we would have made in the lumberyard. I worked graveyard shift so I got paid time and a half. For a kid from Butte where wages were meager, a kid who was sure he was going to prison for life, I thought I had stepped into heaven. A very big cobweb turned out to be brimming with rainbows and, very definitely, led to victory, wouldn't you agree?

George Hardisty

George knew from the time that he was in the third grade that he wanted to be an attorney. After his father died, as well as three other fathers in the neighborhood (within a few months of each other), he had to step into the role of man, even though he had just turned 14.

George and his Meyer lemons

As a Marine officer, he served his country. After he married Margaret, and she became an author, he joined her in giving marriage seminars across the United States. He is the author of the book Plan Your Estate; and has co-authored How to Enrich Your Marriage as well as Everlasting Love.

To keep fit when he isn't in his office, he works vigorously on their acreage on a daily basis.

He is known for his positive outlook on life.

Below: Leaning against one of his Redwood trees

View George's follow-up video on our website: www.RainbowsInCobwebs.com

Rainbows In Cobwebs

*Success in the affairs of life often serves to
hide one's abilities whereas adversity frequently
gives one an opportunity to discover them.*

HORACE (QUINTAS HORATIUS FLACCUS)
(*ROMAN LYRIC POET – 65 BC – 8 BC*)

Calls in the Night

A Tuesday night in August, 2012

It was 10:20 at night when the phone rang. Jeanie and I had arrived at a condo in the North Carolina mountains five hours before. She was asleep; I was absorbed in reading.

I was surprised to hear the voice of our grandson, Graham, sounding very concerned. "Gagi," he said, using his special name for me, "Dad has had a stroke. He's at Carolinas Medical Center."

Craig? Our son-in-law doctor? My heart lurched. How could he have a stroke at 55? We had been concerned about the stress of his schedule, especially the night calls as an ob/gyn physician, but he was in good health.

What to do? I didn't want to awaken Jeanie, but I also didn't want Graham to be in the hospital dealing with this alone. His mother and sister were in California on a brief vacation, Graham had said, and now were trying frantically to get an overnight flight home.

I went to the condo next door where our son, Kevin, was staying. He was fast asleep and jumped when I touched him. We talked over the options and decided I would pack up and head to Charlotte. He would tell his mother first thing in the morning and drive her back to Charlotte.

So many times I have driven that lovely, curving mountain road.

At midnight it was darkness around, and near darkness within. My eyes were on the road while my heart was lifted in prayer, not knowing what I would find when I got to that emergency room.

If "déjà vu" means to see something again, then perhaps "déjà ecoute" means to hear something again. For me it was the sound of another late night ringing. And another long ride.

A Wednesday night in November, 1981

Jeanie and I were lying in bed reading. The phone rang. When I picked it up it was a strange voice. "Dr. Ford?"

"Yes."

"This is Dr. Brazeal calling from the Carolinas Medical Center in Chapel Hill. You have a son, Sandy?"

"Yes, what's happening?"

She quickly told me that our 21-year old son was in the emergency room with a rapid heartbeat. It was under control but they needed to keep him there for observation.

Jeanie and I had looked at each other in disbelief. Seven years before that, Sandy had experienced a heart arrhythmia due to an abnormal electrical circuit in his heart. A relatively new surgery at Duke Medical Center had seemed to solve the problem. He had been an excellent long distance runner, but now, once again, when he was out running his heart took off at a life-threatening rate.

The next day we made the long drive to Chapel Hill where Sandy was a third-year student at the University of North Carolina. Over the next week it became clear that he needed a second surgery to divide an electrical pathway in his heart. The doctors said their techniques had improved and they were very hopeful that his condition would be remedied.

So, early on the day after Thanksgiving we went to his room at Duke Medical Center. I walked with him to the door of the operating room, gave him a hug, and said, "See you later, Pal."

We knew it would be an extensive surgery, but as we waited, the time moved more and more slowly. After twelve interminably long hours the doctors came to the room where Jeanie, Debbie, our daughter, and I were waiting. They walked in wearily with somber faces.

"We fixed the abnormal pathway in his heart," said the surgeon, "but we couldn't get him off the table. His heart wouldn't start."

Numbness – Disbelief - Awareness

Suddenly our world had changed. We had known the surgery might not locate the faulty circuit, but we had not imagined he wouldn't survive. He was gone. Full of life, of love, of vision, our son was gone. A leader in the cause of Christ at the university. An honor student. In love. And at twenty-one...gone.

We made the three hour drive back to Charlotte, the numbness having taken over. I looked at Jeanie. Her face was white and drawn. "Well, either there is a God," she said finally. "And he is good. Or there is no God. It's as stark a choice as that."

At Sandy's memorial service, Craig, who had married Debbie only six months before, somehow found the strength to sing: "Christ for me is to live, to die is to gain." Then he dissolved into tears.

The loss was very deeply felt, especially as we looked for a place to bury him. What parent expects to do this for a child? To love deeply is to grieve deeply and we did just that in the months that followed.

Then at last, the "gain" to us began to emerge. Letters by the hundreds from friends Sandy had touched now touched us far more than we had known. When someone said, "His life was too short," I began to ask myself, How long is long enough? If not twenty-one, then forty-one? Sixty-one? There's no answer to that. The real question is not how long, but how full a life is. And Sandy's life was full to overflowing.

So – What Was Next?

Months later, after leaving home reluctantly to fly to Australia for a speaking tour, I seemed to sense a voice saying: Perhaps the next step in your ministry is to help the younger generation of leaders to run their race for Christ.

So we began to move in that direction. We founded the Sandy Ford

Fund through which hundreds and hundreds of young leaders have received scholarships to prepare for ministry. I wrote the book *Sandy: A Heart for God*, telling his story. It has been a best-selling book that continues to help both young people and their parents.

I had been with the Billy Graham organization for years. Eventually, with my new vision, I left Billy's organization to found Leighton Ford Ministries. Through it, we help young leaders around the world to lead like Jesus, for Jesus and to Jesus. The Arrow Leadership Program which I founded (later led by one of the men I mentored) has had an international impact on emerging leaders. And to this day I continue to mentor men and women involved in ministry leadership as a friend on their journeys.

I often think of the words of our Lord: "...unless a seed of wheat falls into the ground and dies, it stays alone. But if it dies, it multiplies."

The loss we feel for Sandy is still great. We would love to have him back again. But we also have discovered that it is often through love and loss that God's work grows.

August 2012

That first late night call, thirty one years ago, was very much in my mind as I drove by myself to Charlotte. It was nearly one a.m. when I walked into Craig's room in intensive care. It was full of people. Graham was there, of course, as well as several friends, a nurse, and a doctor. Craig was drinking some water and listening to the doctor explaining that he was not having a classical stroke, but the symptoms were similar. That included several seizures. An MRI was scheduled in the next hour to pinpoint the problem.

After the others left, I sat next to Craig. Holding his hand, I reminded him of the time when he had come to my bedside ten years before. I'd had a heart attack, and he had stayed with me then.

He then shared his story of what had happened that landed him in the hospital. He had been playing tennis with Graham. It was a hot afternoon. Suddenly, he realized that he couldn't pick up the balls. His left arm began to twitch out of control. Alarmed, they called 911 and the medics rushed him to emergency.

Despite what the doctor had said, Craig was still very anxious. His greatest worry was that he might have to have brain surgery, and that there might be a tumor. We talked about Sandy, and all the trauma our family had faced, including Debbie's two episodes of breast cancer. A wonderful Filipino nurse came in then to take care of him, monitor his vitals and lift our spirits.

When they took him for his MRI, I left with a hug and a prayer, and wearily went home. I knew that Debbie and Christine, her daughter, had managed to get the last two seats on a red-eye flight from Seattle; and our grandson, Ben, was coming the next morning from his summer job in Minnesota.

In all our minds, though, was the question: How serious is this event? If not life-threatening, how will it affect Craig's life...his practice?

The News: Good and Not So Good

By the next day we were told that there was no tumor, and no life-threatening problem. The seizures came from an abnormal blood vein in his brain that may have been there for years and which began to bleed under some kind of stress. Surgery to remove the small vessel was possible, but not desirable. The bleeding could be controlled by meds, and over time the seizures should go away.

All that was positive. But then Craig began to realize the restrictions that lay ahead. Now he is in a waiting time, with no driving or surgery for awhile, as he recovers.

Craig is a wonderful husband, father, son-in-law and physician. He is known as the doctor who prays with the parents when a baby is born. In fact, earlier that afternoon of his attack, one of his patients, a young mother with brain cancer, had asked him to come be with her. Although it was his day off, he went. He talked to her about the Lord, and led her to Christ in prayer. He truly is as he often says, "a minister in disguise."

So now he has been waiting, taking slow walks, enjoying time with Debbie, and wondering what is ahead. Is there a different plan for him?

A Friend in a Time of Need

Jeanie and I are asking those same questions. Recently I called a close and long time friend in Canada whose son also is a doctor. I told him about Craig and what had happened. He listened sympathetically, stunned by the news, and said he would keep Craig and us in his prayers. Then he reminded me of something very important.

"Do you remember what you wrote to me years ago when you were in Australia?"

No, I didn't remember. "What was that?" I asked.

"It was soon after Sandy died," he said. "I was supposed to go with you to the meetings in Australia but I couldn't make it. I still have the card you sent. You wrote, 'I sense that God is using me in a very special way, and that he is using Sandy's death to touch people's hearts.'

"You see," he continued, "it's one thing to speak to people's heads. It's more important to speak to their hearts. And even more basic, to speak to them out of our lives." Then he reminded me of how God used Sandy's death; and how he will use Craig in ways we cannot yet see.

Craig will be back soon to driving, and seeing patients again. But what is very clear is that he still will be able to say what he sang at Sandy's memorial service: "For me to live is Christ …" and out of his life, God will speak in ways we have yet to see. For Jesus' words are true:

Unless a grain of wheat falls into the earth and dies, it remains just a single grain; but if it dies, it bears much fruit. (John 12:24)

A View from the Sky

Two years ago at sunset, Jeanie and I were flying from Fort Myers on the west coast of Florida, to Charlotte. From the left side of the plane, over the gulf, we could see the sun, a great blazing ball suspended just above the water. It paused there in its radiance, and then in a few seconds, sank below the horizon.

At that moment the light spread widely across the sky in a glorious mix of the most radiant colors, seeming to light up the coast and fill the evening sky.

"Oh, look," I said to Jeanie, my heart filling with emotion. "That makes me think of Sandy. He was like a bright shining sun focused right where he was, glowing in the moment, reflecting the glory of his Lord. Then, and now, his life still shines more widely, more deeply than ever, in the lives he touched."

So we recall Sandy, and we wait with Craig, to see how the light of Christ will shine in ways we have yet to see.

Leighton Ford

Founder and President of Leighton Ford Ministries.

Author of books:
  Sandy: A Heart for God
  Transforming Leadership
  The Attentive Life

Dr. Ford's focus in recent years has been the mentoring of men and women who minister in leadership. Before starting Leighton Ford Ministries he preached the good news of Jesus Christ around the world. Now he is known as an artist of the soul and a friend on the journey.

A note from Vance: It was my privilege to attend an Arrowhead Leadership Conference led by Dr. Ford. Designed to help young leaders be more effective, it was a powerful influence in my life.

Fire is the test of gold; adversity, of strong men.

SENECA (LUCIUS ANNAEUS SENECA
(*ROMAN PHILOSOPHER & PLAYWRIGHT*
4 BC – AD 65)

Fire!

It was Easter Sunday morning, April 19, 1992. My husband, Roy, and I had driven into town from our ranch to attend church. The Easter Lilies that had been placed near the altar were especially lovely, I thought.

We had lived on the farm in Nebraska for years and had friends who attended that church and others that didn't. In our community, everyone seemed to know everyone else and if there was any trouble or need, most of them rushed to be of aid.

Many of our friends and acquaintances lived in the country, as we did. We'd reared our three children there and watched as our grand-children enjoyed the fresh air, farm work and sunflowers. Economics changed from time to time and so did the crops we planted, harvested and sold. It was hard work, but a good life.

The Unexpected

That our lives were about to be changed radically that Easter morn-ing, never entered our minds. But as the service proceeded, suddenly the telephone rang in the office that was situated adjacent to the pulpit. Phone calls are usually ignored on Sundays but it kept ringing, so the liturgist, Don Sampson, finally answered it. A moment later, he abruptly rushed out of the office.

"Roy! Trudy!" he shouted with alarm. "Your house is on fire!"

There was a collective gasp throughout the congregation and cries of dismay. Roy and I jumped up, raced to our car and drove out to the farm.

Even from a distance, we could see that a strong northerly wind was driving the flames into the three beautiful oak trees south of the house. We got there before the fire department, and yes, not only were the trees burning, but so was the house. We felt helpless. It was too far along for us to do anything. So we just sat in the car and watched it burn.

Caring People

Our neighbor had come over and had driven Roy's pickup away from the house. As soon as they heard, our son, John, and his wife, Millie, came, as well. Word had raced through the community. The Red Cross had arrived with sandwiches for everyone and they were shocked that Roy and I were so calm about it all. I think we were just numb. We simply could not believe what was happening.

We finally figured out what had caused the fire. I had made a casserole to share with John and Millie for Easter dinner. Roy plugged in our grill instead of the toaster oven to cook the casserole while we were in church. Not the thing to do. The fire started.

The fire department did everything it could and by early evening things were under control.

The Aftermath

We stayed with John and Millie until our insurance company found an apartment for us in Central City, a town of about 3,000. We found out what it was like to live in the "city" but we both agreed that country life was much better. We lived in the furnished apartment for five months and Roy drove out to the farm every day.

Our daughters, Paula, a nurse, and Julie, an attorney, came from Kansas and California. They went through a lot of stuff for us and salvaged some things. We felt so blessed that many of our photos were on the shelf in our bedroom so they didn't get too badly damaged.

For me the saddest part of all was that the quilts I had made over the past few years were destroyed. Many hours of work had gone into each one that I had carefully designed.

I tried to save my wedding dress. I took it to the cleaners, but it still smelled like smoke.   On Monday morning, Millie took me to a thrift shop in Columbus and found some clothes for us. I kept thinking of all the things we lost but I was fully aware that they were just that: things.

A friendship club I had attended held a personal shower for me and I got so many lovely gifts. The church also gave us a shower. In fact, the whole community participated with so much generosity that we were overwhelmed. I never had to buy another towel or kitchen or bath set.

By June the contractors started building our new home. We made some changes. For instance, we'd had a fireplace that didn't work, so we put in a wood stove which was great. It really put out the heat, just like I remember Grandpa's furnace used to do.

By September we moved into our second new home here. What a blessing.

Trudy Creutzberg

Trudy's quilts were absolute treasures that won prizes at fairs. It is a shame that they were lost. She has made a number of them since then, though, helping to keep one of America's heritages alive. She also crochets lovely afghans and other items.

Trudy and Roy, shown on the left, are now retired and live in Central City, Nebraska.

Rainbows In Cobwebs

*The thing that impresses me the most about America is
the way parents obey their children.*

KING EDWARD VIII
(*LATER THE DUKE OF WINDSOR
1894 - 1972*)

Mikie

Mental retardation, schizophrenia, multiple personality disorder and autism were just a few of the many labels given to Mikie, a three year old being evaluated for his variety of bizarre behavior patterns, including not talking. These labels came from doctors, pediatricians and child psychologists.

What in the world was I doing sitting on this medical review board for the state of Washington? At age twenty-three I was the newest and youngest professional called to be on the board. As well as intimidated, initially I was shocked listening to these experts giving their diagnoses and conclusions to their observations.

On the Spot

All attention was focused on me as I was introduced as Miss Volny, Speech Pathologist from the Seattle Hearing and Speech Center. It was my turn to give my report and recommendations after my own extensive battery of testing of the child they had just labeled; testing that I had done just a month prior.

Suddenly I became energized fighting for Mikie, because I didn't agree with any of the labels being placed on him. I was confident that I knew the answer to the confusion regarding the boy. I didn't and wouldn't label Mikie. Instead, in my reporting, I would present his level of child development skills.

"Mikie is three but he has the speech of a one year old," I said, looking straight into the eyes of the medical professionals who were evaluating me. "He is able to get his way and control his environment through non verbal means. Mikie has developed a unique pattern of communication without the use of speech. That's what causes all his erratic behavior. He isn't deaf or retarded, as proved by my testing, but rather, quite bright. That's not untypical of the many children I see and have worked with. And, quite frankly, I've achieved remarkable results."

"So…your recommendations, Miss Volny?" the Chairman asked.

"My recommendation," I said, "is that I treat Mikie for speech and language therapy twice a week at the Seattle Speech and Hearing Center. He, along with his parents and older siblings will receive the needed help in behavior modification skills that require Mikie to talk so they all will understand the therapy and apply it at home in order to have complete success."

After reviewing the reports from all the members of the board present, they unanimously voted that I get started immediately. After six months there would be an update hearing on his progress. I was thrilled with the decision and arranged for therapy to start the following week.

Leaping Into Battle

Tuesday morning. The battle was on. I took Mikie, screaming and kicking, up a ramp to my therapy room on the second floor. There were no elevators. His mom watched with concern from the reception room. The same thing happened on four subsequent visits.

My colleagues' explanation to visitors who were troubled about his disruptive clamoring was, "Oh it's only Vicky…at it again. He must be a new client."

The Process

In my therapy room, Mikie had one distraction and one choice. Before him was a small chair and table strategically set up with a Fischer Price toy barn along with many plastic animals.

I made him sit in the chair. Initially, the toys distracted him and he stopped crying. However, when I began some interaction with him, followed by a simple request, he blatantly threw the toys onto the floor. I picked up one toy and told him to pick up another. He was angry and not about to comply. He anxiously began walking around the room, banging the walls and yelling again. I ignored his behavior so as not to reinforce it with any attention.

He noticed when I walked over to a cupboard. Out came my primary reinforcements: Chocolate M&M's. That caught his interest, immediately. He had watched me get the candy from the shelf. This time when I told him what to do, he complied. He sat in his chair and got an M&M. He picked up each toy from the floor and. each toy netted another M&M. He followed other simple commands I gave him and again, he was rewarded with an M&M. He was having fun.

Hope

Mikie didn't know it, but step one of a six-month journey had begun. I had won the battle already with that first scrimmage. Our first therapy session was a huge success. Mikie was teachable. Now there was hope.

His mom was invited up to the room to join us for a few minutes to talk about the day's results. As soon as she walked in the door, Mikie changed his behavior. He ran around screaming and hitting the walls again. She hugged him. "Mommy is here," she said soothingly. "I'll make it all better." I was witnessing Mom as a trigger for Mikie's meltdowns, followed by lots of reinforcement that was enabling his patterns of behavior. I knew she was struggling with a decision. To her credit, and I think desperation, she believed me on how well her son had done. She would return again in two days as arranged.

More Progress

For the next four sessions, Mikie continued screaming and fighting when separating from Mom in the reception room. However, he stopped at the fifth. Another battle won. He had learned that no matter what he did we were still going up the ramp. He couldn't change my decision, or

Mom's. His mother was rewarded on the fifth visit as she watched her son holding my hand while quietly walking up the ramp.

I arranged for her to watch every therapy session from then on – through a one-way mirror. She was stunned by what she saw. Mikie was listening, following commands and beginning to talk. We were making great progress in therapy. The commands had changed from following directions to talking. He started with vowels, consonants and syllables. As he graduated to words, saying them correctly, I would give him that object or a picture of it as the reinforcement. As his vocabulary increased, I used more pictures and stickers. These became prizes which he took home with him.

Mikie was learning quickly that talking is needed in order to get what he wanted from me in therapy. Now my goal was to transition these lessons to the outside. His family needed to get Mikie talking at home.

Solving the Home Problem

Since Mikie was the baby in the household, his older siblings had always guessed his needs and desires and would give things to him without his asking. At meals he walked around the table, taking what he wanted off everyone else's plates. He wasn't required to ask for anything. It was time for a change.

I gave Mom her first assignment when I felt Mikie was ready. I told her to make him say at least a one-syllable word in order to get dessert that evening. I urged her to look him in the eye, making sure he understood exactly what she wanted him to do. And no matter what he or others did she must not give him the treat until he said at least one syllable.

The story Mom related to me at our next session has become my signature story of hope and blessing for my work.

"I had cookies for dessert," she said. "I asked everyone to say, 'Cookie,' in order to get one. Dad, and the three older children said, 'Cookie,' and got one. Mikie wanted a cookie. He put out his hand… then screamed…ran around the house…and hit his head on the wall when I didn't give it to him. He kept up the behavior for quite a while.

The other children started crying, telling me that I was mean and that Mikie couldn't say, 'Cookie.' I let them know he could and he would have to in order to get one."

The fight was still going on while she was standing at the sink doing dishes. Mikie then came and stood beside her pulling at her dress so she would look down at him. With face scowling he shouted out very clearly, "COOKIE!" and stamped his foot. She handed him a cookie, he ran away, and she finished the dishes, smiling.

The Review

By the time Mikie's case came up for review by the medical board, he was functioning at his age level. His behavior was one hundred percent improved. He was communicating now with short sentences. He was a well-adjusted and happy little boy with a family who loved him enough that they were willing to learn alongside him, while showing tough love and achieving wonderful results.

Mikie passed the review board with flying colors. All his labels disappeared. File closed.

Vicky Burgess

MSPA (Master of Speech Pathology and Audiology), Speaker, Writer, Teacher.

Author of: Kisses From God: A Mother's Story About The Faithfulness of God After The Death Of Her Son

For years, Vicky taught large classes of women at EV Free Church in Fullerton, CA. and is a popular speaker elsewhere on various subjects.

She resides in Southern California with her husband, Brian, who has retired from his law practice.

Vicky shares more of her delightful self in her video. View it on www. RainbowsInCobwebs.com.

Rainbows In Cobwebs

The best way out is always through.

ROBERT FROST
(*AMERICAN POET 1874-1963*)

I Am Not My Past

Sixteen going on seventeen was a fascinating age for me. I knew everything and yet, comprehended so little. It was a time when I listened to my mother and others in my life but didn't hear what they were trying to tell me. That led to lying, wrong decisions, deceiving myself and finally, a shattered heart.

Manny was a major player in that episode of my life. He gave a testimony in the church I attended by sharing his story about life on the streets, joining a gang, going to prison and how God turned it all around. As I was sitting there listening to him, I remember thinking, *Well, if God can do it for him, He can do it for me, too. I'm not that bad.*

The Mistake

I was so excited about the possibility of change that I asked Manny to do a Bible Study with me. Looking back, I realize I should have found a woman to ask, instead. And I should have listened to my mom when she said, "Valerie, don't do it." Thinking I knew better, I dismissed her warning. Big mistake.

Manny moved quickly into a personal relationship with me, telling me he loved me, assuring me that we would be together forever and, finally, saying that he was going to marry me. Slowly but surely, I started isolating myself from others, ending friendships and pushing everyone away, including my mom, until Manny was my only friend. My world revolved around him, God, church and school.

There were other warning signs. He had an explosive temper, for one thing. For another, he always needed money – mine. It was clear that Manny was not the person I should have been with. But, unfortunately, like many women (young and old), I made excuses for him, rationalized his behavior and stayed.

The Proposal

One evening, in an empty diner in the 42nd Street Terminal in New York, Manny proposed and I said, "Yes." That was it. No fuss, no grand romantic gesture…nothing.

As I was getting ready for the wedding, it was clear to everyone except me that I was making a mistake. But they said nothing because they weren't sure how I would respond. The closer I got to the wedding, the more doubts I started having because of the many things that I was noticing in Manny.

The Warning

One Sunday after church I was walking across the street when one of the leaders came up to me and said, "Separation is not divorce." That's it. No explanation. Nothing. Just, "Separation is not divorce." For whatever reason, that made sense to me, and it was like an answer to my prayers. Still, I hesitated. As I was deciding whether or not to end my engagement and cancel all the wedding plans, there were so many things that coursed through my mind. I didn't want people to talk about me, for one thing; and I was afraid of what they would think. I didn't want to be single again, either, and have to restart the dating process. I didn't want to be the reason that Manny gave up and went back to the life he left behind. I didn't want to lose all the emotional down payments I had made toward our relationship.

In life you have to learn when to let go and cut your losses, because holding on when you should have let go sometimes means losing so much more, and it can mean losing yourself.

One Problem Too Many

I thought things would get better, but I was wrong. The final straw came when I discovered that a significant amount of money was missing from my account. I called Manny to ask him what happened to the money. "I went shopping," he said. I was dumbfounded. So of course I asked him the next "logical" question. "Well, did you get me anything?" "No," he said.

I called the church leader who had told me that separation was not divorce. When he picked up the phone, it was as though a dam broke. I shared four and a half years of frustration and disappointments in about an hour. When I was finished, his one piece of advice to me was to call Manny back and make it clear that I wanted out.

So that's exactly what I did. Manny knew that I was serious and he was livid. "I am coming over right now to get all my stuff!" he said angrily. He was at my house within the hour. I was greeted with a flow of curses and insults. The whole time he was yelling, I just kept looking at him and thinking, "Oh dear God. I can't believe I did it. I can't believe I made it out. It's really over." It took everything in me to restrain my smile. It was finally over.

It Will Get Better

Going through the breakup was like going through a divorce. I felt lost. I was heartbroken. More than that, I was shattered. I had spent so long trying to be what Manny wanted me to be, and who others thought I should be, that I didn't know who I was anymore.

There were times when I thought I didn't want to live – and yet I knew I did.

"I wish I could fast forward my life and see if I actually made it through."

Sexting in Suburbia, Lifetime Movie

Those were among the last words of a girl who committed suicide after being bullied by her schoolmates because of a mistake she made that they wouldn't let her forget.

Can I tell you a secret, that's not really a secret? As long as you have breath in you, you have life. At this very moment, you are alive, and it is possible for things to turn around. I learned that things do get better and that the best is yet to come.

There are a lot of people who have gone through tough times and attempted suicide but they survived and today they are living to testify that it gets better. They can say with an assurance that suicide would have been a permanent, deadly solution to a temporary problem.

It's easy to forget who you are when you've been scared for so long, pretending and trying to fit someone else's image of you. The journey to discovering who you are, and who you want to be, starts with a decision, a decision to realize that you are so much more than you know.

Never Alone

You want to know why I love Jesus and hold on so tenaciously to my faith? One of the reasons is because when no one else was there, when it seemed like no one else cared and no one understood, I could ALWAYS turn to God and cry and talk and write; and then there would be this peace, this knowing inside of me that everything was going to be all right. Little things would happen that would just let me know that He heard me, whether it was a package in the mail, an unexpected hug, a note or word of encouragement from a stranger. Encouragement.

When I needed Him most, He was not this Awesome God that sat on His throne looking down at me and indulging me. He was my friend that stuck closer than a brother and who loved me at all times, no matter what. There were certain times when I couldn't explain to people what I was feeling, because I didn't even know myself; but my Friend knew and understood.

Turning Points

Working through and gradually shedding my fears took time and brave steps forward. Turning points in my life were:

- Becoming a Christian, because that's when I learned that I was created in God's image and that I was fearfully and wonderfully made and loved;

- Ending my engagement, which freed me from people's opinions because I stood up for myself and made a decision for myself without permission from anyone;

- Studying abroad in Paris, which I did after the breakup because for the first time I was on my own and away from everything that I knew. That was the time that I defined for myself what I wanted and who I wanted to be. It was also the time I decided that I was going to live on the other side of fear, no longer seeking the approval of others.

And more. Other steps forward included a month of study in Spain; going to conferences; getting my Bachelors and then my Masters Degrees in Social Work; and starting my own business.

Yes, I had other relationships, and yes, I would like to be married; but I came to the conclusion that I didn't need to be married to be free and fulfilled. I am enjoying life and all that it has to offer.

If you're single, be assured that your time to walk down the aisle and say, "I do," may someday come, but if it does, don't do it prematurely, and don't do it out of desperation or for liberation. Whatever your relationship status is, appreciate the beauty that this stage of your life is offering, and know that it is possible to be whole and content. I am!

Valerie Jeannis

Valerie Jeannis is one woman on a
mission to capture the hearts and
imaginations of young women,
    to inspire them to say yes to their lives,
       take action toward achieving their dreams
       and realize success earlier in life. She
          continues to partner with others to bring
            the message that all of that is possible.

She is the author of:
I Am Beautiful – Changing the Way You See Yourself
Valerie lives in New York, NY

Rainbows In Cobwebs

*Music must take rank as the highest of the fine arts – as the one which,
more than any other, ministers to human welfare.*

HERBERT SPENCER
(ENGLISH PHILOSOPHER 1820-1903)

Archie and Me

Archie (his preferred name) or Art, as I called him, really was a good man. We simply were completely different people. He came into our family at a time when Mom really needed his love and companionship. Like many children today, and being the youngest of three, I was a self-centered and protected child who was born with exceptional talents in music. These talents were encouraged and nurtured by the family, at times to a fault.

Previous Challenges

Archie had no formal education beyond the 4th or 5th grade; and quite frankly, even as a teenager, I held that against him. However, he came from a poor family and it was not unusual for children of his status to enter the work force early, with no time or extra money to attend school. There were other setbacks for him, too. Like me, when he was very young, his Dad died. His mother spent her later years in a mental institution, as did his sister.

After leaving his home on a farm in the Bitterroot Mountains in Montana, he worked much of his life in the Butte Copper mines. He was actually my second cousin through marriage and met Mom through the family. After they married, he stopped working in the mines because Mom insisted. She was afraid he would die of "miner's con," or miner's consumption, a severe asthma that was very common among men in that kind of work.

A Substitute for Mining

Mom taught Archie the photography business that she had learned from her father. Her father, in turn, had learned it from his father. Through the generations photography was a family profession and Mom and Archie entered a partnership of earning a living that way. She knew he didn't have the natural ability to see the detail and beauty in photographs, so she remained the artist in that partnership. He specialized in taking professional pictures at weddings.

My Aunt Martha lived with her family across the street from us in Butte. They also were professional photographers and that added an interesting and competitive dimension to life most of the time.

Mom took pictures for customers in our front basement and then stayed up all night to process the "sittings," as they were called. We lived with pictures washing in the bathtub, and hanging all over the house to dry. I would fall asleep in the living room watching her hand paint the enlargements for early delivery the next day.

Creating Beauty

Neither Mom nor her sister ever learned to drive a car. Since Mom didn't drive, Archie took her everywhere, including trips into the mountains to take pictures that were processed into "Kodachrome" slides for transferring to printed postcards. Their business in postcards thrived throughout the Northwest. Later, they learned to develop and print their own colored photography, also in our basement.

While they traveled the roads of the Northwest to take thousands of pictures, Mom's emphasis was on flowers and skies, but Archie wanted pictures of bridges and roads which, by the way, were often the best selling postcards.

Together they worked it out, but not without some conflict. Mom had a natural ability to fall asleep as they drove down the road. Suddenly she would wake up just as they were passing flowers. 'STOP!" she would shout. "I want to snap those wild flowers along the road."

Of course, it was often too dangerous to stop, so Art would get frustrated as she insisted and they would proceed to argue. He would pull over when possible; but often they would need to wait hours for clouds to move into beautiful formations, or for the sun to shine with proper lighting. Since I frequently went along on their jaunts, I tried to understand these loud encounters, but it was easier to relate to Mom's point of view because I also wanted those particular pictures to be taken.

Opposites

When he wasn't in the mines or doing photography, Archie was, among other things, a hunter and farmer by nature. I neither enjoyed killing animals nor cared much for the value of growing and eating vegetables. I especially disliked weeding the garden in the Montana summers in Butte. However, I was encouraged to do it because payment was included in my allowances.

There was another dimension to the weeding and being outside: I could hear music in the movement of the weeds and trees blowing in the wind. Unlike Archie, I was artistically minded and always looked for beauty in nature.

In music, Archie liked Roy Rogers, Gene Autry and other country greats while, at that time, I didn't. I remember leaving the room when their music was played. Since then, having had a life-long profession in music, I can understand and appreciate most all genres of music and art. I became extremely successful in teaching classes of music appreciation that focused on the values of jazz, rock, popular and "cowboy" music as well as classical.

My Escape

When my brother would call me to work around the yard or do chores, such as hanging paper on the walls of the garage he was converting to an apartment for family rental income, my escape was to get approval immediately from my mother to practice the piano.

Later, when I was in my teens, I built a stereo system encompassing the old family radio for an amplifier for playing classical LP records. I would turn the volume up just as loud as possible on various symphonies, like Beethoven's Fifth, to demonstrate the effectiveness of the large corner speakers I had built and installed in every corner of the living room. That never went over well with either Mom or Archie. They would say, "Turn that music down!" So it was piano practicing that again was my break away from the realities of the moment that seemed debilitating to a kid growing up from age six through the teen years.

I don't think Archie ever understood my need for music. Nor did the frictions between us end until I went to the University of Montana at Missoula to become a music major. There I was encouraged to practice the bassoon and piano whenever time allowed. They became my majors in undergraduate studies, and later I turned to theory and composition and the love of teaching others about the importance of music in their lives.

Some Bonding

Archie and I did have some common experiences on which to build our father-son relationship. We both loved animals, specifically dogs and horses. I was given a very young horse by my Aunt Adele when I was eight years old. She and her husband also lived across the street in Butte. They were not photographers but they were concerned about us.

The colt, not yet weaned from his mare that was to be killed for food at the local slaughterhouse, cost my aunt the huge sum (in those days) of $10.00. She thought I needed the experience to mature properly.

Archie, having been raised on a farm, had trained his own horses. We have pictures of him performing tricks with these favored animals. In fact, the most serious injury in his life came when his most beloved horse fell on him and broke Archie's back. He never blamed the horse! "It wasn't his fault," he'd say. "It was my own careless-ness that caused me to get hurt." To this day, I greatly admire him for those unselfish thoughts.

His broken back, that never mended properly, caused him to be bent forward the rest of his life. He would never get an operation; and the way he walked made his pants bag in the back so they hung practically down to his knees, similar to the young people today. At the time, and even now, I dislike that look that can reflect visual impressions related to the character of a man.

Cubby's Misadventures

When I was confronted with raising the colt in our backyard, Archie came to my rescue. "Come on, Mertz," he said, calling me by my mother's maiden name which also was my middle name. "We'll build a small barn for him." Archie was extremely helpful in obtaining the wood and constructing a home for the colt. It was needed, especially during the cold Montana winters that could reach 60 degrees below zero.

Cubby became the horse's affectionate name, but he wasn't popular in the Floral Boulevard neighborhood where we lived. In fact, he was disliked intensely because he would step over the fence adjacent to his barn that was supposed to keep him jailed, and have a great time roaming around helping himself to fresh green grass from various well groomed lawns nearby. He always would end up at home at feeding time and a night of sleep, though, through every kind of weather.

When the time came to break and ride Cubby, it was my job to do it! The neighbors all gathered around to see me get bucked off. They were ready to enjoy the sight with laughter. I had no saddle, for I couldn't afford one, so I eased up onto the colt's back. Cubby turned his head around and didn't make a move. It was as if he was saying: "What took you so long to take your first ride, Kid?" Needless to say, we had become good friends over the years.

A Generous Offer

Archie reached out to me in other ways, too. He saw to it that I had his beautiful and coveted 1935 Ford Coupe to drive to Missoula for my freshman year in college. It had mechanical brakes that never worked correctly and the car was a real devil to drive down the highway over those 120 miles of winter highway between Butte and Missoula. I wish I had that car now, though, because I understand values in the field of collectibles.

Sorrow

Study at the University, as wonderful as it was for me, also brought some sadness from home. After I left, Cubby disappeared. No one would tell me what happened to my much-loved horse. Archie had promised to take him to a nearby farm to spend out his days in the fields. But as far as I ever knew, he just wandered off. I never heard differently and assumed he had a good life clear to the end. Maybe I will see him again one day. Who knows?

I Was Fortunate

All in all, Archie was a very good man and stepfather. He portrayed masculinity and was a male role model for me. He was hard working and knowledgeable in practical ways that, even though they weren't always in my fields of interest, they were important for me to observe and evaluate. We were truly fortunate to have him come into our lives and especially to care for Mom to the end of her life.

The environment in which a person grows, and the circumstances into which we are thrown or choose, require emotional and intellectual adjustments throughout our time on earth. If we could start out in life knowing ahead of time what we discover as the years move us along, our perspectives might be completely different.

Would they be better? That certainly is difficult to determine. Here's what Mark Twain said on the subject: "Life would be infinitely happier if we could only be born at the age of 80, and gradually approach 18."

Don Hardisty

Owner, Don's Collectibles. Factory Certified Expert in everything Bossons. Specializing in Authentication, procurement and sales of Bossons, Hummels and U.S. Coins.

Music Professor Emeritus New Mexico State University (1969-1998) BME, MME, University of Montana (1955-56). Doctor of Music Arts (DMA), Eastman School of University of Rochester (1969).

Don served in the United States Army as a Specialist in the field of music – two years in active duty performing in bands on the West Coast, and then in the Second Army Band where he also was Associate Director of the 2nd Army Choral Group at Ft. Meade, MD. performing mostly in D.C. and all over the East Coast.

Rainbows In Cobwebs

Hope is like the sun, which, as we journey toward it,
casts the shadow of our burden behind us.

SAMUEL SMILES
(SCOTTISH AUTHOR & REFORMER 1812-1904)

Angels Spread a Cushion

"I think God allowed this awful thing in your life to prevent you from being too pretty, Lynn," my mom blurted out one day. She was referring to a serious eye accident I had sustained at the age of seven. A nine-year-old neighbor boy had tried to pop the bubbles in a friend's bubble hat with a grape stake fence stick. He hit my eye instead.

Intending to comfort me with her statement, it only caused me to question the goodness of God. In an amazing coincidence, my dear Grandma had suffered a similar fate in her twenties when she was chopping wood on the farm. I never realized she had lost her vision in one eye, though, because her positive, sweet, godly spirit pervaded everything she did.

A Turn Around

Two years later, my brother and I spent a month in the summer on my grandparents' farm a thousand miles away. During a church service one Wednesday night, the pastor summoned anyone who wanted peace and joy in her/his life to come forward to the altar and pray with him.

These two attributes were definitely what Grandma had, and I wanted them also, so I went forward and asked Jesus to take control of my life. I told him I was sorry for rebelling against him and I wanted to accept his promise of living with him forever.

Thereafter, Grandma encouraged my love of music and started

teaching me the hymns she sang around the house. Fortunately, my parents were also very musical. Dad was a choir director in church; and Mom was an organist and vocalist. We lived in Anaheim, California. When I was asked to be a church soloist in Long Beach, despite their duties at their church, they dutifully drove me back and forth to and from Anaheim every Sunday – for $5 a week.

After Mom believed she couldn't teach me much more vocally, I started studying with a coach in Santa Ana. I won many vocal awards and eventually auditioned for the Metropolitan Opera in Los Angeles. I reached the semifinals at age 18.

Then I Fell in Love

I met Dave at the church where I had sung for years. I was a junior in college and he had just finished his sophomore final exams in pre-med. I adored him but he already had two strikes against him. He was younger than I; and he wanted to practice medicine. I didn't want to marry a future doctor. Yet I couldn't deny our feelings for one another. Would I be willing to put my music career on hold so I could teach and support him through medical school? Would I be willing to wait even longer to have kids?

You guessed right. In two years, we graduated, and were married.

Roadblock

Our marriage took place in 1970 when reverse discrimination was occurring. That meant that minorities were accepted into medical school before Caucasians. Thus, Dave was forced to register for medical school out of the country – in Mexico – where American wives were not allowed to work.

So we reacted the most prudent way we could: he went to Mexico for school and I moved back in with my parents and kept my teaching position. Not a fun year for either of us, but Dave passed what seemed to be the impossible medical boards after the first year and was accepted by Temple Medical School in Philadelphia.

Also, amazingly, I found a music specialist teaching position in the suburbs two weeks after we arrived there. We were able to move into the student apartments after a few months and though barely making ends meet, we discovered most of our neighbors had the same problem.

Something Was Missing

In three years Dave graduated and was accepted for internship at Los Angeles County USC Medical Center, so we bought a little home in Norwalk, midway between the medical center and our parents in Orange County. There our children, Kathleen and Mike, were born, just two years apart.

It was at that point that we started to sense a void in our spiritual lives and realized that we didn't have the tools to lead our children and ourselves in the right direction.

With friends' encouragement we began to search the Bible for more guidance in how the Lord wanted us to live and interact with the kids. Dave was at the hospital so much we rarely saw him, so these were learning and growing years. Later, we moved into a large home.

I wish I could say that from then on, it was mostly uphill. Unfortunately, I can't. Rather, in just a few years, we would step onto a sled of trouble that would take us careening downhill at breakneck speed.

The Summer of 1985

I was struggling with my balance. I experienced extreme difficulty climbing our three flights of stairs in the house. At my husband's insistence, I sought the advice of a neurologist friend of his. The diagnosis was not good: Multiple Sclerosis!

The only people I knew with the disease had extreme cases, which caused me to feel hopeless. That same summer Dave and I were invited to step into leadership positions at Forest Home Summer Camp in the San Bernardino Mountains – as camp doctor and soloist, respectively.

Miraculous Encounter

One afternoon, as I went to my favorite rock to pray and meditate, I fell asleep. I dreamt that I was sitting in a wheelchair, singing, with my hands raised in praise to God. All of a sudden I awakened and sadly questioned: How could I be praising God in a wheelchair?

As audibly as I am talking to you right now, I heard a voice calmly say, "Lynn, whatever condition you are in, I will use you." There was no doubt in my mind that it was the Lord Jesus Christ speaking to me. Then I realized the significance of II Corinthians, Chapter 12, verse 9 in the Bible that gives the account of Jesus saying to the Apostle Paul: "My grace is sufficient for you, for my power is perfected in weakness." I believed that promise. It meant that Christ was not limited by my disabilities.

Over the next ten years, my legs began to weaken to the point of needing a cane. Then came the walker. And finally a wheelchair. Through it all, I discovered that the Lord's promises have remained faithful.

Do you remember how I didn't want to marry a future doctor? Now, I saw why it was essential that I did, because after contracting MS, the initial expense and incapacity of the disease required someone who could afford the specialized equipment and medication it required. My husband has never griped about the requirements, even the need to carry me at times.

Angels Spread a Cushion

MS didn't prevent the onset of other maladies. In 2010 I was diagnosed with breast cancer. That required a double mastectomy. While I was anticipating my final reconstruction surgery, a frightening and ghastly incident took place.

I was in my small scooter and I pressed the button for the elevator in our home. The door opened, I pushed forward and wheeled into... space!

I only recall being lowered to the ground gently, like angels were cushioning my fall. I was catapulted fifteen feet through nothingness to the ground floor and there was no way I could have survived had I not had divine intervention.

Our tenant heard the fall, thank God, and because Dave was at work, called 911. I was unaware of any injuries initially. X-rays showed, though, that I had sustained a compound femur fracture and several broken toes. That was it! Humanly speaking, it should have been much worse. A week in the hospital plus three weeks in rehab, and I was on my way to a full recovery from the accident.

Rainbows? Hope? Victory? Where?

Where? I saw hope and victory in every miserable situation. There were the special times, too. After all, it isn't everyone who hears the audible voice of the Lord Jesus Christ, speaking directly to her. It isn't everyone who can fall down an elevator shaft with MS and cancer having ravaged her body and still survive. It's a wondrous thing to be touched by angels.

In the meantime, our two kids gave us seven grandchildren, whom we adore, and my husband still has his position as an Emergency Room Physician. I continue to sing with arms uplifted (when the song inspires it) from my position in a wheelchair.

Life has held more than I ever anticipated. It didn't evolve the way I expected but I wouldn't trade my experiences for anything in the world; and I mean that sincerely.

You see, I discovered that I could rely on God's leading and in the process rise above life's circumstances.

Lynn Reid, Vocalist and Speaker

*If you go to our website, you will see Lynn's **video**. Click on it to hear her additions to this story. She even sang for us spontaneously. You'll hear that, too.*

Also, you'll be led to her website, where you can get her music CD of wonderful hymn medleys and original songs called Shadow of His Wings, as well as various musings (blogs). She adds articles to the website on a regular basis.

Note from Margaret: I've been in Lynn's beautiful home twice now. Despite all she has been through, her self-confidence, sweet spirit and giftedness are evident. I also had the pleasure of meeting her accomplished husband.

Rainbows in Cobwebs
Stories of Hope in the Storms of Life

IV

IMPRESSIVE

LIGHTNING & THUNDER

Lightning and thunder can...

Frighten animals and children (and maybe – you);
Be destructive to buildings, animals and people;
Destroy forests;
Be a warning of worse things to come;
Electrify the air.

Lightning and thunder also can...

Be exciting;
Provide great entertainment;
Fill the heart with wonder and awe;
Place life in perspective;
Bring out the noble and caring in people;
Inspire people to create art, writing, cinema;
Inspire others to accomplish great feats.

When you are frightened by something in

your life, find peace in the realization that

this, too, will pass. Meet it with bravado

and faith, looking up, knowing that you

aren't alone.

Rainbows In Cobwebs

*…Laughter and Memories, and
a few regrets…*

HILAIRE BELLOC
(ANGLO-FRENCH WRITER & HISTORIAN
1870-1953)

Number Two

In 1940, when I was five years old, my dad built a small house deep in a eucalyptus grove at the edge of Castro Valley, California. He cleared an area of poison oak, weeds, and a few saplings; then set about doing the job alone.

Contractors that Dad had met through contacts at his job donated their scraps. He hauled most of the goods tied onto the roof or fenders of our 1937 Model A Ford and worked on the house in the evenings and on weekends.

The project began with his erecting a two-seater outhouse that sat well back in the woods. The home itself gradually took shape. Soon, Mom, Dad, my three sisters, and I moved in. The outside wall of the house was still covered with tarpaper, and there was no gas, no electricity, and no water. But we were in our own home. No more crowded apartments.

Manly Tasks

As the only boy in the family, I was allowed to take on the title of "Mom's Little Helper." It was my mother, of course, who bestowed this auspicious honor. Among other things, I hauled water to the house by the half-bucket full from the pump outside (I was too small to handle a full pail).

The girls had less joyful tasks and never were called, "Mom's Little Helper," although I seem to recall Mom sometimes referring to my sister, Mary, as "Momma's Monday Helper." That was on laundry day, a much lower status job than mine; because I was the one who walked all the way out to the roadway by myself to check our mailbox each day. I could even walk a half-mile to the store and bring back one or two items that Mom needed.

But mostly I just hauled buckets of water to the house. Soon, a different kind of water bucket would tumble me from my newfound sense of importance.

From Texas to California

My mother was accustomed to living without household utilities—she had done so in her one-room house in Meadow, Texas, where she and Dad had lived after their wedding. A year later, after Mary was born and had achieved the robust age of two months, Mom braved the trip to California with her baby.

She traveled with other passengers in a Pierce-Arrow touring car. It stopped overnight at scarce travel lodges or cabins for passengers to alight and try to get a few hours' sleep.

Baby Mary was not too happy about the journey. She let her feelings be known concerning road conditions and the vehicle's clunky suspension system. Her complaints continued through the night – just to be sure that Mom got the message.

Dad followed in relative comfort, caring for cattle aboard a freight train.

A Better Plan

It was after a series of apartments, and three more kids, that Dad got the idea to buy a lot and build a house.

I was never aware that we were deprived, somehow, in that tarpaper shack. When Dad got home from work, he would sometimes play games with us and go along with the constant changes we made to the rules. Sometimes he would light one more kerosene lantern, take out his guitar and sing songs that he had learned in Texas. Some were sad; others were ditties with a confusion of rhyming lyrics; all were stories told to music.

The Bucket

One day two of my sisters, while playing in the woods, got into the poison oak. The girls were miserable for days. My dad set out to eliminate poison oak from an area within a wide swath of our house. He worked alone pulling vines off the trees and raking them into a pile to be burned.

I had my problems, too. While we were visiting a new neighbor, I needed to use their outhouse. When I told my mom, she whispered my dilemma to the lady of the house. That lady, a big woman with a brood of kids of her own, took me out to her back porch and asked, "Number one or number two?"

Now, I had never in all my five years of life, ever heard those terms in the connection she intended. I automatically guessed at her meaning, an early failing that plagues me to this day. I assumed she wanted to know how many poops I would make; and I thought, surely no more than one. When I said, "One," she pointed to a large bucket there on the back porch, and promptly left me to my privacy.

I stared at that bucket, which was almost full of water, and wondered how in the world I was going to sit on the thing. While studying the matter, my one and only poop made its appearance in my pants.

My mother was mortified. She rushed me home, stripped her little helper, and doused me with a pail of water that I had brought to the house earlier. Once I was scrubbed and clothed, she asked me what had happened. I didn't have a chance to answer because at that moment my dad stumbled into the house groaning.

Extreme Misery

Dad had earlier announced that the fire he had lit to burn the poison oak, was out. But apparently, during his forestry experiment, the wind had shifted. A massive dose of poison oak smoke wafted into his lungs, and deposited poison oak oil all over his body. The aftermath had just kicked in.

Later, when Mom sent me to his bedside. I was awe-struck to see my father lying there with multiple blisters on his forehead, neck, and arms. It might have been my imagination, but I swear I saw those blisters undulate on his legs and chest as I watched. Worse, a layer of white death covered every visible portion of his body. (Later, I learned it was just calamine lotion, but I had never before seen so much of it.)

"Sonny," he rasped, "I feel the fires of hell, and I won't be around long. You have to be the man of the house."

I stood there, stunned. I had been elevated from "Mom's Little Helper," all the way to "Man of the House," yet I hadn't even been able to handle a Number Two situation.

A New Future

Dad got over his misery, but his sense of the dramatic stayed around for years. A few months and a few more poison oak infections later, he sold the house. The water was turned on in the tarpaper shack for the first time on that final day as we were leaving.

Mom's last action was to print our house number in chalk on the tarpaper near the front door. She did it with flair, and a look of satisfaction. Dad snapped her picture. Mom probably was thinking good riddance to a tarpaper shack that had been nothing but hard work. But perhaps that was simply her way of putting the lid on a year of miserable itches and ugly skin eruptions for everyone but me. I was the only one in our family who never got the slightest bit of poison oak. In my mind, that made up a little for the poop calamity.

Hoyt Huggins
Author: Wingate's Spaceship

A little more information:

At age 17, I joined the United States Air Force as a high school dropout, and retired 22 years later as a Major with a college degree. I am a walking ad for what a military career can do for an energetic and curious person eager to learn and serve.

I had fascinating assignments in Britain, France, Germany, Pakistan, and Japan. In the States I served at bases in California, Wyoming, Missouri, Minnesota, Texas, and Oklahoma. My final assignment was as Wing Chief of Supply and Supply Squadron Commander at RAF Lakenheath England.

After finishing my Air Force career, I enrolled in an MBA course in Kansas City, Missouri. Midway through the course I took a job with a small firm and helped it grow to a multi-national company. I led the team that received two patents on an automatic order-filling system producing a 600-percent increase in order fulfillment productivity.

Ah, memories and laughter. You'll be glad to hear that Major Huggins has written another story for us that will be in our next book.

Major Huggins lives in Brentwood, California, with his wife, Audrey, and their rescue dog, Trampas.

Rainbows In Cobwebs

...Jesus...said to them, "With men this is impossible, but with God all things are possible."

(THE BIBLE – MATTHEW 19:26)

You Know You Died, Don't You?

On December 23, 2011, I didn't feel well and thought I had a virus. I was sick for two days but I was hoping I'd be all right so I could enjoy Christmas. On Christmas morning, though, I felt an incredible pain in my jaw. It was so bad that I asked a friend to take me to emergency at University Medical Center in Las Vegas, Nevada.

The news wasn't good. "You've had a heart attack," the doctor who attended me said. Heart attack? That was a shock...but on Tuesday they put a stent in my heart. I was released on December 29.

On December 30, at 6 AM in the morning, I awakened and it seemed as if I heard the Lord's voice say to me: *a sound mind*. I knew that Scripture and I repeated it. "I have the mind of Christ." Almost immediately, it seemed as if I heard those words again: *a sound mind*. I didn't know what to make of that unusual experience, but later I realized that I was being prepared for what was about to take place.

It Happened Quickly

That afternoon, I felt a wave of weakness come over me and I fainted. When I came out of it, I fainted again. Then it happened a third time. I called my son, William, and told him. Within five minutes, he was there.

He held me as we walked to the bathroom. That's all I remember. William frantically performed CPR on me as he called 911.

Paramedics arrived and they proceeded to give me shock treatments. I was unaware of it, because I was not cognizant of anything. Three times, as they rushed me to the hospital, their shock waves coursed through my body.

Astonishing

When my eyes opened and I was breathing normally, one of the paramedics looked me directly in the eyes and said something neither William nor I will ever forget.

"You know you died, don't you?"

By the time we arrived at the hospital, word of what had happened had preceded us. A nurse met us at the door. "You are a miracle," she said.

I knew Who had used William and the paramedics to save me, and I let the hospital staff know, too. As they carried me down the hallway, I was worshiping Jesus out loud and thanking them for giving me back my life.

Telling the World

On New Year's Day, January 1, 2012, I aired my Moments of Meditation radio broadcast from my hospital room. They had given me a big private room that became my chapel. I had the opportunity to talk about my miracle, about the Lord, and to pray for doctors, nurses and patients. Word got around. Nurses would come to my room asking me to pray for them.

I have never felt any kind of chest pain. Every day has been full of joy. Every time doctors walked into my room I welcomed them with laughter and didn't hesitate to talk to them about Jesus.

Let's Acknowledge It

God restored my life. We serve a miracle working God, who is still doing wonders. I frequently quote a verse from the Old Testament of the

Bible, Jeremiah, Chapter 29, verses 11 through 14: *...for I know the plans I have for you says the Lord. They are plans for good and not for disaster to give you a future and a hope. In those days when you will pray, I will listen. If you look for me wholeheartedly, you will find me. I will be found of you. Thus says the Lord.*

I shall not die but live to show forth the glory of the Lord.

Eloise Carey

Eloise Carey has recently completed a new CD entitled: Multi-Millionaire.

From 1981 to 2009, with the help of friends and local churches, she started the House of Prayer International, a unique ministry that touched the community of Oakland, CA, as she sheltered, fed and clothed those in need.

Through her organization Eloise has a local broadcast in Las Vegas, NV, KKVV 1060 am.

Rainbows In Cobwebs

A pine tree stands so lonely
In the North, where the high winds blow,
He sleeps; and the whitest blanket
Wraps him in ice and snow

HEINRICH HEINE
(*GERMAN POET 1797-1856*)

Ice Storm

At dawn, I threw off the covers, excitedly nudging my sleepy sister. "Lorraine, look outside. Everything is covered with ice." We leaped out of bed, rushed to the window and gasped in delight. We had awakened to a fairyland. In one night our world at Hill Brook Farms had changed. Freezing rain had pelted the windows of our farmhouse throughout the night. Bushes laden with ice hugged close to the ground. Irregular crystal ice daggers hung along trees, gutters, downspouts and wires.

We dressed hurriedly, ate breakfast and looked out the window again.

No Relief

The freezing rain continued. By mid-afternoon electrical and telephone lines had snapped under the burden of ice. Without electrical power, our farmhouse was chilly.

We did have a fireplace in the living room, though, so our mother quickly got things under control: "Lorraine, you and Emma start a fire. It'll warm part of the house. We'll have to cook our meals over it, too."

Lorraine and I crunched up newspapers, arranged them in the fireplace, then added kindling. We placed heavy logs on top, and lit the pile. In seconds, we had a delightful blaze, hissing, crackling, and wonderfully warm. Our two younger sisters brought in more wood from the supply on the porch. To keep the heat concentrated in the living room, we closed the door to the kitchen.

At 12 years of age, Lorraine was the oldest of us four children while I was a mere ten, so we were pleased that Mom trusted us with this task.

Meal Preparation

Now that the fire was going, Mom discussed our limitations in preparing food for supper. "What about macaroni and cheese?" I asked. It was my favorite meal.

"No," Mom said, "we don't have the use of the oven."

Lorraine suggested chili. "Good idea," Mom said. "Let's get the ingredients."

How four girls and a mother managed to work over a cast iron pot in the fireplace, without someone getting burned or the food being ruined, I'm not sure, but it went well. After we located the ground beef and got it sizzling in the pot, we separated it into small pieces with a long handled fork. We then added chopped onions, seasonings, quarts of canned tomatoes and cans of kidney beans. Soon it all was bubbling and releasing a wonderful aroma.

Hot cocoa would be served, too. The recipe was on the can. We would stir the cocoa together with sugar and a pinch of salt and then add milk.

Another Challenge

Our water supply was running out. "Lorraine, you and Emma bundle up, take some pails and go out front to the hand pump," our mother directed. "Be careful on those steps."

Sleet pelted us as we stepped outside. We were delighted. Giggling, and with pails in hand, we slid on our feet down the treacherous front steps, holding on to the rail with all our might to keep from falling. The pump was covered with ice, so we climbed onto the base and cracked the ice off with a stone and began pumping, taking turns.

Still laughing, our faces bright red from the stinging sleet, we crept up the icy steps with the heavy pails, water sloshing out as we went. It was great fun, but we knew that the steps needed sand poured over them before someone got hurt. We would tell Daddy.

Precious Moments

Late in the afternoon, our father came in from the barn, wearily stomping his heavy farm boots. The hired hand joined us. He was a neighboring teenager who needed work. He lived in the wash house next to our farm house. Dad was glad to have his help.

All seven of us huddled around the fireplace for an early supper. The chili, served with crackers, was delicious. Steaming from the hearth, the hot cocoa topped off a perfect meal. Daddy was a man of few words, but his eyes twinkled as he gave us an appreciative smile.

Isolation

It occurred to me that our crank-style telephone hanging on the wall was strangely silent. Usually it rang incessantly all day because there were five people on the party line. Sometimes when we answered our ring – one-long and two-shorts – we could hear deep breathing from a curious eavesdropping neighbor. That's when we immediately would turn our conversation into a vague one containing few details, and cut the call short.

But on this frozen day, we didn't have to worry about nosy neighbors. The phone wasn't making a sound, and it seemed as if we were isolated in a frozen world.

Cows Won't Wait

With the milking machines down because the electricity was off, and since we had no generator or auxiliary power, Daddy and the hired man would need help to get the cows milked and fed. That meant we older girls were on call. So out to the barn we trudged. There was a strange warm glow in the sky and the wind whistled from the north as the fury of freezing rain continued. Although we were digging our boot heels into the crunchy ice to keep from falling, Lorraine and I half slid along the treacherous walk.

Surprisingly, heat from the cows made the barn warm and inviting. Daddy hung kerosene lanterns from the beams so there was no chance of a cow kicking one over and starting a fire. The lanterns cast eerie shadows against the rafters and the whitewashed stone walls.

We climbed up to the hay mow and used flashlights to see so we could throw hay bales down the steps to the main floor. Then we forked ensilage from the silo. We gave each cow a shovel full, dumping it on the concrete in front of her stanchion, and topping it with a scoop of ground grain. I always figured, that to cows, grain was their dessert, the same way that I loved hot fudge topping on my ice cream. After that, we pulled out hay from the compressed bales and forked it on top of the grain. The cows would munch on the hay while they were being milked. It smelled sweet and pungent, reminiscent of the summer clover fields.

There were 25 cows and they each had to be milked by hand in this time of emergency. That was no easy task. My father told us what he expected us to do next.

We were used to barn chores, but tending to the cows was a challenge. One of us had to wash their udders with a cloth. Unfortunately, the water we used, treated with a disinfectant, was ice cold. They didn't like that – at all! They were used to being milked by suction cup milking machines. Once the cold water hit their udders, they kicked, fussed and slashed their tails full of you-know-what in our faces. Somehow, though, we didn't mind these annoyances because we had a mission to accomplish. We were needed.

Our father finished the job to be sure the cows didn't get mastitis – inflammation of the udder.

Welcome Relief

We were nearing the end of our work when, suddenly, the barn door opened and our neighbor, Charlie, walked in.

"Hello," he called out cheerily with a grin. "I figured you could use some help."

What a welcome sight he was, with his congenial manner and concern. We weren't so isolated after all. We also knew that his coming meant that he had wrestled with chains at his house, putting them on his truck tires. Then he had driven, sliding and slipping, over four miles of hilly frozen roads to assist us.

The milking and feeding took four hours instead of the normal one-and-a-half, and all of us were feeling the strain. It was 8:00 o'clock that night when we returned to the farmhouse, weary but with a sense of accomplishment. The fireplace was a welcome and warming sight, glowing brightly as the logs burned and spit their sparks.

My father's old clock chimed from the mantel, keeping perfect time as it had for many years. It had been a wedding gift to his great grandparents in 1893. Candles glowed on the mantelpiece and around the room, giving us enough light along with the fire to eat sandwiches, play a few games of Pit, and drink the rest of the hot cocoa.

After prayers, we children crawled into our beds, each next to the warmth of a sister. Only our cold noses stuck out from under several layers of blankets.

Ahhh...Sunshine

By the next day the freezing rain stopped. But another day passed before the sun came out and the electricity was restored. It was a relief to have power again.

Reflecting now on this ice storm, I believe that, at best, it was a nuisance to my father and mother...at worst, a nightmare. But to me it was an adventure. It seems to be my most treasured after-Christmas memory from my past. It far exceeded the traditions and expectations of the holiday we had treasured just a week before it happened.

What I remember most vividly was the toasty fire that brought sustenance, and the simple glow of the candles as they cast their shadows against the fireplace wall and around the room. It was family togetherness through isolation, a sense of being needed, of working for a common cause we had to achieve. That was reward enough.

Emma Westerman

Raised on a large dairy farm near Bangor, Pennsylvania, Emma received both a B.S. and M.S. from Pennsylvania State University, University Park. She lives in Pine Grove Mills, near State College, PA with her husband, Melvin. Her articles have been published in magazines and devotional books.

Besides writing and painting, she quilts and creates crafts for sale at local shows and businesses. Other interests include church, the Daughters of the American Revolution and family activities related to their farm heritage.

Get better acquainted with Emma by watching her video on www. RainbowsInCobwebs.com.

Rainbows In Cobwebs

The endearing elegance of female friendship.

SAMUEL JOHNSON
(ENGLISH WRITER – 1709-1784)

Questions...
Answer!

My dearest friend, living in another state, shared via e-mail that she had been diagnosed with breast cancer. She said that her two sisters died of lung cancer after years of smoking cigarettes, so she understood cause and effect – but then she asked, "How do I explain my cancer?"

You're Asking Me?

I didn't know what to say. I searched endlessly for advice to give her and words of comfort to offer as she underwent surgery and treatment. My thoughts centered on the battle that my mother had fought...and lost...against the same miserable disease; but instead of finding answers - more and more questions surfaced and weighed down my soul. I began slipping, inch by inch, to the end of my rope. Dangling at the end of my rope, grasping the last knot - I finally looked up for help.

And there He was. It was almost as if I actually could see him standing with outstretched arms, waiting until I asked for his help. Then it seemed as if he lifted me, slowly drawing me closer to him while gently prompting me to focus only on him. He assured me that he was working out his good purposes, and he urged me to drop my thoughts and focus only on him. He is The Answer.

Friendship in Perspective

I wrote my experience down in poem form, and referred to it frequently – especially when circumstances and questions threatened to pull my focus away from Him. Through the process, I learned that a true friend is one who listens and turns you toward God, rather than trying to solve your problems. I entitled the poem:

The Answer . . .

Why? What's the cause? How to explain it?
No answers I find ... I hit a dead end.
Searching my "self" brings silence, not hope,
so I slide - inch by inch - to the end of my rope.

Dangling ... I weaken ... can only look up . . .
That's when I see You - Your arms reaching out.
Questions abandoned, I whisper, "Help ... please ..."
You lift, calling gently:
Just focus on Me ...
Look in My eyes ...
See the smile on My face ...
I love you, My precious ...
Trust in My grace ...

Bask in My presence ...
My Promises guard you ...
My Word lights your path
and provides every clue.

Ask <u>Me</u> your questions,
for
I Am **The Answer ...**
the all-knowing, up-lifting Savior of you.

Take your thoughts captive, whatever they be,
Look up instead - focus only on Me

for
I Am The Answer ...
whatever your questions,
Just focus on Me,
Focus only on
Me

When my friend and I visited the last time, we took a short walk in the warm sun and rested on a bench while rehashing some of the highlights of our long friendship. I gave her a copy of the poem that evolved from her seemingly unanswerable question, and encouraged her to read it often. "Rather than circumstances, concentrate on him," I said. "No matter what we may think – he is in total control. He wants us to put ourselves in his presence, call our thoughts captive, and focus only on him. He promises to handle the rest."

She smiled and said quietly, "You know, I needed to hear that."

God's timing is perfect.

Andee Wise

Andee is a Legal Executive Assistant in Pleasant Hill, CA. and is very active in her church. Among other things, she assists in the preparation of actors for large, public dramatic presentations that the church gives, such as a gripping 4th of July production in a park, attended every year by thousands.

From Margaret: The Hardistys are aware of several big cobwebs in Andee's life that she hasn't visited in this book. I mention it, because just watching her and listening to her, we have been delighted with her ability to concentrate on the rainbows that have been there.

Furthermore, she has turned them into victories. Her positive outlook and laughter, despite everything, are infectious.

Rainbows In Cobwebs

Go confidently in the direction of your
dreams. Live the life you have imagined.

HENRY DAVID THOREAU
(AMERICAN AUTHOR 1817-1862)

Warrior Cowboy

I have learned that if a plan doesn't work out, there's often a very good reason. As a new college grad with two degrees under my belt, I couldn't wait to get into the real world. I was fortunate enough to have the opportunity to major in Music Business and Sound Recording. It always has been a dream of mine to work in the music business.

After all, I had overcome the many obstacles of being severely physically disabled with cerebral palsy from the time I was born, but I experienced great success in my college career. My grades were high, I discovered hidden talents and skills, and made a lot of friends with both students and faculty.

I had successful internships where I proved my skills and even spearheaded a very successful marketing campaign for a new album. One of the songs from the album was featured on a major network television series. I had killer recommendations and even connections to executives of record labels and high ranking officials in some of the top ten companies in the world. So I thought I was good to go with finding a decent job out of college.

I was wrong. Very wrong.

As I started to do interviews at these companies for positions that I was well qualified for, one of two things kept happening. The interview would either go very well, or the interview would be cancelled if they found out I had a disability. In every single case, I never heard from the recruiters or anybody from any of those companies again, no matter how I tried to get through. The same thing occurred at least thirty five times in a two month period. So I started to get a little discouraged.

Rainbows Lead to Victory

Then, one day, my phone rang. It was a college buddy of mine, asking if I would be interested in producing a live double album that they were about to record. I had worked with the band before, doing projects with them since we were in the same classes together. They loved my work, and knew I had a talent for mixing. I immediately agreed, and spent the next few months at my home studio inside my parent's house.

So, how did I do it? In fact, how do I manage to do anything, given the fact that I can barely control any part of my body and I live in a wheelchair? God had blessed me by allowing me to discover my life purpose at the young age of 12 when I was awakened by the power of music and the positive life-changing impact that a song can have on a person.

Since then, I have devoted my life to earning a successful music career. In addition, it is my mission to serve as living proof that, although everyone has his/her own unique struggles and challenges in life, each of us has a unique life purpose – and has the ability within ourselves to overcome the roadblocks on our journey to fulfilling that purpose.

Meeting Challenges

I also have a tremendous work ethic, as well as a certainty that I can do anything I set my mind to do. My dad is a great role model. He always told my brother and me to give 100% to everything we did. In fact, I've had a lot of incredible people in my life who have been supportive and who encouraged me to reach high and far; my mom and dad, my brother, my grandmother and countless others.

For example, one of my teachers, Ms. Stolfi, was sure I could ride a horse when I was in the sixth grade. Although I was hesitant, she and my mother encouraged me to join an after school horseback riding program. Within weeks, to my surprise, I was able to sit on a horse without falling off.

What happened at the conclusion of that program is what changed my life and rocked my world. In the closing ceremonies, we all rode out to Garth Brooks' song Standing Outside the Fire. It was an earth-shattering moment for me. It was as though every word in that song was written for me at that very instant. As I rode that horse with the music playing and people cheering, I knew then that country music was to be a major part of my life purpose.

Warrior Cowboy

I've been writing songs ever since. My debut album I Will Stand will be out soon and yes, I did the mixing on it. I wrote the album's lead single "Warrior Cowboy" in honor of wounded soldiers who have fought for our freedom.

I've been disabled all my life – it's all I know – but it's new for them. The bridge in the song sums up my approach to life: "I don't need to kneel to say a prayer, to thank God that I'm still here."

We all, in one way or another, fight for what we believe in and have battle scars. No matter how wounded we get, we still have our spirit which can never be destroyed.

Precious Memories

Dad worked to provide for the family, so I spent a lot of time at home with my mom. She played a very significant role in my life. Not only did she encourage me to pursue music and my dreams, she also invested a lot of time and energy to helping me with everything from personal care to getting me from place to place for the first three years of my college career.

She drove me to the campus, which was 45 minutes from where we lived. She did this four to five times a week, and was always there if I needed help with something. She was such a positive force. As I was working on an album for my buddy's band, we were both really excited about this being my first project in the real world music industry. It also enabled me to spend some quality time with Mom. I would take breaks to eat meals and we'd often watch television. We had a lot of laughs.

One time, as we were watching television, she looked at me, and said, "I'm proud of you."

She was fighting a hidden battle with cancer – little did I know that would be one of our last times together. A few days later, she was hospitalized from what everyone thought was the flu. The cancer had spread suddenly into her liver. Within a week, she passed away.

I now realize that being rejected from all of those companies was the greatest gift I have ever gotten, because it enabled me to be home and spend time with my mom during the last weeks of her life. It's also very comforting to know that she was able to see my entrepreneurial career being born. It validated all of the time and energy that she put into my life preparing me to live and survive in the real world.

Shane Michael Taylor

*Featured on CBS and ABC, country music artist Shane Michael Taylor is a motivational speaker and the author of Living This Rodeo: A Journey from Fantasy to Reality, which details the journey that led to his career as a country music artist. His debut album is titled **I Will Stand**. His lead single "Warrior Cowboy" is garnering national attention.*

*Take calculated risks. That is
quite different from being rash.*

GEORGE S. PATTON
(*GENERAL-UNITED STATES ARMY 1885-1945*)

Drug Deal and the Snitch

As a narcotics detective, I had served a search warrant on a guy who was both buying and selling heroin. They found heroin in his house. Part of what we do to get to the bigger fish, the guys who are dealing drugs on a wider scale, is to tell the guy we caught with heroin, that if he wants to work this case off, then he has to give us the names of a lot of bigger fish up the line. "If you do that," we tell them, "then we'll go to the District Attorney and cut you a break." The DA usually goes along with that if the heroin addict comes through with good names.

The guy I was telling you about agreed to do that. We had to have actual proof, so we set up an undercover buy. He was to make his contacts and arrange to meet them in a motel room. He'd introduce me as a friend who wanted to buy a bunch of heroin. The other part of the plan was to have a swat team waiting in the parking lot to come to his aid if the whole plan went south.

In the Moment

At the scheduled time, I pick the guy up. He is dressed like he's from a Hells Angels clubhouse. He has a long beard, long hair, and looks really rough. I take him over to the motel room where he and his drug contacts are going to do the deal.

Out in the parking lot are six guys stuffed in a van dressed up in black swat uniforms and armed to the hilt. I'm wired for sound and have a gun stuffed down the back of my pants. I have my radio hidden.

We go to the motel room to wait. Drug dealers are notoriously late. I'm not sure why, but there is never a drug deal that goes down on time. Nothing is happening yet, so I shut off my wire and the radio to preserve the battery.

Surprise Visitor

All of a sudden, the Lord comes up. I don't mean that he walks into the room and I see him, and I don't quite know how it happens; but it's just one of those things when I know, without a doubt, that the Lord is prompting me and he's not taking, "No," for an answer.

I'd love to be the hero in this story like I really was obeying God, but I wasn't. I was the uncooperative vehicle that he was dragging along.

I fight it. I keep telling God, silently of course, that I am going to buy heroin in just a few minutes and there is going to be a drug dealer walk in through the door and this really is not the way things should be working.

Does He Listen? No

All the while I'm trying to reason with the Lord, I am talking – sort of – with the addict. Before I know it, I am talking about the Lord. I don't do any great job of it. I am more doing it so that I can soothe my conscience, pat myself on the back when I walk out of the room and say that I told the guy about the Lord.

God has other plans. Here the addict and I are talking a little about the Lord, and I am asking how he got to be a heroin user, and then I ask him if he knows anything about Jesus.

"Well, there was this one thing that happened in jail one time," the guy says. "I was locked up in a cell. I was totally high on heroin and this voice came to me and said, 'That's not your blood you're corrupting. It's mine.'"

I am blown away and I realize that I need to get this thing going. So

I talk about the blood of Christ and ask him if he would like to accept Jesus as his Savior.

"Yes," the guy says. Just like that.

Obviously, this would not go over well in police circles. Here we are in a Motel 6, waiting to buy heroin, sitting on the bed holding hands with our heads bowed, going through a prayer to have him accept Jesus as his Savior.

I've got a gun sticking out of my pants. I'm wired. I'm hoping the whole time that my wire isn't actually on. If it is, the six swat guys that are waiting for me in the parking lot with their M-16s will be listening and thinking: What in the world is this crazy guy doing?

Now What?

When we finish praying, I think…well, gosh, what do we do now? After all, I still am a cop and this still is a drug dealer. So we hug and five minutes later, there is a knock on the door. I turn my wire on, these guys come in with a bunch of drugs and I buy them.

The drug dealers leave and the guys outside follow them to find out who they are working for.

I shake the snitch's hand – and never see him again.

Name withheld *

*The writer of this story wants his name and photo withheld for obvious reasons. Such men are keeping your lives safer day by day and seldom seek personal glory.

These woods are lovely, dark and deep,
But I have promises to keep,
And miles to go before I sleep,
And miles to go before I sleep.

ROBERT FROST
(*AMERICAN POET 1874-1963*)

Salt Princess

This story requires a bit of history so that the full impact of what happened will be felt. That takes us back to civilizations that no longer exist but whose influence has lasted throughout the centuries.

People have been traveling long distances to trade with one another for thousands of years. Caravans of donkeys and camels made their way from Babylon to Egypt. Abraham and Sarah went from Ur of the Chaldees to Canaan on one of these caravan trails. Abraham became the parent of Ishmael and his descendents – all of the Arabs – and he and Sarah the parents of Isaac and his descendents – all of the children of Israel. You can read about it in Genesis, the first book of the Bible. And that brings us to...

The Silk Road

In China it was discovered that they could unwind the cocoon of a silk worm, spin thread, weave cloth of great beauty, and sell it in exchange for goods of immense value – such as spices. Pepper, cloves, cinnamon, turmeric, ginger, and cardamom were easy to carry and brought high prices. The spices grew in India, across the Himalaya Mountains.

The route from China to India was called, universally, the Silk Road, even though the road was used to carry spices and sometimes precious stones, as well as silk.

The Silk Road was nothing more than a path winding through the mountains, barely wide enough for a fat donkey with a pack saddle full of goods. In some places the road followed a broad river bed. In some places it was cut into the side of a cliff to form a half tunnel. Sometimes it crossed a narrow, scary, suspension bridge, high above the river below. If a donkey didn't like the bridge, the driver would place a blindfold on him and lead him across.

The road is so old that no one remembers who cut it, how they chipped away the stone, or who lived in the caves above the road, even though it is obvious that someone did.

The mountains, including Mt. Everest, are the tallest in the world, but travelers don't have to scale them. A river, the Kali Ghandaki, cuts across the mountains. When we traveled through the area, we followed the rustic path that existed along the river. Not that it was easy. It wasn't. Actually, it was hard work – but fun, too. There were marvelous things to see.

A Highly Coveted Spice

To go from China to India, those who followed the Silk Road had to cross Tibet. High on Tibet's cold plateau are salt mines left by a dried-up ocean. Although silk was valuable in India, so was salt. In fact, it was so precious that people named their children after it: Salt.

This story is about a little girl whose home was close by the Silk Road. Her name was Nuna Kumari, which means: Salt Princess. Nuna was born not far from the town of Sanja. Sanja is in the country of Nepal, about two hours' ride by bus from another town, Tansen, where the Tansen Mission Hospital is – the hospital in which I practiced.

The town of Sanja has gained some fame because Nirmala Pradhan's family came from there. When Mother Theresa died, Nirmala took her place. Although thousands of missionaries have given their lives to help others, Mother Theresa was probably the most famous female missionary of all time, thanks to the exposure afforded her by the Catholic Church, the media and Hollywood.

Tragedy Visits a Home

In Nepal there is no such thing as central heating or a furnace, not even in upscale hotels in the larger cities. Some people have small kerosene heaters. In the towns there may be electric space heaters if and when the electricity works. But most people build a wood fire in the floor of the house. The floor is made of dried mud, so it doesn't catch fire. When the weather gets cold, the entire family sleeps around the fire. They place the babies between the fire and the grownups, so they don't freeze in the shadow of their parents.

The sad part of that is, sometimes the babies roll into the fire, suffer serious burns or even die. Nuna Kumari rolled into the fire when she was only one. She was burned severely behind her right knee, on the front of her right ankle, and on the side of her left ankle.

Almost Beyond Description

It's difficult to describe Nuna's condition that developed as time went on. Serious scars formed, shortening and bending her right leg backwards at a 90 degree angle until her heel touched her buttocks. Her right foot bent up until it grew inside of her leg. Her left foot rolled upside down so that the top of the foot was on the bottom and the sole of her foot pointed up.

Using a stick, she could stand up on her left foot, but that was painful, because she was standing on what was meant to be the top of the foot. It was easier to crawl on all fours like a baby.

An Attempt to Cope

When she was old enough to go to school, she crawled to school. There weren't any school buses. There wasn't even a road in her village – just a foot path. After school she crawled home. Over time, the crawling caused thick calluses to form on her hands and knees.

Once she was home she helped her mother with housework while sitting down: grinding cornmeal, cooking rice, washing dishes, knitting and sewing.

Nuna learned to read and write, quite amazing because many girls didn't even get to go to school. She even learned a little English.

Worry About the Future

When she was sixteen years old, though, Nuna began to contemplate the future. "What will become of me in life?" she thought. "1 live in my father's and mother's house now, but when they die, 1 will have no place at all. No one will marry a cripple like me. I'll probably just lie beside the road and die like an animal that has been hit by a truck. Unless…" A light came into her eyes. "Unless they could help me at the Tansen Mission Hospital. Yes. I need to try."

Our hospital had gained recognition because of our work with patients, saving lives, patching up bodies, and helping those in need.

By this time, a new road for cars and buses had been built on the old Silk Road and it ran through Sanja. Nuna crawled to Sanja, got on a bus, and when the bus stopped in Tansen, she crawled again into the hospital.

Unscrambling the Puzzle

We took X-rays, studied the scars, and planned how to unscramble the puzzle of Nuna's crooked legs. Then the work began. A formidable task that was my job.

Can a surgeon adequately explain in writing what he had to do to make wrong things right so it makes sense to the reader? I only can try.

First, I cut away the scars. Next, I cut, patched, and grafted her leg and thigh bones.

After that, I cut all of the foot bones out of the right leg – except the heel bone (not possible if she ever were to walk at all again). Then I turned the left foot right side up, and grafted skin to cover the places that had been hard scar tissue.

The Outcome

The operations left her with no right knee, and just one bone from hip to heel. The right leg was six inches shorter than the left. Still, the right heel was there to bear her weight. Compared to what she had before, it was like a miracle.

With an artificial leg to make the right leg longer, she could walk almost like a normal person. For the first time in her life she could wear shoes. With shoes and a skirt, she looked just like the other girls.

Her legs weren't very strong, however. She needed a walking stick. She couldn't do farm work like other girls and women. She couldn't carry a sixty-pound basket of manure to the fields, or carry hay to the cattle.

She Had to Make a Living

We thought that perhaps she could teach. She already could read and write. With more education… So we enrolled her in a nearby boarding school, just a mile from the hospital; but she was behind her age group in everything. She did fit in with the younger students because she was small.

In Nepal, all good teachers know three languages, Nepalese; their own tribal language (Nuna's was Magar); and English. Nuna really was behind in English. To help her catch up in English, my wife, June, walked to the school every morning at eight o'clock. It was winter and cold, so the two of them sat in the sunshine on the schoolhouse steps for the lesson.

They could bundle up everything but their hands which they needed for writing. Nuna was left-handed, and June, right-handed. June had a pair of warm gloves. Nuna had none. So June sat on the left, Nuna on the right, each with a glove on the outside hand, a pen in the inside hand.

When it Doesn't Work

Nuna seemed intelligent enough and she was determined. She just wasn't an academic. The English lessons weren't working.

What to do? We talked it over. Her hands were nimble. She could knit, sew, and crochet like a whiz. We decided to send her to a girl's tailoring school in Kathmandu for a year to learn to make all sorts of clothes by hand. That, too, was a boarding school.

When, at last, she had learned all that the sewing school had to teach her, she was able to move back to Sanja near her home village and family. We bought a sewing machine for her and she opened a little shop. She was on her own, no longer a crawling beggar, but an independent lady.

Happy/Sad/Happy

Does this story have a happy ending? We don't know. Over time we discovered that Nuna had bipolar disorder with episodes of severe depression and, at times, hallucinations (she saw frightening things that weren't really there). When she was well and on medications, she did fine. When she was depressed, she was helpless.

Earlier in this story, I told you about Nirmala from Sanja, who took Mother Theresa's place when she died. When Nuna was born, it was legal for Nepalese men to become British soldiers in what they called the Gurkha Regiments. Nirmala's father became a Captain in the British army in India before India became an independent democracy. Nirmala began working with the Sisters, became a Roman Catholic and then a nun. Eventually, she was appointed Mother Superior of the entire Missionaries of Charity.

When that happened, we thought, "Hurrah!" But how ironic! In her own country, Nepal, Nirmala couldn't legally have become a Christian, but in India, she became a leader of Christians through the Missionaries of Charity.

However, at about the same time that Nuna had her first operation, it became legal to be a Christian in Nepal, so the Missionaries of Charity began working in Sanja. They watched over Nuna, made sure she could get the medications that she needed, and that no one was taking advantage of her.

Nuna had gone to church with us, knew the hymns, and had a Bible to read. We don't know if she really understood what being a Christian meant, but she did understand that loving your neighbor heals the heart. Jesus said that people who love one another are the salt of the earth. We think, in that statement, he included the Salt Princess.

Keith and June Fleshman

Keith is a retired Orthopedist.

He and June live in Salem, Oregon.

Note from Margaret:

I have known Dr. Fleshman for a long time. He served many years in Nepal with his wife, helping the helpless, selflessly giving up any idea of living a comfortable life as an Orthopedic surgeon in the United States.

As you read other stories in this book, you will find additional tales of sacrificial giving that will inspire and amaze you as this one has.

Rainbows In Cobwebs

When morning broke, and day
Smiled up across the tide
Here in the harbor safe she lay,
Her rescue by her side!

MARK ANTONY DE WOLFE HOWE
(*AMERICAN EDITOR & AUTHOR 1864-1960*)

Who'll Catch You
When You Fall Off the Cliff?

People often ask me if I think my entrepreneurial spirit is the result of nurture or nature. I have thought about this a lot, because I have thrown myself headlong into a wide variety of industries, often with little or no expertise in the field. I learned on the job.

I've had extraordinary success, and more good fortune than I can believe possible. But everything I've taken on has been crazy frightening, at least in the beginning. I think my resilient enthusiasm for adventure is a result of both environment and opportunity, but not for the reasons you might expect.

Turbulent Times

I was born in the suburbs of Venice, California. But my parents moved to, and then separated in, British Hong Kong. If you've ever been to British Hong Kong you'll know it's a disparate blend of extreme wealth and poverty. When I lived there it was a massively populated patch of island and scrap of mainland, acting as the eye-of-the-needle gateway between mysterious communist China and the rest of the world.

In this city fortunes were made quickly, and lost. Risks were taken daily (just crossing the street), and there were possibilities everywhere. Your driver or 'ahmah' could own the block of apartments you live in and you might never know it!

My father abandoned us in this wild world, took a new wife and most of our possessions. My mother was thrust into poverty and fear. She never fully let that go; holding on to a healthy respect for every dollar, living with a lean and disciplined budget.

She married again and we had a good life. Her husband had a solid job with benefits and housing. We all worked extra jobs to have spending money; just enough.

Resisting the Conventional

My teachers told me I'd make a great writer, or legal barrister. But my parents were firm in pushing me into practical interests, like cooking, sewing and typing…so I would have skills to fall back on. They said university would be wasted on me. I'd be married and rear children. That was enough.

I built businesses, anyway. Especially once I was married. I worked full time and claimed my college education at night. Without my parents' disapproval and words of doom and gloom, I was free to take on run-down businesses and build them up. I had small wins, and then larger ones. The successes grew in momentum.

Another Fascination

Once we had enough money coming in for me to stay home with our babies, I pursued my passion for writing and began to fashion novels. Whenever I would start writing a book, though, I would confide in my mother about it, and she would tell me, "Be realistic. Even if you did get your book published, it's highly unlikely that anyone would ever buy it." Her words would evoke doubt and fears, and I would lose interest in the project and go back to something else.

Always, it seemed that it was my mother's voice stopping me from living my current dream. I blamed her for holding me back; for spoiling my creative endeavors. That is, if I wasn't blaming my husband.

Stoically, despite my reluctance, Mom helped me renovate my home and rear my children with abundant love and attention. For 10 years she worked at my side, making clothes and selling them at market stalls, so that we could have spending money while my husband worked hard to build his company.

Was I Grateful?

When my husband and I grew apart and divorced, my mother moved her home to be close to the children and me. That's when I turned on her. I let her know that I thought she was interfering and domineering. I shut her out of my life and set about showing what I could do without anyone holding me back.

I bought houses and renovated them, collecting them like trophies. I invested in businesses. I bought stock and became a day trader. I hired expensive advisers and got publishing contracts to write books. I had become the success I always dreamed of being. Next stop on my list – TV personality!

Humiliation

On advice from a financial adviser, I had tied up my cash in retirement and managed funds. When the real estate market began to fall, I liquidated as fast as I could; but there was no cash to hold my position. I chose to sell everything, the best assets first, which amounted to millions in property and shares. To add insult to injury, the managed and retirement funds were decimated.

I felt humiliated. Devastated. I fell into clinical depression. My friends avoided me.

My boyfriend left me, shattering my heart. My lawyers lectured me. And my home had to be sold. In order to make it saleable, it needed to be immaculate to stand out to buyers, for the market was weak. I had no energy to do what needed to be done.

An Angel Appears

Who do you think showed up to see me through it all? Who took control and dragged me out of bed each day? Who brought in her friends to do the carpentry and the landscaping? Who pulled out the sewing machine to decorate every window? Who sang and teased, cheered me and got me through it? Who do you think rescued me in my darkest hours and told me how proud she was of me? Who took me in after the house was sold?

My mother, that's who.

Starting Over

With all this encouragement, I decided to rebuild. I would make it happen smarter and faster than the first time. For that I needed new knowledge, so I spent 100 hours interviewing millionaires to find out how to create recurring income in this new era.

And when I took on too much, who do you think helped me write my first published books? Who sat with me, laughing and continuing to tease, spending weeks stripping 1500 pages of interview transcripts down to 200 pages of gold and wisdom?

Who do you think survived the market crash, losing only a little equity in her own real estate portfolio?

Yes, my mother. My mother, my greatest critic. The one I blamed every time I quit. The one I thought had held me back. The one I was sure had held me down. She's now my best friend, my rescuer, my cheer leader, and my most loyal supporter. She always was, really. I just didn't realize it.

I had pushed until I hit my limits. I fell, and then I found out where my safety net lay.

If I haven't told you lately, Mom, thank you! You are truly amazing. You lived through much tougher challenges than I ever did, and you taught me to how to be a champion in life. I just didn't appreciate the foundation you were building until I landed on it.

Cydney O'Sullivan

Carolyn Deigan, Cydney O'Sullivan, Anne McKevitt, Billionaire Consultant

Cydney O'Sullivan is from Los Angeles, California, but spent most of her childhood in Colonial Hong Kong during the 1960's and '70's. Starting her first job as a voice actor at the age of eight, and moving into television and radio before entering the corporate world, Cydney worked in multiple industries and management roles. Taking every opportunity to travel, in 1987 she decided that Sydney, Australia, was the land of beauty and opportunity and settled in to make the most of it.

She has earned millions in business, real estate and investments; is Associate Editor at Social Media Mags International; and is the best-selling author of the book Social Marketing Superstars and How to Be Wealthy NOW!

V

STORMS
STRENGTHEN RESOLVE

Storms can...

Be very destructive;
Frighten almost everyone;
Reduce buildings and areas to rubble;
Kill and maim.

Storms also can...

Bring rain that is needed;
Cause people to be thankful for shelter;
Last only for a short while;
Place things in perspective;
Be exciting;
Bring out the noble and caring in people;
Inspire men and women to create art, writing, cinema;
Lead people to accomplishment of great feats.

When a big storm invades your life,

look for ways for it to bring out the

very best in your spirit. Call upon God

to protect you; and then go forth to

clean up and conquer.

Rainbows In Cobwebs

Doubt is the vestibule which all must pass before they can enter the temple of wisdom.

CHARLES CALEB COLTON
(*ENGLISH CLERIC & WRITER 1780-1832*)

Order to Appear

It was the second time in my 18 year old life that I had entered the courthouse.

"She'll work off the fine," my grandfather had said the year before when the judge gave the option of paying $45.00 or doing a day's work at the courthouse. My crime had been driving forty five in a residential zone.

This time I had misplaced a parking ticket and forgotten about it until an order to appear at court had arrived. It terrified me. How could I have let a simple parking ticket turn into a court case? Too ashamed to ask my grandfather to go with me this time, I nervously entered the courtroom alone…and 20 minutes early.

A Wiser Older Man

I got a big break. A wiser older man, who was at least 20, sat next to me watching the other citizens go before the judge for their crimes. "Just look at that guy!" he sneered. "No respect for the judge. Look how he's standing there, slouching. Can you believe it?"

Before I could be sure whether I believed it, Wiser Older Man continued, "Ohh, he's gonna' get it. Did you see the look the judge gave him?"

Nodding, I felt something like panic settle into my chest. Suddenly I'd forgotten how to breathe.

"Listen, what did you do?" He looked into my face as he asked. I started to stammer my reply, but he rushed on. "Doesn't matter. Whatever you do, when you get up there, show respect. You need to really mean it and show it, got that?"

"Yes!" I meant it with all my heart.

"When you get before the judge, look him in the eye. Don't slouch. Be respectful. If you do that, he'll go easy on you. It's all about showing respect! If you don't, it could go bad for you!"

My mind was whirling. I could barely think. I rehearsed in my mind how I would walk up to the bench. But that couldn't happen because my legs had become ice water.

My name was called. My advisor nudged me, repeating, "Show respect! You'll be fine."

I went before the judge. He stated my name for me to confirm. I mustered my courage.

"Yes, your Majesty!"

I was not beheaded.

Kathy Young

Kathy enjoys managing a privately owned Executive Suite business in Dublin, CA.

She home educated two sons and assisted her husband, Lance, in his construction business. Prior to having children, Kathy worked in real estate related fields in a variety of capacities. She graduated magna cum laude with a B.A. degree in Home Economics and a secondary teaching credential at San Francisco State University in 1978. Kathy and Lance live in Walnut Creek, California. Kathy has written another entertaining story in this book for you to enjoy: Reagan at the Rexall.

Sow good services; sweet remembrances will grow them.

MADAME DE STAEL
(*FRENCH WOMAN OF LETTERS 1766-1817*)

Orly

"I Have Light"

Holding the carefully wrapped baby in his arms, the father entered the train station. Tianjin was one of China's five most populous cities, so the station was noisy and teeming with people. With throngs of strangers pressing past each other, it was the perfect place to leave the tiny girl. *What have we done to so offend our ancestors,* the father wondered, as he had many times, *that the one child the government allowed us to have should be born a female? That is bad enough, but for her to have a serious birth defect as well, is worse.*

But this was a problem that could be solved, he and his family had decided. If they abandoned the baby before she was registered, the government wouldn't be the wiser and they could have another child. Perhaps the next time the ancestors would bless them and they would get what they really hoped for – a healthy boy.

The father was fully aware of the fact that what he was doing was against the law, even though abandonment of special needs children and girls was commonplace. He glanced around the station, getting his bearings.

Trying to appear nonchalant, he slipped into one of the bathrooms with the child and waited; but each time when he thought the room was empty, another man would enter. Fifteen long minutes went by – then twenty. Finally, after 25 minutes, he and the baby were the only ones there. He acted quickly. Setting her against the wall, he surreptitiously scurried toward the door, slipped out, blended into the crowd and made his escape.

He knew it wouldn't be long before the little girl would be discovered and reported to the station police – who would turn her over to the Tianjin orphanage. They would publish a lost-child notice in the Tianjin newspaper for the amount of time required by law. When no one came to claim her, she officially would be classified as an orphan.

An Uncertain Future

Although the earthly father was certain that he was not noticed as he abandoned his child, there was One who did notice: God. As the human father distanced himself from what he had done, the Heavenly Father set plans in motion to rescue the unwanted baby.

The first step was the government orphanage; but soon she was transferred to a Christian orphanage in another city – Langfang – where all the orphans had special needs of varying kinds. There, Christian missionaries, Mike and Elisa, received her gladly and named her Miao Miao. She received food, a crib and love.

There she would fit in and not feel different because of her affliction. The missionaries would correct her problems surgically, if at all possible, before she became old enough to understand or feel that she was "broken." There, those who reached out to the rejected and unwanted little ones, believed in following the Biblical admonition:

Pure religion in the sight of God is this – to visit
orphans and widows in their affliction and to
keep oneself unspotted by the world.

JAMES, CHAPTER ONE, VERSE 27

Hope Blossoms

As Miao Miao grew a bit older, she became aware that families who lived outside of the orphanage usually had a mother and father. The older children talked about their longing of being adopted by one of these families; and soon, a similar longing stirred in Miao Miao's heart.

And why not? She vaguely was aware that teams of visitors to the orphanage liked her. Hadn't Mike and Elisa told her she was a favorite? They also called her a little mother hen, because she helped them with the other children so much.

So it was no surprise to her when she was given the name and a picture of a family who wanted her. She was ecstatic. She would have a family of her own. But the day came when Mike told her that it wasn't going to happen, after all. The government was not going to allow it.

Awareness

How much a three year old is aware of what is going on in her life is uncertain. It's possible that she might have heard the term, spina bifida. With spina bifida the bones in the spine don't grow properly. In time the missionaries would arrange for her to have surgery, an expensive operation that the Chinese government would not pay for and birth parents can't afford, but she wasn't aware of that.

Miao Miao's hope was renewed when she received the name and picture of another family that wanted to adopt her; but once again that hope was dashed when the proposed adoption fell through.

Hope Disappears

When, at last, a lovely Christian family sent her a teddy bear and a picture that Mike attached to her crib, he and she thought: This is it! This time it will happen. Once again, though, the government said, "No."

"Honey, don't lose heart," Mike said when he told her the disappointing news. "God is going to give you a family."

Miao Miao looked up at Mike, her dark eyes piercing his. "I don't believe God," she said quietly. After that, she refused to mix with the other children and avoided contact with anyone else. Now, besides the spina bifida, she had another serious problem: Reactive Attachment Disorder – RAD, for short. To add to the problem, although she had the spina bifida operation there in China, her spine became retethered. That caused her to walk hunched over.

My Heart Was Moved

We continued to pray over and over as a team for Miao Miao. "God, this little girl really needs a family," I'd say. Imagine my surprise when it seemed that God answered me very clearly. "Yes," I was sure he said, "and you are the one I have chosen to adopt her."

So I acted on that. With the idea of officially making her our own child, I brought her home to live with us. She was thrilled, right? Wrong. Her RAD caused her to act out in disobedient and bizarre ways. I tried everything I could think of – different forms of discipline; love; talking; punishment; threats…nothing worked.

I talked with several people who were renowned parenting experts. "No," they all said, "don't adopt her. You have so much going on in your life. You are living by faith – no salary or support. You have a lot on your plate as the leader of this missionary organization and this little girl has serious emotional issues."

It made sense. After all, I already had five adopted children. I was homeschooling and had another child who was so badly burned that at that time he was a special needs child. How in the world would we have any more time and attention for a sixth child, and a troublesome one at that?

"So what do you want me to do, God?" I prayed. I opened my Bible to I John 4:

And so we know and rely on the love God has for us. God is love. Whoever lives in love lives in God, and God in him. In this way, love is made complete among us so that we will have confidence on the Day of Judgment, because in this world we are like him. There is no fear in love. But perfect love drives out fear, because fear has to do with punishment. The one who fears is not made perfect in love.

It was the phrase, "we know and rely on the love God has for us," that grabbed me.

I felt that I'd had a direct communication from God Almighty, my precious Father, Abba (Daddy). God had heard my concerns, they were legitimate, and I knew that I was to set everything aside and rely upon his love. This revelation was so gripping that I made the decision to proceed with the adoption.

Rainbow #1 – Victory #1

What was happening to Miao Miao was God's providence. The only door he opened was the one that was the best for her – not to live in the United States, but to be adopted by a missionary living in China. Once I made the decision to adopt her, no matter what, it was as if a light switch was flipped on in heaven. Almost overnight, Miao Miao's RAD disappeared. Miraculously, she became a sweet, obedient, charming little girl. A miracle? There was no other way to explain a 180 degree change in a child's behavior.

Rainbow #2 – Victory #2

I gave Miao Miao a new name: Orly…which in Hebrew means, "I have light." Light she was to us and we, to her. I was so encouraged by the changes in her behavior that I went to our insurance company to ask about a second spina bifida operation so Orly could stand and walk erect. I was told that they wouldn't cover it because it was a pre-existing condition.

Then I heard about a group of physicians from UCLA who were going to China to do surgery on children. I told them about Orly. They said the magic words: What resulted was a whirlwind of blessings:

1) We flew to Shanghai, and gracious friends put us up in a beautiful hotel.

2) The surgery was performed successfully, free of charge.

3) Then, of all things, the doctors covered our family's incidentals while we were there.

4) Not only that, but Steven Curtis and the Mary Beth Chapman's foundation, "ShowHope," gave me a $3,000 grant to help with my adoption expenses. God – and I can only attribute it to God – provided the rest of our needs through a series of miracles. In the end, I received all the money necessary to cover the entire cost of the adoption and other expenses.

Orly Today

My daughter is a lovely teenager now, beautiful inside and out, although she seems oblivious to that. She is an "A" student, a favorite of her teachers, and she continues to care for others. She is always loving and helpful around the house.

And for her dad, who years ago asked God whether adopting her would spread my love too thin, the answer is an unequivocal, "Absolutely not." I love each of my children and others wholeheartedly. A significant portion of that is because of Orly, who now is free of the spina bifida and loved and cared for by her family. Miracles still happen, as you can see.

Dr. John Bentley

Dr. Bentley holds a BA in History from UCLA, an MS in Administration from Central Michigan University and a Juris Doctor from Regent University.

He is a former Army officer and Gulf War veteran.

Media guest appearances include Focus on the Family, Prime Time America, the Joni Show, Celebration with Marcus and Joni Lamb, Moody Radio Network's Morning Ride with Mark Elfstrand and numerous other radio interviews in the U.S. and Canada.

1st Picture: Orly with her dad.

2nd picture: Orly as a small child with orphanage visitor, famed professional performer, Steven Curtis Chapman

John Bentley, a former attorney who gave up his practice to serve God by serving children, has set up

orphanages in other countries besides China – such as Cambodia. Go to our website for the fascinating video he shot that will tell you more.

Dr. Bentley's story and Harmony's work has been featured in several of Max Lucado's books including Fearless, Every Day Deserves a Chance, and You Changed My Life.

To the left: John with four 10 year old Ethiopian girls who are or were living with their mothers in prison. The government asked John to help. His organization has acquired three and soon to be four homes near the prison to take care of these adorable children and so they can visit their mothers.

Rainbows In Cobwebs

A day of horrific human tragedy
A day of extraordinary human service

DOUG MACSWAN
(*WRITER OF THIS STORY*)

September 11, 2001

In 2001, my family and I lived in a small town, Windham, New Hampshire, about 40 miles north of Boston. During that time, I would often travel to New York City on business and that's where I was on September 11, totally unsuspecting of the tragedy that would play out that day.

Business as Usual

Monday, September 10, was just another business day. I took an early morning Delta Shuttle flight out of Boston's Logan Airport to La Guardia in New York. I had meetings in mid-town so I stayed in a hotel that was conveniently located.

On Tuesday morning, I left the hotel to catch the subway downtown for a 10 A.M. meeting at AIG, the large insurance company. As I walked down 45th Street, I noticed what a clear, sunny day it was. The bright blue sky was just beautiful. I caught an express train at Grand Central but as I rode, I became aware that the ride was taking too long. I glanced at my watch. I should have been at my destination in 10 minutes, yet 30 minutes had already gone by.

When the train approached Fulton Street Station. where I planned to get out, I grasped my briefcase. Just then an announcement came over the loud speaker: *This train will not be stopping at Fulton but will continue on to Wall Street Station.* Similar things had happened before, so I settled back, not giving it another thought.

A Jolt

I got to the Wall Street station about 9:45, climbed the stairs and stepped onto the walk in front of the church that was situated there on Broadway. A crowd was standing in the street looking up into the sky behind me. I turned and looked up, too, and I was stunned! I saw large flames and smoke billowing out of both the World Trade Center towers.

There was a man standing next to me looking in the same direction. I turned and said to him, "Wow, that's pretty scary!" "Yes," he said, "I'm late for work, and my co-workers are up there." He told me he worked on the 104th floor of the south tower at Aon Corporation.

I remembered my 10am meeting and started walking up Broadway. I took a right toward Chase Plaza to get to 80 Pine Street, the meeting location.

Panic

Suddenly, with the towers directly behind me, I heard people screaming. As I glanced over my shoulder, I saw that they were running toward me in the direction that I was walking. I didn't know what they were running from, but it had to be something bigger than all of us. So…it was just a gut reaction…I started running, too. Somehow I knew that the panic had to do with the towers that were spewing out fire and smoke. What had happened? Was something falling?

Instantly, the world as I knew it disappeared. Without warning, I was wrapped in what seemed like a huge black blanket. I couldn't see and I had to cover my mouth with my hand to try to breathe.

Then, everything became eerily quiet… and I became disoriented.

Where am I? I wondered, standing still. I pulled my suit jacket over my head to try to create an air pocket so I could breathe, and I crouched down, leaning against a metal railing to my right. Then I started thinking that whatever was falling was coming down on top of me. What a stupid place for me to die, I thought. I live in New Hampshire and I'm going to die in downtown New York. I'm going to get buried under a pile of rubble. Will they ever find my body?

Thinking back on my reactions that day, it's surprising that neither of those thoughts really bothered me that much. Maybe my mind had just gone into survival mode, blocking out emotions that were not productive. But then I envisioned the faces of my young daughters and my next thought was: They're going to grow up without a dad! That really scared me and jolted a desperate prayer out of me: "Please Lord…" were the words that shot toward heaven, while all the time I was thinking – don't let me die here. I needed help to get out of there.

A Heavenly Answer?

A church bell started ringing. It was close – right near me. Later I found out it was from a Catholic Church, Our Lady of Victory.

And actually, I was a little stunned. Did God hear my prayer? I wondered. I lifted my suit coat from in front of my face and at that very second, I saw a beam of light moving in front of me, along to my left. I jumped up and put my briefcase on my shoulder. I could make out a form – a man carrying a flashlight to light his way. A woman had her right hand on his left shoulder, walking in his footsteps. I rushed to them, put my hand on her shoulder and followed them. I also reached over and gave the man a pat on the back for his good work leading us out of there. It wasn't long before he stopped and shined his light on a revolving glass door that opened into a building. The woman went in. I went in. The man kept going.

Later, when my emotions had settled, I wondered how many people in downtown New York carry a flashlight – like the one the man had – on a bright, sunny summer day. Practicality took over in my mind. I guessed he was probably a firefighter or police officer. He may have saved my life. I still don't know who he was or if he lived through that day.

War Zone

When I got through the revolving door, I realized I was in a small restaurant called Bull Run, near the New York Stock Exchange. I walked up a few stairs and then turned and looked behind me. It was quite a sight. Many people were streaming in through the revolving door to get away from the pandemonium outside. It truly looked like a war zone with all the dust and soot that covered them.

One waiter was motioning to those still outside that they could not all come in; but another waiter was doing the opposite. He was motioning for them to come in.

Most people walked past these two men toward the back of the restaurant. I followed. I noticed a number of sinks along the back wall with water running and people were rinsing their faces, and hacking from the dust and soot that had invaded their lungs. It was a dramatic and shocking sight.

I used one of the sinks and then moved out of the kitchen through a doorway to a lounge area in the Club Quarters hotel that was connected to the restaurant. There was a TV there. People were crowded around, watching as the scenes of the disaster were replayed. Many people stood there stunned; a few were sobbing. Still in shock, it was very bewildering for me to watch all this and wonder what was happening. Then the reality of it began to penetrate.

So that's it, I thought, as I watched the pictures of two planes flying into the twin towers.

One of the towers had fallen. I started to wonder if the gas pipes and other underground utility lines could become a danger to the building that we were in and that was a scary thought.

My family. I have to call my family. Fortunately I found a public telephone. I called my wife in New Hampshire. No one answered. I left a message that I was okay, but that in case anything else happened, I loved her and my three daughters and really hoped to see them soon. I still felt that I might not see my family again and that made me extremely sad.

Not long after that, about 10:30 A.M., the second tower fell and I saw that happen on TV. That was just another shocking sight among so many on that day.

More Human Kindness

Later on, a restaurant worker was walking around handing out free bottles of Evian water to anyone who wanted it. The restaurant also gave out cloth napkins so those who went outside could cover their noses and mouths.

As it got to be about 12 noon, some people started to leave the building where we had taken shelter. At about 1:30 P.M, I started to see a little daylight out the windows. Shortly after that, I left and started walking north.

As I walked out of the Wall Street area, some people reached out to help those who had been through some difficult experiences. When I went by a hospital, I saw nurses and doctors outside, offering to check people who were coming out of the downtown area. News reporters were also there asking many of us questions about our experiences.

Once I was out of the area where there was smoke in the air, I spotted a restaurant with a table out on the sidewalk. Cups of water had been placed there for people to take. Because my hotel was a long way from downtown, I kept walking north. After awhile I came to a subway station that was open and I went in. As I stood on the platform waiting, four construction workers were nearby talking. One of them looked at me and sort of whispered to his friends, "I think he may have come from there."

I felt that he was trying to be sensitive to my situation so I walked over and joined the conversation. We talked for a few minutes and one of the men made a profound statement: "This is going to change things," he said. "Things will never be the same again after what happened today." I was impressed with that thought. How true it was – and is.

A little later as I was getting close to my hotel, I met a few more people who were in New York because, they told me, they were part of the group traveling with Michael Jackson, since he was there that week to do a concert. They were very friendly and pleasant.

Many people reached out to me and to others to be friendly and to help in countless ways. Small kindnesses that they did that day have stayed with me ever since September 11 – kindnesses that made a huge positive difference in spite of the terrorist attack.

I'll Always Be Grateful

Finally, the commitment, the service and the sacrifice of firefighters, police officers, military personnel and others became clear to me. They showed how heroic they were on September 11. I appreciated it in a much deeper way than I ever had before. I valued every one of them, no matter who or where they were.

So, on the Saturday after September 11, I went to my local police station in the town where I lived in New Hampshire. "Thank you for being here for everyone. I appreciate it," I said to the first officer I saw at the station.

I went to visit the local fire station, too. I just wanted to say thank you to those people for being ready to sacrifice themselves for others. I spent a few minutes with the firefighters and I was saying that it was amazing to me that their job could involve running into a burning building. One of the Lieutenants just chuckled, and said, "Well, that's our training."

Burning building? There may be people in there - I'm going in. That's what I do.

That was one of those stunning moments for me, to realize that where I lived, and pretty much wherever we are in our country, there are people who have decided that they will be there for others and sacrifice themselves, no matter what. That kind of service ethic and commitment always will inspire me and I always will remember it.

On that day of the terrorist attack, I experienced the horror of thinking that my three daughters would grow up without a dad; and yet I was delivered from that terrifying situation. At the same time, my heart goes out to everyone who suffered a loss that day and still is dealing with that loss today – thousands of people.

According to New York magazine, 3051 is the estimated number of children who lost a parent on September 11. Below are more details on the number of people killed and other information related to the attacks in New York.

- Total number killed in attacks in New York: 2,753
- Number of firefighters and paramedics killed: 343
- Number of NYPD officers: 23
- Number of Port Authority police officers: 37
- Number of WTC companies in the towers that lost people: 128
- Number of employees who died in Tower One: 1,402
- Number of employees who died in Tower Two: 614
- Number of employees lost at Cantor Fitzgerald: 658
- Number of U.S. troops killed in Operation Enduring Freedom: 2,108
- Number of nations whose citizens were killed in attacks: 115
- Ratio of men to women who died: 3:1
- Age of the greatest number who died: between 35 and 39
- Bodies found "intact": 291
- Remains found: 21,744
- Number of families who received no remains: 1,717
- Estimated units of blood donated to the New York Blood Center: 36,000
- Total units of donated blood actually used: 258
- Number of people who lost a spouse or partner in the attacks: 1,609
- Estimated number of children who lost a parent: 3,051
- Percentage of Americans who knew someone hurt or killed in the attacks: 20

Source: http://nymag.com/news/articles/wtc/1year/numbers.htm

Doug MacSwan

Doug MacSwan has worked as a sales and marketing executive in the information technology industry since earning his MBA from Harvard Business School in 1984. He works with clients in banking, insurance and other industries who want to improve their business results. He welcomes inquiries related to these topics.

Doug and his wife, Sally, have three daughters in college and live in Fairfield County, CT.

Sally has an unrelated story that comes up next, entitled: Surprised by Hope.

The Hardistys met the MacSwans at a conference in Connecticut and were so impressed with them and their experiences that we asked them to write their stories for this book. I'm sure you're glad that they did. We are.

Another 9/11 story was submitted to us by Sam Bradley, who was sent to New York to apply her skills to help those who needed it during the chaos that followed the terrorist attack. It will appear in our second book in this series. Meanwhile, you can read her first fascinating story in this volume, entitled A Paramedic's Tale.

If you need further encouragement and help after reading the stories in this book, go to our website where you can find emotional and spiritual support.

Rainbows In Cobwebs

Where there is love there is life.

MAHATMA GANDHI
(*LEADER OF INDIAN NATIONALISM*
1869-1948)

Surprised by Hope

"How old are you, Emily?" Dad asks as Emily bounces into the living room on her tiptoes, dressed in her clown costume. Trying to get her attention, he repeats the question several times, as she eagerly examines a pile of random toys on the floor and begins to line them up.

"Ma nam' i' fo e ol!" she responds with a gleeful smile. It's a mispronunciation of: "My name is four years old."

Laughing, Dad asks once more, "Emily, how old are you?"

This time, with a little smirk on her face, and in an almost surprised tone of voice, she says, "Ma nam' i' fo!"

This was Emily captured on video on her fourth birthday. At this point in her life, she was just learning how to put words together in short, memorized phrases, often not understanding their meaning.

Earlier Symptoms of Trouble

Even as a newborn, Emily was clearly different from her older and younger sisters. In fact, she was different than any child we had ever known. She didn't seem to get hungry, and it took a lot of coaxing to get her to nurse or take a bottle. The slightest noise or movement would distract her, and she would stop eating. When she finally finished, she wouldn't fall asleep in my arms, but would squirm and cry until I laid her down; then she would fall asleep.

It Didn't Get Better

Over the next three years it became more evident that Emily was dissimilar. Although she was clearly hungry, for example, it continued to be difficult to get her to eat. She ate less than a dozen different foods.

I somehow figured out that when she was strapped tightly in her highchair, with the tray pulled close against her, she calmed down. If she watched Barney on TV and had a toy to feel on her tray, I could feed her by standing behind her. I reached in front of her, and when she felt the spoon on her lips she would open her mouth and take a bite. If I fed her from the front she would squeal and turn away when the spoon came toward her.

I also found a way wherein she would feed herself. If I put several Cheerios on her tray, she would quickly brush them off onto the floor with her hand. But if I put just one Cheerio on her tray, she would pick it up, examine it, then eat it. Eventually, she did the same thing with two or three other finger foods.

She continued to resist being held and moved constantly, prancing around on her toes, climbing, running, exploring and feeling objects. Always moving. She was a happy little girl, but for no apparent reason, she often would throw tantrums and appear panicked.

Other Challenges

Emily preferred to wear no clothes – just her diaper. She would squeal and run away and even go into a tantrum when I tried to dress her. I solved this problem. After she fell asleep at night, I would dress her in the clothes she would wear the next day.

She would let me undress her so she could take her bath but she was afraid to get into the bathtub. Nor would she sit in a sink full of water. But if I held her firmly, she would stand up in the sink and let me pour water over her with a cup. Combing her hair, brushing her teeth, and using soap or sunscreen would cause her to panic.

Even at age three, she barely spoke; and more importantly, she didn't understand what was said. She could point to objects of interest, or things she wanted. "Dat," she would say. Or she would repeat two word phrases over and over, such as, "Hi Momma; Hi Momma." Or, "Awww..da; Awww..da" (all done). She sometimes jabbered to herself, and appeared to mimic the actions of others.

Diagnosed

We knew that these behaviors were not normal. What we didn't know was that they all were related. Grouped together, they were common signs of autistic spectrum disorder. When she had just turned three, she was diagnosed with that disorder.

Autism was a term we knew little about 21 years ago. Typical of many parents of children with autism, we had no idea of the magnitude of the problem. Even the professionals are limited in their understanding. Autism is a foreign world where so much is unknown and unpredictable – moment to moment – and looking years down the road. We were told that the challenges parents have in dealing with autism often destroy marriages and tear families apart.

Persistence paid off

To our advantage, we had spent the past three years loving Emily and getting to know her. We had learned much about how to take care of her and provide for her basic needs and desires. Actually, she was a delight to be around, and her high level of energy and enthusiasm was contagious. She was fascinated with sights, sounds and objects that we hardly knew existed. She opened our eyes and ears to a world we had never known before.

One thing was unmistakably clear – Emily was a priceless addition to our family. We loved her beyond measure, and she loved us.

A Revelation

An unimaginable breakthrough in Emily's development took place shortly after she was diagnosed with autism. We moved to a different state where we had access to a beautiful indoor pool. Since I swam competitively in college, I knew that with three girls, ages four and under, swimming was a near to perfect activity for our family.

We began swimming every day. By swimming with them, I taught Emily and her older sister to swim on their own in a couple of weeks. For a child who had resisted bathwater, it was amazing to see her delight in this activity. It was difficult for Emily to transition from the pool room to the water, however. But once she was in the pool, it was as if she were released. She loved to go under, as deep as she could go. As a result, she mostly swam underwater. On the other hand, she also liked to stand at the edge of the pool, jump high into the air and then plunge into the pool.

Another trait: she would "stand" in the deep water with her face barely emerged, and would spin around and around, always with a huge smile on her face. She also loved it when I stood in the pool and would throw her into the air as high as I could, then catch her in the water and push her under as far as I could. "Gin, gin", she would say as I did this over and over (Again. Again.).

Astonishing

Physical activity was a big part of our family on a daily basis. But it was within days of swimming that we began to notice significant changes in Emily. She slept better; and it was easier to get her to eat. She was calmer, transitions were easier for her, and she had fewer tantrums and panic attacks. Most remarkably, she began to use words, and even started to interact with others.

If we missed even a day of swimming, she seemed to regress. So we swam seven days a week. We couldn't afford to miss a day. The more we swam, the more Emily's behavior and development seemed to improve. The doctors called this progress nothing short of a miracle. It was as if the wall surrounding Emily was slowly crumbling. Swimming was the key that unlocked the world with which she felt so disconnected.

Two years later, we were still swimming with Emily seven days a week.

A Scientific Explanation

When Emily was five, she had an extensive evaluation at a world famous children's hospital. There we learned the apparent reason for the miraculous changes in her.

"With autism," the doctor explained to us, "sensory input to the brain is not integrated and processed properly. The billions of pathways in the brain are not connected in normal ways. Numerous studies indicate that if the correct sensory stimuli can be applied, especially within the first several years of life, permanent neurological change results." Furthermore, we learned that, even if the neural pathways are not connected properly, resulting in a host of problems and limitations, the pathways can reconnect permanently in proper ways.

The doctors explained to us that swimming was the stimulus that produced this effect and result in Emily's young brain. "You don't want to know where she would be right now without the swimming," they explained.

Direction

Now that we had a scientific basis and explanation as to why swimming was so important for her, we continued to make it a top priority. When Emily was in first grade, all three girls joined a recreational swim team where sportsmanship, swimming technique, teamwork, a spirit of healthy competition and fun were emphasized. Emily blossomed. As part of the team, she became more comfortable around people and developed a few close friendships.

She also was fast. By the time she was in high school, she was one of the best all-around swimmers on the varsity swim team, and she was made captain her senior year. As an unpretentious leader, she was accepting, kind, supportive, and made everyone feel essential to the team, even the swimmers who were just beginning in the sport.

In a similar way, she began to develop her social and leadership skills in the classroom. She took the initiative to help tutor students who also had disabilities. Some of them went from having failing grades to performing well.

"You have an extraordinary gift, Emily," one teacher told her.

Reaching Higher

During her entire junior year, Emily focused on discovering all she could about countless institutions of higher learning, so she could find her "perfect college." She was very private —almost secretive — about her intensive search. In the spring, she announced that she had found the ideal school, which just happened to be a sixteen hour drive from home. We had huge reservations about the distance, but we let her apply and further encouraged her to apply for merit scholarships. In the fall of her senior year, she not only was admitted to her top college but she received a full tuition merit scholarship as well.

Emily is currently studying at this top-ranked university, where she receives outstanding support and accommodations that address her specific special needs. She plans to graduate with a degree that will enable her to help children and adults with autism and other disabilities.

A Thrilling Truth

Emily went from being an utterly dependent child to a confident, independent, and resourceful young adult. As she grew, we had the privilege of seeing the unique ways she expressed herself as well as the depth of her understanding, emotion, and kindness.

Sally MacSwan

After graduating from the University of Michigan, Sally MacSwan worked in clinical dental research for 16 years until she and her husband had their first child. Since then she has been a stay-at-home mom rearing three daughters.

Sally and Emily

All three daughters are currently in college. Sally now works with families who have children with autism and helps them address their challenges. She welcomes inquiries related to this topic. She and her husband, Doug, currently live in Fairfield County, CT.

From Sally: When Emily was in fifth grade, I found, in her backpack, a poem she had written. We're including it, as she wrote it, because I think it reveals who she was then and who she continues to be.

Glowing Star

Star, oh star,
You are a glowing, golden thing.
You are something I don't know about.
But all I know is that you are something
Special, and Warm,
And something that lights up the night sky.

How come you glow, as if you were a flashlight
Sitting there
Just lighting the night sky, gazing upon the Houses
The cities,
And the ocean
Below.

Do you ever see yourself, how
Beautiful you are?
Do you ever think that anyone cares about
You, or that anyone thinks that you are a
Unique flashing shape? You are a great
Special glowing thing that is so unique.
You are a glowing jewel in the sky.

Rainbows In Cobwebs

Every great dream begins with a dreamer.
Always remember, you have within you the
strength, the patience, and the passion to
reach for the stars to change the world.

HARRIET TUBMAN
(*AFRICAN-AMERICAN ABOLITIONIST 1820-1913*)

My American Guardian Angel

The plane landed with a thump. As the pilot brought it to a stop, I looked at my girlfriends, Madalina and Andreea. We were very excited and anxious, all at the same time. We're in America! We're actually in America!! We couldn't believe it; it was as if we were trying to catch up with reality. After a long flight from Romania, we had started our first American experience at JFK airport in the great city of New York. We had finally arrived in the Promised Land. It was going to be wonderful. After all, this was the country of all opportunity.

We followed the signs and the crowd to pick up our luggage and made our way outside.

The excitement I felt quickly turned to apprehension. I was only 21. I realized that the world was much bigger than I had thought. Masses of people were milling around everywhere.

"Where do we go from here?" we asked ourselves. We had the address for the motel that had been prearranged for us by our summer employer. It was written on a slip of paper, but we had absolutely no idea how to get there. There were a lot of cab drivers and shady looking people who offered to give us a ride, but fear took over. It felt like a jungle.

"There's an information desk inside," we said to each other. "Let's ask there."

We were told that the easiest and cheapest way to get to the motel was on a shuttle. A shuttle driver assured us that he knew where the motel was. We paid the fare and an hour later arrived at our destination.

Not Exactly Ideal

It was now night outside and the motel looked similar to what I had seen in the movies: an Indian front desk clerk who eyed us rather oddly and then led us to a dark, cold and shabby room. This would be our home away from home for the next seven days. I fell asleep thinking of what the next morning would have in store for us.

I woke up very early, not knowing where I was. Confusion soon became reality. I was ten thousand miles from home. The day brought some discouraging news, too. We already had jobs lined up at an amusement park but found out that we'd have to take two buses over two hours to get there. Four hours of traveling each day! But we were glad for the job, so we took the long, multiple bus rides, signed up and received our assignment.

The job wasn't as much fun as we thought it would be. The rides were scary to watch and the food was very unhealthy.

Shock and Sorrow

To make it worse – much worse – after just a few days of working at the park, someone, somehow, fell out of one of the rides and was killed! That sobered the crowds and they soon dispersed, leaving the park almost empty and us without many working hours on the schedule.
We eventually were told that we'd have to leave…that they'd call us if the crowds started coming back. This meant that our only source of income was now gone and the pocket money that we had brought from Romania was fast running out.

Days later, we still were waiting for that phone call. We compared our finances.

"We're out of money," we agreed. "We can't even pay for another week here at the motel."

More Challenges

Thankfully, the call we'd been waiting for came from the amusement park. We could go back to work the next morning. Hope came rushing back. "Be on time," the voice said.

We boarded the bus which always stopped in Port Chester, New York, where we had to change to another one. To our horror, we missed the connection. We fought back the tears and our words tumbled over each other. "We'll be late." "They'll fire us for sure."

We knew that we would have to find other work. But how? "There has to be a newspaper here in America that lists jobs in it," we told ourselves, "like in Romania." "We have two hours before the next bus comes for the amusement park. Let's spend the time looking for work."

A young man was sitting on a bench, and we went over to him. "Excuse us…"

"No understand English," he said, and started talking fast in Spanish. Combining our poor Spanish with sign language, we tried to get our message across to him. "Newspaper." "Job." "Place to live." Finally he smiled and nodded. "Si… Si… Notebooks," he said in Spanish. "Jobs. Place to live. Church." He pointed down the road and held up two fingers.

"Two blocks away? They have two notebooks in front of the church? Gracias."

We hurried up the street to the church. Once in front of it, we couldn't see anything that resembled notebooks. There were no newspapers, either. We knocked on a door. An older man opened it. He said he was a deacon, asked how he could help us and invited us into his office.

Our story of woe tumbled out, ending with, "In just a few days we're going to be homeless if we don't find a place to stay."

"I'll see if there's anything I can do," he said. He made some calls. One of them was to someone whom he called, "Father." Obviously he was speaking to the head priest of the church.

We waited for an answer, wondering if we'd soon be on the street, or not.

Amazing Turn of Events

The deacon smiled. "The priest told me of a man by the name of Frankie, whose wife died many years ago. He's very lonely. The priest called him and told him your problem. He lives in a large house here in Port Chester and would be happy to have three young ladies stay there for the summer. So, how many days do you still have at the motel?

"Two," we said, our delight showing.

"Okay, tomorrow I am going to come to your motel to pick up your things and drive you to Frankie's house." We were elated. After making arrangements with him, we returned to the bus stop and made our way to the amusement park, apologizing for being late. For the rest of that day, we walked around as if on a cloud. We were in a state of happy astonishment.

Frankie

The deacon did just as he had promised, and then drove us to Frankie's house. It was a big, two story home on a corner… mysterious looking, yet comforting.

Frankie met us at his front door and welcomed us. He then proceeded to show us around. The place was beautiful, sunny and immaculate. It felt like a sanctuary. "Here are the washer and dryer," he said and showed us how they worked. "Here's your bedroom and bathroom. All I ask of you is that you keep the kitchen clean."

Frankie gave us so much more than he asked in return. He even made breakfast for us each morning and then drove us to work. Yes, we were able to keep our jobs. From that point forward, it was as if the clouds cleared, the sun shone and our American experience started living up to – and even exceeding – our expectations. The rest of our summer was wonderful. What's more, when the summer was over and we had to head back to Romania, Frankie handed us a key to his house. "Whenever you come back to America, just view my home as yours. Stay here anytime you want."

Would we ever come back to America? We didn't know at that time; but we did know that we had a friend and a home waiting for us if we did.

Five Years Later

Because of that experience I did decide to return to America, and even though this happened five years ago, I still keep in touch with Frankie; and whenever I go to Port Chester, we have breakfast together. He is my family in America. He's my guardian angel.

Diana Doroftei

Diana is a Romanian-born writer now based in the United States. She holds a degree in Economics, Business & Finance and contributes to the work of Leadership Alliance, an international management and strategy organization that works with Fortune 100 companies worldwide.

Since she moved to America, Diana has been committed to sharing the wisdom and culture of her mystical homeland, Romania. Her passion led to her first book The Little Book of Romanian Wisdom, which is like an ambassador for her homeland, best known as "Dracula's Land."

From the Hardistys: You'll find a story in this book about Romania: We Survived Communism. The writer is Lydia Popa. Fascinating account.

Rainbows In Cobwebs

The steps of faith fall on the seeming void,
But find the rock beneath.

JOHN GREENLEAF WHITTIER
(*AMERICAN QUAKER POET*
& ABOLITIONIST 1807-1892)

Tragic Loss – Amazing Victory

It was my first week on the campus of Bob Jones University, Greenville, S.C. After breakfast my new roommate and I were standing together watching the new girls leave the dining hall. A very petite, pretty girl walked by carrying her books to her first class.

My roommate challenged me, saying, "I'll give you a dollar if you can get a date with her." At Bob Jones, you could look but not touch. It was a challenge and being shy wasn't one of my weaknesses. I walked up to her and, like a gentleman, offered to carry her books. I found out that her name was Marcia and that she was from Chicago, like me. I asked her for a date. She said, "Yes." But my cheap, or broke, roommate never gave me the dollar he owed me.

I got much more than a date. I fell in love with this hundred-pound sweet, kind person named Marcia, and a few years later we were married. She was the love of my life! We served seven churches as pastor and wife. Those great years brought three sons into our family. What a deal!

The Shock

After thirty-two years of marriage, we resigned as the pastor of a church in Boulder, Colorado, to join Dr. Paul Cedar in launching the Mission America Coalition. During that month of resignation, this hundred pound wife suddenly looked like she was four months pregnant.

Alarmed, I sought professional help. In three days, doctors did exploratory surgery.

My sons and I sat in the waiting room together with a few dozen church members and neighboring pastors. In a short time, the two surgeons came out with a shocking statement. My Marcia was completely impacted with ovarian cancer. She was inoperable! She would have but a few weeks to live.

That was the worst news of my life. My head was in a fog. Nothing was computing.

A few hours later when Marcia was slowly waking up from the anesthesia, I was holding her hand. The doctors came into her room and gave her the same message. After they left, she looked at me and said, "I feel so sorry for you." I stared at her, unbelieving. I was feeling totally sorry for her. I had no thought about myself. She was going to leave this world much too young. All of our life together, if she had a problem, I took care of it. Now, I was helpless.

I spent the last hours of the evening with her, hugging, kissing and talking about dying and the future. "I believe in Heaven," she said at one point. "Why would I resist going there?"

Angry

As I drove home it was nearly midnight. I cried most of the way. Likely I should not have been driving. During that tearful drive, I did two theologically stupid things. First, I said aloud to God, "I'm ticked! You're getting an angel and I'm losing mine." Later I thought how dumb I was telling God I was ticked. But I reckon He knew that anyway. I didn't need to inform Him of that fact. Second, I spoke to Him, suggesting, "If you want her in Heaven, you can take her to Heaven." Like she was mine and He needed my permission.

Later, I was ashamed of my poor theology; after all, I was a seminary graduate. I had served thirty some years as a pastor and should have known better. But I needed to tell Him. I know He understood.

The Chair

I have a comfortable prayer chair at home. The very next morning after receiving Marcia's diagnosis, I sat in it to pray. But I couldn't. The words...the petitions...the praise...none of it was there. All I heard was, *your wife is dying; your wife is dying.* I would try again, but even though I could get a few phrases out, the only thing my mind heard was, *your wife is dying.*

I determined that every day I simply would sit in my prayer chair, anyway. I begged God to tell me how long my little angel would live. No answer. Finally, though, I received a strong impression that He was saying, "You don't want to know. It would not be good for you to know." Amazingly she lived another eight years, not just a few weeks.

Wonder of Wonders

Then the time came when Marcia left me. I continued to sit in my prayer chair each day. Weeks went by, the funeral was behind me, and sadly, folks were forgetting about her.

That's when it happened. My Heavenly Father started talking with me. Oh, Silly, not in English or Greek; but He started a communication with me that was clearer than language. This continues right up to today.

So, out of incredible heartbreak of losing my beloved came this incredible blessing. I learned that private prayer was not just words that start with, "Dear God," and end with, "Amen." It is not a one-way communication where I do all the talking and God does all the listening. I learned that if I quieted myself, He would talk to me. I learned to quiet myself before the Lord through the pain and heartbreak and sadness of losing someone I loved and who loved me unconditionally.

Folks frequently ask me what God talks about. I'm embarrassed to respond – it's kind of personal, you know? But so far He only talks to me about His business, never mine. During my prayer times, I discovered that He wants me to listen; and when I am ready to really listen, He will talk, not about my stuff, as I said, but about His stuff—His Kingdom. If you and I should be sitting together to pray, and Jesus came to sit with us, I wouldn't say a word—I would just listen! What about you?

God talks to me regarding four things. Things He wants me to do. They are: 1) the media; 2) education; 3) government; and 4) the business community. Amazingly, He has moved me into positions to serve Him in those capacities.

For example: government: I co-founded the Presidential Prayer Team, an online service that has over three million households promising to pray daily for the President of the United States.

Out of the cobwebs of my misery and heartbreak came a powerful life-giving relationship with the King of Kings! Today, Marcia is in Heaven, joyfully serving the same King of Kings! We were married 40 years. I will always miss her. But she is in Heaven; and I? Well, I'll be there someday, but for now I am blessed to have this ability to listen and speak with our Lord.

Since that loss, the Lord has given to me a wonderfully kind, loving wife whose heart is one that wants to serve others and bring happiness into their lives. Ginger and I have been married six years now. God is good all the time!

Dr. Cornell (Corkie) Haan

Dr. Haan is the National Facilitator for Mission America Coalition and the Co-founder of the Presidential Prayer Team. The Presidential Prayer Team website is available worldwide for those who wish to join others in praying for individuals in our government as well as certain issues.

*He and his wife, Ginger, who also has a story in this book, reside in Arizona. Hear more from Dr. Haan in his **video** on our website.*

Rainbows In Cobwebs

It is well to think well; it is Divine to act well.

HORACE MANN
(*POLITICIAN & EDUCATION*
REFORMER 1796-1859)

I Had to Lose Weight…or Die

"You idiot!" I thought to myself as I realized how completely out of breath I was from walking up a flight of stairs at the Round Hill Country Club in Alamo, California. I was hoping that the pounding in my chest wasn't a heart attack. Wow. I had somehow grown to a chubby 230 pounds and was no longer the athletic guy I once was.

I had grown up wearing shorts for most of the year – no shoes or shirt – thinking that I was Tarzan. Making a hearty Tarzan yell and diving into the swimming pool off the roof was a trademark of mine as a teenager. I was always running around with a very fit body – proud to have developed muscles at an early age and enjoying the attention it brought.

Now, here I was at 44 years of age, huffing and puffing just from a short walk up a flight of stairs. What a wake-up moment. I had several friends and relatives who had died from heart attacks and now it was my turn…or was it?

How could I reverse this situation and reclaim my health? I decided to do what I've done for so many other projects. I'd start researching how my body works and find the best approach to getting healthy again. Physically, I was a mess. I had been having progressively worse and more frequent headaches. The doctors were giving me additional powerful pain killers to try to manage them. I also had digestive problems that, after a series of very invasive tests, the doctors could not give me a treatment for or an explanation of what caused the problems.

Part 1 – The Research

Digging into my research material and talking to others about what was working for them was the catalyst that changed my health. A conversation with a friend who mentioned that she had stopped eating wheat and had instant results was a huge piece of the puzzle. I started a no-wheat diet that day and, amazingly, six-years later I have not had another digestive problem. I was raised on bread, cookies, cakes and cereal and found them surprisingly easy to drop after getting results so quickly. Part 1 was solved!

Part 2 – The Headaches

Part-2 was trying to find a trigger for my headaches. If wheat was responsible for my digestive problems, what could be causing the headaches? My research kept pointing to sugar as a probable cause of inflammation, which triggers headaches. Could it be that simple? Could cutting out a few foods change my life drastically? Why didn't the doctors talk about this if it was this uncomplicated? I'd try it for 30 days to see if I noticed a difference.

In the first 30 days the headaches all but disappeared. Part-2 solved!

Part 3 – The Weight

Part-3 was to take off the weight I had gained – permanently. A major part of reclaiming my health was to drop 50 or 60 pounds and get back to the 175 pounds I weighed for most of my adult life. The challenge was that I didn't want to go on a crash diet only to have the weight come back. I have watched many people do this and didn't want to fall into that trap.

With wheat and sugar already out of my diet, the next step was to figure out what to eat to drop the weight. I experimented with different foods to see which ones made me feel the fullest for the longest period of time. I discovered that protein lasted for three to four hours, while carbohydrates (carbs) would only last an hour or two until I was hungry again.

I worked with a 1,200 calorie 'bank account' each day and logged everything I ate. I broke everything down to numbers – my body needed about 2,200 calories per day to function. If I ate 1,200 calories, then 1,000 calories would have to come from somewhere else. I figured that if a pound is 3,500 calories, then I would lose two-pounds per week if I cut 1,000 calories per day out of my food intake. Seven days X 1,000 calories per day = 7,000 calories divided by 3,500 calories per pound = two-pounds per week.

My menu became a bit of turkey, a chicken breast or a small burger: lean protein two times a day. About 150 calories per serving. Then...

Breakfast: Oatmeal and blueberries (there is no gluten in oatmeal);

Snack: An apple at 10 a.m. to keep my blood sugar stable;

Lunch: Lean protein and some veggies;

Snack: A banana at 3 p.m.;

Dinner: Lean protein, a small salad and some veggies around 6 p.m.

All calories had to have a purpose. No empty calories from sodas or sugars. Through trial and error, I had figured out what high-nutrition foods I liked and kept me the fullest. My one splurge was a bit of bar-beque sauce to keep my taste buds happy.

I also read that the body 'eats' protein first, before it 'eats' our fat cells. This meant that my body would consume muscle before it consumed fat. I needed to maintain my muscle mass in order to get my body to focus on eating the fat cells.

A quick 15-minute routine with dumbbells in my bedroom twice a day was all I needed to do in order to maintain my muscle mass. I added walking to increase my circulation and build my lung capacity and heart strength. 20 or 30 minutes every day on a slow paced hike was perfect.

Was It Working?

At the start of each month I would weigh myself and give myself the option of continuing on or stopping the program. I was losing 8 to 10 pounds per month and I was never hungry – not once. I kept going. I was having fun with the whole process of reclaiming my health! At the end of six months I had dropped my 60 pounds and was back down to my perfect weight.

The heart attack warning that day was scary at the time. Changing my perspective on it made it one of the most important shifts in my life and will probably add years – or decades – of extra time to my life.

Has It Lasted?

It is now six years later and the changes I made are still effective. I consistently weigh 175 pounds. I continue to maintain a wheat-free and limited sugar diet. During that time, I have never needed drugs for blood pressure, diabetes, heart problems or headaches.

Funny how a life-changing moment like a heart attack scare can turn into a fantastic opportunity for a new life!

Kevin O'Brien

Kevin is a happy-go-lucky Irish guy who loves exploring new parts of the world and making a difference in people's lives. As a Realtor, he is in the $50-million club and handles million dollar transactions on a regular basis.

To keep the balance, Kevin always wears a Mickey Mouse tie as a statement of his personal values about the importance of family. He has 20 of these ties and has dozens of Mickey Mouse items in his office — all cherished mementos given to him by many of his clients.

He is an avid hiker, skier, scuba diver and licensed pilot.

Dear Reader: Do you see why we are interested in hearing of your cobwebs, rainbows and victories and how they can help others as they journey through life?

That's what this book is all about – helping others. If that's your desire, we have a link on our website www.RainbowsInCobwebs that will take you to our guidelines about submitting your wonderful life experience.

Rainbows in Cobwebs
Stories of Hope in the Storms of Life

VI

SURPRISING

COBWEBS

Cobwebs (synonym: spider's webs), can...

Look awful, especially inside a home;
Make a clean room look unkempt;
Form a trap for unsuspecting "good" insects;
Remind us of spiders – creepy crawly things;
Stick to hair and skin.

Cobwebs also...

Trap unwanted and harmful insects;
Astonish us as an architectural wonder;
Are made of one of the strongest natural materials known to man;
Often are used by hummingbirds to form their nests;
Can be beautiful when the light shines on them just right;
Form miniature rainbows when raindrops adorn them.

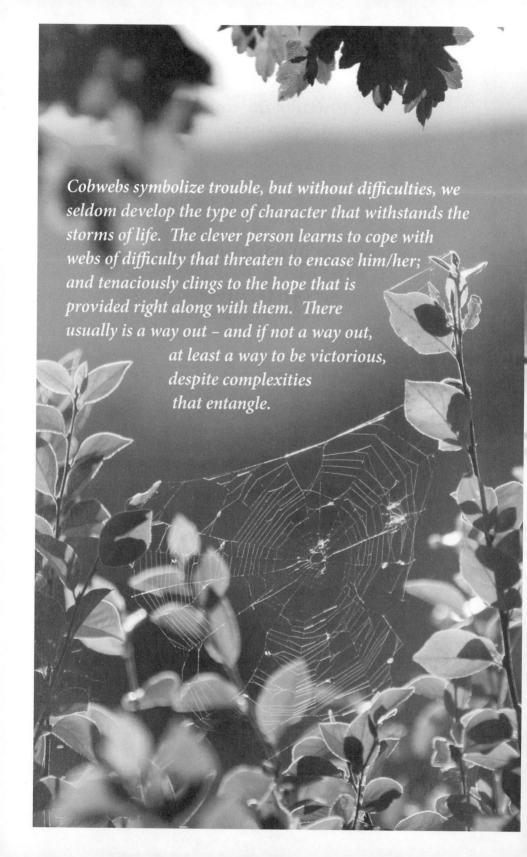

Cobwebs symbolize trouble, but without difficulties, we seldom develop the type of character that withstands the storms of life. The clever person learns to cope with webs of difficulty that threaten to encase him/her; and tenaciously clings to the hope that is provided right along with them. There usually is a way out – and if not a way out, at least a way to be victorious, despite complexities that entangle.

Rainbows In Cobwebs

Talent does what it can;
genius does what it must.

EDWARD GEORGE BULWER-LYTTON
(*ENGLISH POLITICIAN & WRITER 1803-1873*)

Go Mobile

It wasn't that I was without intelligence. Or uneducated. I had graduated from Azusa Pacific University in California with two Masters degrees – an MBA and an MHOD (Master of Human Organizational Development). And that was with straight A's. I hadn't messed up my life with drugs or other things that some my age did, either.

So why wasn't my business taking off like they said it should? Why wasn't I realizing my dreams? Why was I, at 25, still working at a steakhouse making minimum wage, asking such inane questions as, "How would you like that steak cooked?" "Do you want some ketchup?" "A little mayonnaise or steak sauce?"

Don't get me wrong. AJ Spurs served great steak and I did a pretty good job of serving it, or they wouldn't have kept me on for five years. And the people were nice; but they'd heard about my dream. They knew I had an MBA. And they were just trying to be friendly when year after year they asked, "So, how's that new business going?" "Did you ever open that gelato shop?" It was embarrassing! I'd try to crack a joke about not giving up, but I'd struck out - over and over; and the only reason I was there serving steak was because I needed to pay my bills.

There were a lot of times I was tempted to give up, but I couldn't get rid of this passion, this dream I had.

Italy – the Place of Dreams

My parents weren't wealthy, and they worked hard to help me get through school. I had traveled, too. By the time I was 22, I had visited 51 countries. A lot of that was with World Vision, a Christian organization that is built on giving life in all its fullness to every man, woman and child. I was amazed at the extent of their outreach and proud to be part of their effort.

One of the countries I visited was Italy. It was there the dream materialized. Here was a way I could have my own business and help people, too! Since I was a Christian and came from a family that believed, not only in prayer, but that God directs us in what he wants us to do if we stay open to his guidance, I felt certain that this new passion was from him.

"Okay, so now God is into ice cream?" some asked me with a smile. Well, yes, I was quite sure he was. Italian ice cream called gelato – less fat, less sugar, creamier– and delicious. And I was determined to take it to America.

Not that it wasn't already in America. Others had discovered it, as well, and gelato shops were opening up in many places. Still, I had my dream. I could see it. I could smell it. And, I had every reason to be optimistic. It was 2005. The market was booming. Money was flowing. Gelato shops were exploding and rolling in dough.

But my shop was going to be the shop of all gelato shops. I had something no one else did. Something I knew people would love – I had committed to give 50% of my profits to charities, to helping kids, to changing the world. That's because of a prayer I read by St Ignatius Loyola (1491-1556). The prayer said this and it changed my life:

Lord Jesus Christ, take all my freedom, my memory, my understanding and my will. All that I have and cherish you have given me. I surrender it all to be guided by your will. Your love and your grace are wealth enough for me. Give me these, Lord Jesus, and I ask for nothing more. Amen.

I remember the prayer like it was just the other day but, really, I was only 12 when I made that commitment to the Lord. Now I was grown and yes, people told me I was crazy, but that was the spark that drove me every day. When this came together, every cone I served, every batch of gelato I mixed would save and impact another life somewhere in the world.

As I took yet another order for steak, "How would you like that cooked?" the question went around and around in my head: *So why isn't anything happening?*

Reality Hurts

I was finding out the bitter truth, of course. For one thing, I was $40,000 in college debt. My only collateral was a great surfboard and a **really** sick mountain bike. Hardly impressive when I tried to get a loan from a bank to open a shop. Did they laugh out loud? No, but I could see it in their eyes. To them I was a joke. But to me, they were a joke. I had to show that I had enough money to do the business before they'd loan me enough money to do the business. Yeah, like that makes sense. And the government Small Business Administration was really laughable.

My parents, who believed in me and my dream, took out a 2nd on their home to give me the initial funds to open my store. Still, despite their help, no one would give me a break.

Yes, I had a business plan – a well thought out business plan that I took to one store front owner after another (30 of them!) with hopes of leasing one of their buildings for my gelato shop. I was turned down or outbid on all 30. "How much are you worth?" they'd ask. "How much cash do you have?"

Like the banks, they were serious on the outside and laughing on the inside. My degrees didn't impress them at all. They thought I was too young. They wanted somebody who was more financially secure – someone who had a ton of money behind him. They didn't want to open up to something that was going to go bankrupt.

"Okay, God," I finally said, "if this passion of mine isn't from you, then put out the fire. If the fire continues to burn, though, I'm assuming that you put it there and it's going to happen. Deal?"

God doesn't speak to me out loud, but he speaks volumes, just the same. My passion for this business stayed and I became convinced that he was saying, "No," for a reason. I soon found out what that reason was:

In 2008, disaster struck. The economy went south. Really south. In some ways it seemed that my dream was even farther away. Yet, my grandma and mother had taught me from the time I was a kid to trust God because he had the best in mind for me, always. Did I fully understand what God was doing at this time in my life? Not completely. Besides, I still was asking, "Do you want a little more ketchup with those fries?"

Why Didn't I Think of That?

Then it happened. Three months after everything collapsed (specifically, the housing bubble finally burst), I was hanging out with a friend who said, "Dude, I've got an idea. Instead of doing a brick and mortar gelato business, why don't you go mobile? You know, take your product on the road." My head snapped up. I stared at him. "Go to events," he said, "like fairs and festivals."

The fire burned hotter inside of me, and not because I was going to be a carnie, either.

My brother drew up plans for a trailer. I mean, we're talking an awesome Roman Coliseum trailer with everything inside necessary to hit the road. We built it out and I got my first gig at a fair. People loved it. They really loved it! I was scooping gelato almost faster than I could make it. The media heard about my 50% profit deal and I ended up in magazines, on radio and TV. As a result, more fairs and events invited us. Then – Disney Downtown!

Way Bigger

Our original projection had been to do $250,000 a year with a retail shop. As I write this, five years have passed since my friend made his suggestion. **We just did $1,000,000 this last year.** And now we are opening up overseas operations.

So God is into ice cream? Yes, it appears that he is.

Can you see why? Can you see why God was telling me to wait? Had I started a brick and mortar business, when the economy went sour I would have lost everything. And because my parents had taken out a 2nd on their home, they would have lost their house. There would have been no worldwide business, and, most importantly, I would never have had the opportunity to pour 50% of all the profits into the lives of others.

Through my own organization, *Working to Give*, and under the auspices of *Faith In Action*, I've been able to travel the world serving in over 80 countries, living my faith out loud, with one goal in mind: to show people God's relentless love through faith in action.

Whether or not this will apply to you, I don't know, but I discovered that when a dream or goal doesn't materialize, first check with God and then check your passion. Yes, God may be telling you to move on to something else. But if your passion is still there, he may be doing with you what he did with us - teaching perseverance and trust in him.

He wanted us to be a blessing to the world. Perhaps he has the same goal for you. If your passion and vision comes from him, then you need to persevere, trust, keep working and watch to see what happens.

Matt Holguin

*Matt is Owner and CEO of Working to Give. You'll want to see the great **video** that he has on our website. Don't miss it. Inspiring.*

Go to: www.RainbowsInCobwebs. com.

The only way out of the labyrinth of suffering is to forgive.

JOHN GREEN
(*AUTHOR: LOOKING FOR ALASKA*)

Redemption

"It's over! Our marriage is over!" These negative words I said to myself catapulted me on a journey I never wanted. I loved Don. We had our problems, but I thought we were making progress. That's when I found out something that shocked and devastated me.

Actually, I had been prepared for that heart-wrenching moment. I knew a year before that we had been drifting apart, and I knew that I was to work on my own problems. In fact, I was brought face-to-face with a Bible verse that changed my course of thinking about love. I Corinthians 13:7 in the Living Bible:

> *"If you love someone, you will be loyal to him no matter what the cost. You will always believe in him, always expect the best of him, and always stand your ground in defending him."*

When I confronted Don, he admitted that he was having an affair. And not just an affair with a woman – but with a man! It was crushing. He had struggled with same sex attraction since his teen years, he said, but had held on to his secret for 14 years of our marriage. He also had a somewhat positive admission: "I've always wanted you to be my best friend."

Bitter Truth

Open, honest communication would have made us best friends. Instead, during those 14 years I had focused on Don's faults and carefully pointed them out to him. I had not yet heard the phrase that we can't change a spouse; we can only change ourselves. My frequent nagging halted his desire to share his deepest secrets with me; and who knows but what it may have contributed to his decision to look for love and acceptance in a man.

It was decision time. Don knew he had to make a choice. "I'm going to a counselor and get some help. I don't want to lose you or the boys." I asked God for strength to love Don unconditionally and thought: *Now, things will get better.*

The **cobweb of blindness** had kept me from seeing the kind of wife I needed to be for 14 years. The **cobweb of deceit** had snared Don into believing that his same sex attraction could only be alleviated by having an affair with a man. He sincerely wanted out of the trap, but the enemy of God knew how to ensnare him time after time.

Floundering

My inclination was to run to God by reading the Bible daily and spending time praying, listening for anything he might be trying to tell me. As a result, I heard his voice in quiet times when I was alone, or sometimes when I was doing an ordinary chore. It wasn't an audible voice but I had learned to be sensitive to what was coming from him rather than from my own desires. So as I went about my life, God was there.

While Don was floundering, I kept praying, *I don't care what it takes. Just make me into the person you want me to be.* More than ever, I realized that God will respond to a genuine plea. One day as I was changing sheets on the bed, I lifted the top sheet into the air. Immediately that familiar, inaudible voice asked a question: *Will you stay with Don?* And I thought, why would God ask a wife such a question? I knew I had grounds for divorce. Obviously life was going to get harder, not easier. These thoughts flashed through my mind quickly. As the sheet floated down on to the bed, tears floated onto my cheeks.

"Yes, Lord," I sobbed, "I love Don and will stay with him as long as you'll help me."

Many Lessons to Learn

I felt sure, in that moment, that God was telling me that he was going to put our family back together, but it came with a warning that the progress would be slow. How long was I willing to wait? I assumed a couple of years, but I had much to learn before the rainbow in my cobweb would appear.

My impatience brought on anger. There was no doubt in my mind that I was in a spiritual battle, not a physical one. It didn't help that Don began leaving the house several nights a week, being gone for hours, and then lying about his destination. My anger grew more intense. I was angry with him. I was angry with God for allowing this to go on for so long. I screamed out, "Why don't you just zap him!" Like I was expecting a bolt of lightning to smack the man. That's when I was sure I heard the Almighty's retort that caused my jaw to drop: *Don's sins are no worse than yours.*

Attitudes

I honestly could not think of one thing I was doing that was wrong. Then I realized, it wasn't what I was doing or not doing, saying or not saying. It was what I was thinking. My thoughts showed up in my attitudes. I call them sins of the heart. No one but God and I could see them, but they were as ugly in his sight as anything Don was doing.

I discovered them one by one. Without warning, my awareness of a heart sin would surface. "Ah, that's one of them," I would say. For example: Pride. I had felt that I was better than Don. Pride spawns many more, like self-righteousness, a critical and judgmental spirit, the poor me syndrome, self-pity. My impatience and anger had been more obvious to me, but I had to deal with these that I kept hidden in my heart, as well.

Finding Release

Getting rid of what was not right in my heart was working. I would admit to a wrong attitude, and then my discernment became more acute the next time it surfaced. A big part of the problem was negative thinking. Whenever my mind was in neutral, I would mentally rehearse what Don had done and was continuing to do.

A popular gospel song came out around that time called *Praise the Lord*. One phrase was: *He can work through those who praise Him, praise the Lord, for our God inhabits praise...* While memorizing those words, I realized that I needed to consciously replace my negative thoughts with praise to God. I knew that he was going to turn this around, but here was yet another lesson I needed to learn before his promise would be fulfilled. Though I watched Don move farther and farther from God, I began saying, "Thank You, God, for what you are going to do. I praise you because you are deserving of all glory and honor and praise."

Despite all of that, after several more years of seeking help, then allowing himself to be trapped yet again, Don finally gave up and left our family. From all appearances, our marriage was over!

Promise Fulfilled

Two years from the day he left, I came home from work and opened the door. Inwardly, I gasped. Don! Don was sitting there on the couch. I was stunned! I also was pleasantly surprised.

"Wh…why are you here?" I asked.

"I got up this morning and decided I was going to move to another state," he said. "I realized that I would never see you or the boys again. As I was packing, a voice came to my mind. It said, 'Go home.' It kept repeating, 'Go home,' over and over. Ginger, I'm home, but I don't know if you even want me here."

Wow! How could I respond to that? I was sure that God had promised to put us back together and I'd struggled with many doubts, but here it was happening. I knew the progress would be slow; but by now it had been seven years! Seven years?

"Of course I want you home," I said, holding back the tears that were near the surface.

Now, here we were on the outset of a new life. God had allowed us to view the rainbows on the glistening threads of our individual cobwebs.

No one else could take credit for putting us back together. However, a long road lay ahead as we tried to rebuild our lives again.

The Fallout

Don fully expected his two wandering sons to come back to their senses but they were involved in worldly pursuits and not about to change their lives, even though they were happy about Dad moving back home. That change would take another seven years.

During those seven years we made a move closer to family members. We began attending a loving, caring church and got involved in the music. Our sons participated occasionally to please us. Then, one moved to another city. The other went through an extensive rehab program. Just as God was faithful to woo Don back to himself, though, he did the same for our sons. With their lives turned around, they moved back home and enrolled in the local university.

Shortly after their college classes began, Don made an announcement. He believed he should go public with his testimony – to share it with the whole congregation. Because our sons had made wonderful changes in their own lives, they agreed to do the same. At a Thanksgiving Day service, our pastor invited us to the platform where we each shared our portion of our story.

The audience rose with a standing ovation.

Don and I began sharing our story at other churches, at small gatherings and with individuals who were struggling.

Frightening Turbulence

However, a storm arose within several months. Don became very sick, finally making an appointment with the doctor. Diagnosis: HIV Positive! He began taking meds, but this ravaging disease continued to bring weakness, loss of energy and appetite, killing off important disease-fighting blood cells. Within two years the HIV became AIDS.

We formed a small group at our church. Most were family members of someone diagnosed with AIDS. Don knew there were times when I wanted to give up on him, so he named the group Hope Ministry. He verbally encouraged family members by saying, "Never give up hope." We met weekly. We encouraged one another and learned vital lessons that helped us as care givers of our sick loved ones.

Through this storm, we slowly saw the web of devastation in our families fill with morning dew, bringing God's peace.

Don lived six years after his HIV+ diagnosis. I cut my work schedule to two days per week, and wonderful friends came over to the house to care for Don, bring meals, mow the lawn and vacuum. On Don's last day on earth, his bed was surrounded by caring, loving family and friends who were praying as he entered his heavenly home.

Tell Others

A few months before Don's death, he told me to continue telling our story. He said he wanted people never to stop praying for their prodigal loved ones, to always believe that God will intervene and turn their heartache into a blessing.

"Blessed be the God and Father of our Lord Jesus Christ, the Father of mercies and God of all comfort, who comforts us in all our tribulations, that we may be able to comfort those who are in any trouble, with the comfort with which we ourselves are comforted by God."

THE BIBLE: II CORINTHIANS, CHAPTER 1, VERSES 3-4

Besides Hope Ministry, I knew I was to become more active, not only in telling Don's story, but to be part of a support group to the larger community. I had to do all I could to inform pastors and leaders of the various ways they could minister to people in their congregations and the workplace, whether they were strugglers who wanted help for their unwanted same-sex attraction, or family members of those who have the problem.

A Gift

Nine years after Don's death, I was presented with a marvelous gift. Corkie Haan came into my life. We both had been widowed, both involved in ministry and both had sons. He became my husband, a wonderful man who has been very supportive of my ministering to others in their pain.

It is often out of our wounded spirits that a ministry comes forth. The webs that people get trapped in can be turned into a thing of beauty. Only God can do this. He invites our cooperation. His promises – as recorded in the Bible – tell us that he will do above and beyond all we can imagine. How true that is.

Rev. Virginia (Ginger) Haan

Reverend Haan has been the Liaison between Exodus International and the Assemblies of God.

She has been active for 10 years in the ex-gay movement and currently is Secretary of the Board of Waiting Room Ministries. Through her own ministry, Kingdom Lifestyle, she counsels with wives whose husbands struggle with homosexuality, as well as families with a gay loved one.

Ginger was in the education field for 35 years, teaching 15 years in elementary school. Ministry-wise, she has taught elementary, college age, and women's Bible studies.

If you have a loved one who is seeking help because of same sex attraction, or you are struggling with it yourself, you'll want to look at this amazing woman's **video** *on our website.*

Ginger and her husband, Dr. Cornell (Corkie) Haan, who also has a story in this book, reside in Arizona.

Rainbows In Cobwebs

How cruelly sweet are the echoes that start
When memory plays an old tune on the heart

ELIZA COOK
(*ENGLISH AUTHOR 1818-1889*}

Remembering a Parent Who Can't

Dear Mother,

This letter is a gift I want to give you even though you are not able to receive it at this time…a remembrance of a milestone of sorts. This is your tenth anniversary in the nursing home. Ten years ago this week is the day that Dad calls, "The worst day in my life." That's when he had to concede defeat in his long hard struggle to care for you. On that day ten years ago, he chose to move you into the Alzheimer's unit of the local nursing home. He still speaks of that day with great sadness, regret and, unfortunately, shame.

However, Mom, as you may know, Dad really had no other good options. He had tried valiantly, for several years, to care for you as you moved ever so steadily into dementia. The time came when he could no longer give you the quality care you so richly deserve. On that day, your life together lurched in a very painful direction. After almost 51 years of marriage, you now were separated under two different roofs.

There Have Been Changes

Mom, so much has changed. However, one of the constants is that Dad still talks with you and feeds you three meals a day. He has missed only those few days when we insisted that he visit his children and grandchildren. Even then, his thoughts were never far from you. He would sit, stare out the window and seem to be by your side, holding your hand. He would talk about his love for you, and your faithful love for him and us children. His goal in life now is to be faithful to the end in caring for you. His greatest concern is that the Lord will take him before he takes you so that he would not be able to complete his watch.

When others note this intense focus on you, he jokingly says, "I spent $2.00 on our marriage license and I'm going to get my money's worth."

Punctuating his daily care of you, last fall you and Dad celebrated your 60th wedding anniversary. It was certainly different from the 50h celebration when you were aware of it all.

The Children

You have missed three of your four grandchildren's graduations from college. One of them married. Two became teachers, like you. One went on three mission trips. Your daughter and son-in-law won awards as "Teacher of the Year" at their respective schools. Your daughter-in-law became a professor and speaker at women's conferences.

And I? I published my first two books and became a full professor.

We would have loved sharing those significant events with you. You played such a vital role in helping us be fruitful in our lives. Thank you.

A Remarkable Woman

Mother, we have seen glimpses of the beauty of your soul in the midst of the brain dementia. We have seen those qualities bubble up in spontaneous eruptions and moments of wry humor that transcend a dysfunctional brain.

You are so much more than your brain. We have seen that over these last ten years. We have sensed that while your brain has not been a willing servant of your soul, nevertheless your soul has continued to function quite well. My sense and my prayer is that your inability to express an awareness of God's tender presence with you has had no effect on his ability to be with you in your struggle. I'm certain that you have never really been alone throughout your experience.

Joy Ahead

Dear Mother, one of our great hopes in the midst of all of the losses is that for you, it is the same as it was with the Apostle Paul when he said, "…to live is Christ, and to die is gain." *

We know that when you depart and are with Christ, it will be very much better. †

We long for you to leave behind your earthly tent and to be clothed with your dwelling from heaven. ‡

Through our tears, we fix our hope on the sowing of your perishable body in weakness…so that God can raise it as an imperishable body in power and glory. §

Anticipating our separation from you, we long for the moment, "…in the twinkling of an eye, at the last trumpet…" "…when all in Christ will be raised imperishable, and we shall be changed…" and, "Death is swallowed up in victory." ** and ††

As that day draws near, we pray, Dear Mother, that you have the unshakeable comfort and confidence that God himself has promised, "I will never desert you, nor will I ever forsake you." ‡‡

May his Spirit whom he has invested in you as a guarantee of the redemption of your body, give you a deep, abiding peace. §§

And so, Mom, through my tears, I give this letter to you even though you cannot comprehend it. Perhaps today will be one of those increasingly rare moments when you recognize Dad for a nanosecond and start to smile. He lives for those moments. We all do.

That's all we have from you until we stand beside you in God's glorious presence. Until then, my prayer is that he graciously would communicate directly to your heart my great love and affection for you.

I love you and miss you very much, dear Mother.

Your son, Walt Russell, Ph.D

Bible References to what I wrote to my mother:

* *Philippians 1:21.*
† *Philippians 1:23b.*
‡ *2 Corinthians 4:16-5:4.*
§ *1 Corinthians 15:42-49.*
** *1 Corinthians 15:52-54.*
†† *1 Corinthians 15:55.*
‡‡ *Hebrews 13:5b.*
§§ *Ephesians 1:13-14; 4:30.*

*Dr. Russell is a Professor
of New Testament & Bible
Exposition at Talbot School
of Theology, Biola University;
and he spent seven years as the
chairman of the Biblical Studies
and Theology Department.
Before coming to Talbot/
Biola in 1990, Walt was a
campus minister, church planter,
pastor, and professor in Texas,
Maryland, and Virginia.*

*In addition to numerous articles and scholarly books, he has published:
Playing with Fire: How the Bible Ignites Change in Your Soul (NavPress)
and is presently finishing a new book that emphasizes the need to equip
Christians. It is entitled: The Organic Church; Growing Ministry around the
Sheep, not just the Shepherds.*

*Are your cobwebs too much for you? Perhaps we can help you find the
rainbows in them and even point you to victory.*

*You'll discover a link on our website that will lead you to where that help
is available. www.RainbowsInCobwebs.com*

*I have sought repose everywhere, and I have found it
only in a little corner with a little book.*

FRANCIS DE SALES
BISHOP OF GENEVA (1567-1622)

On Driving: Asian Style

Yesterday, I went out driving. Oh, this wasn't an ordinary occasion, though. I went out by myself. Alone for the first time. What's this, you say? A 20 year old, single American girl who hasn't driven alone? Wow. Whatever happened to you in the land of independence and freedom?

Well, in the land of the free and the home of the brave, I hold claim to the title of 'Good Driver.' And I had put some serious stake in believing that the rest of the world's streets provided the same basic experience. Moving overseas to Kuala Lumpur, Malaysia? No problem. How is driving in Asia much different anyway? So went my assumptions. They were grossly incorrect.

My theory on driving on Asian streets is comparable to saying that bobbing around in a kiddie pool is swimming… until you're thrown out in the ocean with no choice but to move your legs and arms as fast as you can in deep water that is rough and choppy with the faint, adrenaline-laced hope of survival.

Metaphorically, I have provided you with an accurate description of driving in the U.S. of A, versus Malaysia. I mean, the average driver has only neurons in the brain space that traffic laws should occupy. Malaysia is a world where only the strong drivers (and their cars) survive.

Headed for the Mall

So thus began my first time driving overseas through the streets of Kuala Lumpur. My destination was the new mall. It was only a short mile and right turn away. Simple.

The car that I was blessed to drive was the new Proton. First in the count against it: it was new. I hold a fierce loyalty to old rattletraps. I mean, the new thing's interior retains the reek of a freshly minted upholstery.

Secondly: It BEEPED when it backed up and screamed at me when it got too close to something. My truck back in the 'States wouldn't have protested; in fact, it would have plowed straight into said object, had I requested such a thing. Old rattletraps provide character (also commonly referred to as problems), and unquestioning loyalty (also referred to as lack of technology).

Anyway, I settled for hissing at the Proton to shut up each time it started yelling at me.

The mall ended up being a bit of a disappointment. Seeing as coffee in Malaysia either is disgusting (in my opinion) or terribly expensive, my plan was to use Starbucks as an incentive for a first successful solo drive. The plan proved to be fraught with challenges. Instead of a quiet purchase of a delicious cup of coffee to enjoy in solace, I encountered a lot of stares. As in, very nearly jaw-slack gapes.

Back Off, Please

Dear men of Malaysia, my skin is white; my hair is blonde. Yes, it is within your right to grace such a genetic rarity with a double take. But, please. Just because I am out alone in broad daylight does not mean that you should approach me to get my phone number in your truly mangled English. Take into consideration that I have an honest and sincere way to turn you down, because I don't even know my new Malaysian phone number yet.

My little internal dialogue didn't happen to deflect the insistence of the next man. I was walking out to leave when a nearby restaurant host flagged me down, with waving of menus and hands. Politely, I said,

"Hello," but after that, it got sticky. Maybe he was speaking Singlish, a common variety of Singaporean accents tangled with English pronunciation; or maybe it was the garbled Manglish of Malay and English. Whatever, it was terrible. I finally deciphered his query of whether I was staying in town with my boyfriend. I stupidly responded, "No."

Lesson learned. For the record? If anyone else asks, I left my husband and six young ones back at our little shanty in the rainforest where the children are entertained by monkeys and pythons until they become old enough to send off to college in the U.S..

Because that poor fellow tried so hard to get my phone number and it got so ridiculously absurd in that his English became thicker and thicker, that I began to laugh. Of course, that encouraged him all the more. So I backed away, still laughing, and left the man trying to hand me his pen and paper.

Uh... Where Am I?

I got safely back to my car and was off. Off is right. I took a wrong turn which stuck me on a freeway. Then I took another turn that led me...somewhere. In the U.S., we have wonderful things called "off ramps." Stop taking them for granted.

In Malaysia, you take a road that looks like an off ramp and it only connects you to another freeway heading in yet another direction. The Proton and I took one turn...and another. And one more for good measure.

As I saw the toll gate ahead, it was already too late to get away. A Muslim woman in a head covering greeted me.

"Um, hello!" I said brightly in a friendly fashion. "I'm from the U.S. and I'm lost..." My voice trailed off as she nodded and gave me a ticket. I thanked her, thinking it was a free pass for the toll bridge. Such a kind woman, looking out for the young, lost American.

At least that's what I thought until we reached the next toll bridge where my ticket turned out to be a bill for the money I owed. So much for Malaysian hospitality.

Victorious

After I quit grumbling, by some miracle, I turned down a wrong road that became a right one, which led to home. The Proton complied without screeching once I quit negotiating tight U-turns and backing up in the middle of roads. I think we have reached a good place in our relationship.

Caitlin Halone

Caitlin's studies, at the time of this writing, are with an English major at Treasure Valley Community College; and she currently is taking a year off to travel, staying (and driving) in Malaysia.

"I am madly in love with books," she says, "and a natural with chopsticks."

When she isn't exploring the world, she lives:

"...in a small town in Idaho that no one has ever heard of."

You don't need a million dollar smile like Caitlin's in order to keep your chin lifted, your shoulders back, and your eyes sparkling with hope and expectation. Positive people tend to be happier and more successful at everything in life than those who are negative. They fix their eyes on the rainbows of hope in their cobwebs and look beyond to the victory that soon will be theirs, no matter how long the cobwebs hang around.

Rainbows In Cobwebs

Obstacles are those frightful things you
see when you take your eyes off your goal.

HENRY FORD
(*FOUNDER OF FORD MOTOR COMPANY. 1863-1947*)

Wheels in Action

When I was young I drifted along like all contented kids and genuinely was happy. I had a loving family, lots of friends and plenty of sports and activities to keep me busy. It seemed like nothing was standing in the way of my perfect low key life. I envisioned the future. I would: breeze through school, do low stress work, enjoy vacations once a quarter, and finally retire at age 60.

A Serious Blow

Then my world was turned upside down. At age 17, I was diagnosed with Friedreich's Ataxia (FA). At the time I thought, "Friedreich's Ataxia? What the heck is that?" I could barely pronounce it, let alone know what it would mean for me and my family…for the rest of our lives.

Over the next few years we found out that Friedreich's Ataxia is a genetic, progressive, neuromuscular disease that affects all muscle co-ordination from the toes to the fingertips. We found out that…it would be only a matter of time before I would be in a wheel chair…it would be only a matter of time before I lost all ability to take care of myself…it would be only a matter of time before my heart failed and I would suffer a premature death.

And I was 17 years old! 17 is the pinnacle of optimism! My whole life was in front of me, and I found out that it would be nothing but downhill from there on out. So I lived with those facts for a few years.

Making Time Count

I graduated from high school, went to college at U. C. Davis where I earned a degree in Civil Engineering, and got a good job at Brown and Caldwell in Sacramento.

All the while I was losing the ability to perform in sports. Sports like baseball, basketball, golf, and skiing. When it came time for me to give up my bicycle which I loved, though, I thought, No! That's enough of losing all these sports and activities that mean so much to me. I will find a way to keep riding. What I found was a recumbent tricycle. My first thought was, "That's pretty lame. Tricycles are for clowns and little kids." But there were no other options. I had to take action. So I went for a test ride.

As I was rolling around in the parking lot, I fell in love with the freedom that came with this new machine…a freedom I had not felt in years. That's when I started riding. My first ride was seven miles. I was so proud of myself. I had no idea I had that in me. My next ride was 25 miles. Then 50.

Only four months after my first ride I went for a century ride. What was I thinking? 100 miles in a day? I was the last one on the road at the end of it. All of the other cyclists had finished their ride, packed up their bikes, and were driving home by the time I crossed the finish line. But I had done it! 100 miles in a day! Are you kidding me!? I couldn't even walk down the street. From then on there was no limit to what I could do.

Incredible Distances

From that point on my journeys have included two cross country trips, including Race Across America (RAAM) for which I assembled a four man team. RAAM is known as The World's Toughest Bike Race. It's a 3,000 mile bike race from the pier in Oceanside, CA. to the city dock in Annapolis, MD: 3,000 miles through the desert, over the Rockies, and across the plains. But here's the catch: The team must finish in less than nine days.

This was an insane proposition, considering that two of our teammates (Sean Baumstark and I) have FA – the energy depravation disease that is supposed to keep us from doing things like this. I was the only one on a recumbent. Sean rode a traditional bike, although a little unsteadily. We were in the "open division" which means we were competing against other teams with a mix of bike types. There were over 30 teams in RAAM when we raced.

This is a glimpse into the experience: Wake up at 4 a.m. after about 2 1/2 hours of sleep in a moving RV; scarf a peanut butter and jelly sandwich, broccoli, and Mac 'n cheese; try to find your shoes among the nine other people in the six person RV; get dressed; and ride as fast as you can in the rain, in the dark, in the middle of Kansas.

Our team finished in eight days, eight hours, and 14 minutes.

How Was It Possible?

All of those crazy cycling journeys were completed out of passion. Passion for fitness. Passion for cycling. Passion for all the people in my situation living with FA.

In 2009 I joined the staff of FARA (Friedreich's Ataxia Research Alliance), and we created a national program of fundraising bike rides called Ride Ataxia. The mission of the program is to...

Educate the public about FA

Enable the advancement of FA research, and...

Empower people living with FA

Our first event for this national program was in a Philadelphia location. It welcomed 350 participants (including 12 families living with FA) who raised $125,000 for FA research.

Since then we have added locations in Northern California, Dallas, Orlando, Portland, and Chicago. To date, the ride has reached thousands of people, disabled and able bodied, and has become a main revenue stream for FARA.

Reaching for a Cure

With Ride Ataxia as part of the fuel for the research, FARA is on the fast track to a treatment and a cure for the disease. FARA understands, in detail, the cause of FA and has designed several approaches to solve the problem. Right now FARA is pushing along seven clinical trials in different stages of the process, and we have many basic science projects in the works that will develop into clinical trials. We know some of these approaches will fail – that's just the way it goes. But some of these shots will find the back of the net.

When my journey with FA started I was frozen in fear. However, through action, I was able to move again and build some confidence and momentum. I will continue to take action for myself and the cause. There is no limit to what anyone can accomplish when he or she takes action.

Kyle Bryant

You can help! Go to our website, RaimbowsInCobwebs. com and click on this fantastic man's **video.** *He'll tell you how you can be part of the solution in finding a cure for this disease. A worthwhile cause, those who labor in this field are looking for those who care.*

It is not sufficient to have great qualities;

We must be able to make proper use of them.

Francois de La Rochefoucauld

(*French Author 1613-1680*)

Leaving My Love

You...have...twelve...messages...Beep!

Message...one...2:04 pm... "Renée? I hear you've been seeing Phil Anderson. Is that why you dumped me? I'll bet you were cheating on me! I'm miserable and you're happy." Click. Beep!

Message...two...2:07 pm... "Did I mention how miserable I am? You just dumped me and you already have a new boyfriend. How fair is that?" Click. Beep!

Message...three...2:13 pm... "I am so mad at you! How could you dump me like that?" Click. Beep!

Good grief, I thought as I fast-forwarded through the next five messages. Is he ever going to get tired of this?

Challenge

Message...nine...2:38 pm...

"Hi, it's Lisa. Remember me? I played brunch for you at the Park Hotel a few times last year. I'm supposed to start this harp job in Hong Kong next week but I just got a call for a cruise ship gig. It's around-the-world, and I've always wanted to be a cruise ship musician. I'm hoping you can work the Hong Kong gig for me, or you know another harpist who can. It's only for six months."

My heart thumped as her voice continued. "All transportation for

you and your harp is included. There's free room and board plus salary."
When she named the amount, I listened more intently. "I was supposed
to start this Tuesday, but I've talked with the booking agent and he says
the hotel will let you begin a week later so you can get ready. Please call
me back as soon as you can. OK?"

Beep!

Mind Whirling

Huh? What just happened? Yes, I remembered Lisa. Hong Kong?
The salary she mentioned was nearly twice what I presently made without the free rent and meals. My mind vaulted into hyper-drive as my
excitement grew. I'd never traveled to that part of the globe, and Mr.
Unhappy-Ex would certainly burn out on his phone messages if I did.

I saw WIN in big letters. My inner voices were screaming: Don't
miss this opportunity. Call Lisa right now before she finds someone else!

But Wait

Put on the brakes, Renée. Hadn't I just met the love of my life? Phil
Anderson? **The** Phil Anderson. Racer. Event promoter. My New Boyfriend. That wild bike ride – yes, our first date – the bike ride that ended
in the sweetest kiss that was more of a brush of lips than a kiss. That
had been four months ago. So many bike rides since then…and dinners
out…movies…shared smiles…more kisses that were for real, now.

How could I risk losing him? Six months would be an eternity.

I settled into my recliner, telephone and message pad in hand. Yes,
call Lisa before she finds someone else.

What to Do?

Okay, so my first phone call wouldn't be to Lisa. I needed to hear
Phil's voice. He answered. The words tumbled out of my mouth. "Hey,
Hon? I just got the strangest phone message today. One of my harp
friends called with an opportunity for me to work in Hong Kong because
she was going to do it, then got an offer to be a cruise ship harpist, and

it pays really well, and I could finally get ahead on my bills, and it would look great on my résumé, but I would have to leave by next week and…"

Hearing it out loud made it seem strange, scary and impossible.

"Sweet Renée," Phil's voice said. The twinkle in his eye crackled through the telephone cable. "You need to get more info. We'll meet for lunch tomorrow to figure this out. How about noon at the Taqueria? I love you."

"I love you, too. Good night."

A Moment in Time

Chicken parts dancing in the hot grease made for an appropriate background to our conversation, echoing the raindrops that had begun to fall. We were sitting at "our" table, clutching hands and gazing deeply into each other's eyes. Yes, we had only been together four months. However, the feelings were so intense, how could this not last forever?

"Renée, look at it this way," he said, his voice strong but gentle. "If we are meant to be together, six months will fly by. If we aren't, and you pass this up, then you won't have Hong Kong, either. I'll watch your place for you, collect the mail and stuff. You need to do this."

How could he make so much sense? We made a plan to talk daily by phone. He could come visit at the halfway point. No one would accuse us of having a rebound relationship. Six months wasn't that long. Once again I saw WIN in big letters.

Any Regrets?

Are we sorry that we made that decision? Not for a moment. Today, Phil and I are together on Mt. Diablo. My time in Hong Kong is a distant memory. Yes, the separation had been difficult and lonely; the daily phone calls only serving to remind me of how much I missed everything in California. But we learned so much about each other during those six months…things that might have been overlooked during the daily demands of life.

In this beautiful moment, we're standing in front of family and friends, repeating vows we had recited 20 years earlier, promising ourselves to each other forever.

Renée Roberge-Anderson

Renée lives with her husband, Phil, close to Mt. Diablo in the San Francisco Bay Area. Together they raise Guide Dog puppies-in-training, grow organic vegetables, go to the gym and ride mountain bikes. Renée still plays the harp for weddings and parties.

Rainbows In Cobwebs

Our greatest challenges are our greatest gifts. Lived and embraced by one who once was a wounded warrior; now a wounded healer.

DARA FELDMAN
(WRITER OF THIS STORY)

All Things Are Possible

Who would have thought that being sexually abused at the age of five…then putting on weight in a effort to protect myself…becoming the heaviest kid in elementary school…growing up with an alcoholic mother…marrying an alcoholic…having two children by him…divorcing the man and then watching him die as a homeless alcoholic…would all lead me to success in the journey of life? How about if I break it down a bit to explain?

She Sowed the Seed

Mrs. O'Leary, my third grade teacher, showed me, an eight year old, much compassion and understanding which I desperately needed. I was going through a really rough year. My mom was dealing with her second bout of breast cancer while working on her doctorate. In addition, she was in the beginning stages of alcoholism, so needless to say, she was not very available.

I needed help. Because my babysitter had sexually abused me, I became a compulsive eater and it began to show up as weight on my body. It also affected my behavior. I would sneak into the coat closet to steal food from other kids' lunch boxes as well as sneak back into an empty classroom to steal change from their desks in order to buy ice cream at lunch. As I grew chubbier and chubbier many of my classmates would tease me and call me Bahama Mama. I didn't want to go out to recess because I would be bullied.

Mrs. O'Leary obviously knew I was dealing with serious problems. She allowed me to stay in during recess to help her. I graded papers, made learning centers and created bulletin boards. I loved it…and her! This was the beginning of my passion for education and my desire to help others know their inherent value. I will be forever grateful to her for loving me at a time when I felt unlovable, and modeling for me the importance of developing authentic relationships with others.

As I grew into an adult, though, I developed into the perfect and classic co-dependent, trying to be all things to all people and feeling lower than the scum of the earth in terms of my self-esteem. And of course, as is often true of abused people, I married unwisely. Even though the marriage was not good, I hasten to say without reservation, that we had two wonderful children who grew up to be loving and compassionate people who make the world a better place.

Dealing with Addictions

There was a time when my mother was so ill from a stroke that I indulged in a destructive habit: bulimia. There I was – a parent with two small children and taking care of my mother, working full time and caring for my ex-husband who was undergoing cancer treatment as well as being an alcoholic.

I knew he was an alcoholic when we got engaged; however, I thought if I loved him enough he would stop. Not true. On New Year's Eve of 1990, in a hotel room in San Francisco while we were still married, I suggested to him that "we" give up drinking. He said, "NO," because it made him smarter, better and more creative. My mother, who had gone to Alcoholics Anonymous and had risen above her addiction, suggested that I go to Al-Anon, designed for family members of alcoholics.

When I went, they just encouraged me to, "Keep comin' back." I have been "comin' back" to Al Anon for over 22 years now. I also got help for my bulimia at Overeaters Anonymous and have been free of that miserable habit now for 15 years.

Unwavering Gratitude

So my first rainbow and victorious release from the cobweb of abuse is that I was blessed with an amazingly rich and meaningful career in education; and I've developed a deep sense of compassion and understanding for others. My second rainbow and victory was from Al Anon in dealing with the cobweb of alcoholism. A third rainbow and triumph was mine when I went to Overeaters Anonymous and overcame my eating problems.

A fourth rainbow and achievement comes from knowing what my children and I discovered – that their father took the hard life for all of us to be guided to live a spiritual life of gratitude and service; and that things happen for a reason.

Since it is my passion to help others know and realize their highest potential, a goal I am constantly reaching for in my own life, I now share my story with groups, write and live a joyful life. To top it off, a huge rainbow came into my life when I met the man who is now my husband: Dave.

Dara Feldman

Director of Education, a Master Facilitator and a Board Member for The Virtues Project.

Consultant for the Character Education Partnership.

Character Development Coach at Greencastle ES in Montgomery County Public Schools, MD.

Disney's 2005 Outstanding Elementary Teacher of the Year.

Some cobwebs are so persistent that
their victims can't get rid of them. And almost all
cobwebs, even if they are swept out the door, leave
residues of sorrowful memories, embarrassment, regret,
lost opportunities and more. Our writers have shared
many of theirs with you, baring their hearts. And yet,
despite what they endured, or are enduring,
these men and women triumphed.

As you give serious thought to how
they refused to be defeated, it just might light
the path to victory for you.

VII

GLORIOUS

RAINBOWS

Rainbows can...

Provide hope in the times of storm;

Beam ribbons of beauty to appreciative hearts;

Remind us of God's promises;

Inspire art and stories;

Bring out tenderness and caring in the human heart;

Speak music to the human spirit;

Sparkle in water from sprinklers;

Appear on a wall from light through a window;

Flash from water drops on a lawn;

Form circles and semi-circles;

Appear in prisms.

Look earnestly for the rainbows in whatever trouble that has come your way. They shout HOPE! Grab them, hang on tenaciously and let them shine on the path that will lead you to victory.

Rainbows In Cobwebs

You've gotta dance like there's nobody watching,
Love like you'll never be hurt,
Sing like there's nobody listening,
And live like it's heaven on earth.

WILLIAM PURKEY
(*AMERICAN AUTHOR & PROFESSOR EMERITUS*)

Hollywood or Happiness

Los Angeles called to me in the fall of 1997 and I answered. I had an opportunity to live with a friend of a friend whose mom was an executive producer and worth millions.

"Will Karlee come live with me?" this friend of a friend said. "I need to be around her good attitude and energy." Because she said this after meeting me just once, I was flattered.

I was fresh out of college and not working, so the fact that she wouldn't let me pay rent helped tremendously. Money wasn't an issue with her.

It's interesting how everything flows when it's part of the plan.

I got a job right away as a production assistant at my new roommate's mom's company. I worked over eight hours a day, usually, and made about $300 a week. Although the pay wasn't much, I enjoyed my work. I was happy.

Stars in My Eyes – and Life

My first assignment was working on a Damon Wayne's and David Alan Grier's TV show. They were so much fun. I loved my new life: meeting people, working, learning.

One day I dropped off a script in Damon Wayne's office. "Karlee!"

he said, "Why are you always so happy?" The first thing that came to me was, "I don't know. Why not?"

That was the end of the conversation. I walked away thinking how funny that was. I'm at the bottom of the pecking order. He's at the top. And he just asked me why I'm so happy.

Interesting I thought. And I carried on.

The Other Side of the Coin

Not long after the exchange with Damon Wayne, I ran into my new roommate's mom at work. That was a surprise. It was a big company and she owned it, so I didn't see her often. I wanted to make sure she knew how happy I was and how much I appreciated being there. When I told her this, I will never forget the way she made fun of me by repeating and mimicking what I said; and then she walked away.

People are strange here, I thought. And I carried on.

A Relationship Begins

Not long after that I met Rob Schneider. He was a nice guy. He also was a comedian. We became instant friends. Since I'd had only one boyfriend in my whole life, I was shy and not eager to have another one. However, we did start spending a lot of time together. I taught him yoga and meditation and the ways of the spiritual life with which I was raised. He taught me about Hollywood, acting, writing, and growing up. It was a mutually beneficial exchange.

Hollywood Cobweb

The executive producer who had hired me and took me under his wing, as the new girl on the lot, became jealous of my relationship with Rob and threatened me. Awkward, I thought. Why does this man who has hundreds of staff and TV shows to manage care about me hanging out with Rob Schneider? Was it a control issue? Was he attracted to me?

People are strange here, I thought. And I carried on.

Jealousy, or whatever it was, seemed to be catching. When Rob and I actually began to date, many people became resentful of our happiness.

I couldn't bear the pressure, so I quit that job. I didn't understand why everyone seemed so judgmental of my life instead of focusing on his or her own.

One day Rob asked me if I'd go see a good friend of his since one of their mutual friends had just passed away early that morning. "Of course," I said. "Who's your friend?"

"Adam Sandler," he said.

I nodded, suddenly aware. "Oh, yes! That's the guy in Billy Madison."

Once we were in Adam Sandler's house, I sat there and watched these two grown men enjoy belly laughs as they remembered their dear friend, Chris Farley. Adam played the phone message that Chris Farley had left for him right before he died. It was surreal. Since I was a new friend and not part of their history, I took the supportive role as best as I could. To me, the men's interaction was sweet. I felt lucky to have been included in that evening – just to be there for them.

At one point Adam looked at Rob and said, "I want a girl like Karlee."* It was flattering and nice but I thought...

You're Adam Sandler...I'm just me. Hmm, these people are strange. And I carried on.

A Time of Awareness

Rob and I had a wonderful journey together. The TV show he was working on had been canceled, and I had quit my job. That left us with each other and time to learn and grow. I did everything with him. We went to meetings, talk shows and comedy acts. We traveled a lot. I learned a lot.

"If you could make a movie like your friend, Adam Sandler, what would it be?" I asked him one day.

"I've got this idea about a gigolo; but instead of sleeping with people, he makes their lives better," he said.

"Write it, Rob. It sounds good." He did. In fact, he wrote it about our love story. He wanted me to play the lead girl. I thought that was thoughtful of him; but I wasn't attached to it.

As time went on in my three years of dating and working with Rob, and spending lots of time with Adam Sandler and other celebrities, it began to sink in very clearly: Money and fame do not make you happy.

I'll never forget hanging out with Adam, just the two of us. He shared with me his confusion that, after a premier of one of his productions, he didn't feel fulfilled – like he had worked so hard on this movie, so why wasn't it making him as happy as he thought it would?

The best explanation I remember giving him was this. "You know how women can be needy of men at times and it pushes men away?" I asked. He understood that. "Well, if a woman isn't filled up inside and completely happy on her own, a man will never be able to make her happy. Same with your movies."

I think he got it, because, as he said, when he is doing standup comedy with a live audience, it is fulfilling because of all the energy coming to him; and then afterwards, there is a letdown. He's right. You must fill up on the inside first. Rich and famous people really don't have it all if they don't have it first on the inside.

Strange, I thought, but cool. And I carried on.

Deep Hurts

The opportunity to prove what I had said was about to come my way. We were in Hawaii with Adam Sandler. Rob had just finished his script about the gigolo changing people's lives.

I had the opportunity to tell Adam about the script.

"I'll read it," he said, "and if it's good, I'll make the movie."

Within a few days after Adam read the script, it was green lit. Rob was so happy. He had a job after months of no work and just writing.

"Now that it's a sure thing, Rob," I said, "go for a big name to play the lead actress." He disagreed and assured me that I would play the lead. I went through weeks of auditions. The pressure was heavy.

Then Rob dropped a bombshell. He didn't want me to play the lead, after all. He became distant and non-supportive. It was so hurtful. Hadn't I been by his side supporting him all along? I didn't understand it; but it made me fight harder for the part.

Finally it came down to another girl and me. Adam Sandler said,

"If it's close, we go with Karlee." But Rob had already decided against me and nothing was going to change his mind. I saw the audition tape he did with the other girl and he was cute and encouraging with her; but during the audition I had with him he gave me no energy. It all hurt. What a confusing time. I was young. I only knew people sticking up for each other, not promising them something and then giving up on them.

Rob told me later that he was threatened by me becoming more famous than he if I played the part – and then leaving him.

"Well, I'm not becoming more famous," I said, "and I'm still leaving you." And I did.

It Was For the Best

I left Los Angeles after that and moved to London. That was an experience I'll never forget. My life went in a different direction. Instead of acting in Hollywood where people aren't happy, but are jealous, deceitful and not supportive, I am doing work I love. I am a coach; a wellness teacher, and a trauma practitioner. I get to help people change their lives for the better.

I couldn't ask for a more rewarding and fulfilling job.

Not that I gave up acting totally. I still had acting success with commercials.

I ended up having a lot more than just a movie career. Successful actor friends of mine have told me that they feel like they aren't doing enough to get paid as much as they do. They also have told me that they admire the work I do. Are they being honest? Yes. I know the allure that Hollywood has, but fame and money, as I said, is not what makes you happy.

Funny how you think you really want something; but God has an even better plan for you. And so…I carry on.

Karlee Holden

Karlee Holden: NLP, SEP, Wellness Teacher, Actor, Author

*Adam Sandler did meet a girl like me and married her, like he wanted. I love her. She's amazing!

The Hardistys met Karlee at a conference. We were impressed with her genuine warmth and beauty.

Broken dreams. Life is full of them. Yours are not like Karlee's or like those of any others you read about in this book. No, despite similarities, your crushed hopes are uniquely yours.

It's time to quit obsessing over what you've lost...or never had. Trudging through the mire of hurt is like walking on broken glass in bare feet. The only thing you get out of that is more wounding and bleeding. Throw those glass shards in the garbage, where they belong. Put the incidences of loss out of your mind. Replace them with new dreams, new hope, new circumstances. Change your direction.

Rainbows In Cobwebs

First they ignore you, then they laugh at you,
then they fight you, then you win.

MAHATMA GANDHI
(*LEADER OF INDIAN NATIONALISM*
1869-1948)

Prepared for Battle

I started out in business at the age of eight, selling suckers, hawking pencils, clipping lawns, snowplowing…anything that would earn some money. Then I began to climb the economic ladder. By the time I was 11 years old I was selling paintballs as well as the gear, and I also was organizing paintball outings for up to 50 people.

Despite my success in my business ventures, growing up brought pain, as well. I put on a lot of weight. By the time I was 18, I weighed 225 pounds. Since I was only 5'5" tall, the extra pounds were very noticeable, especially because of my 38 inch waist.

My physical stature affected me in many ways – and it wasn't good. I was very shy and quiet in school. I had some friends, but overall I was out of it socially. If I had to be in front of people to speak on a subject, in class, for example, it was…well, very bad. I stuttered a lot and spoke very quickly, almost to the point of being uncontrollable, and certainly not very understandable.

My Solace

Up until that point, by 13 years of age, I was studying the stock market, stock market activities and what made stocks go up and down. When I was 15, I was trading my own money. I did that via my dad's subaccount through his brokerage account where I turned $1,000 into $16,000 over a five year time period.

In my senior year of high school I asked my economics teacher if he wanted to play the stock market game that was being offered to high schools in the state of New York. Schools form teams and compete against other schools.

"I've never done it before," he admitted, "but if we entered, I'd want us to win. Think we could do it?"

"I know we could," I said. So we entered and played the game. I wasn't surprised when we came in 1st in our County and 2nd in the state of New York. My teacher was ecstatic. It made him look really good.

Law of Attraction

This was the first time I realized that the law of attraction was at work. I didn't know what it was at the time. But I was using it without even knowing.

Today, I would define the law of attraction as: harnessing the power of one's mind to pull the desired outcomes into your reality. So, if you want the million dollar mansion, you need to fully manifest those thoughts and believe that you are going to achieve it.

Visualization is a big part of this technique. Picture the size of your bank account (what you want it to be) and picture yourself moving into your million dollar house that you've always wanted. These images in your mind are so vivid that your mind actually thinks it is reality.

With hard work, perseverance and the power of one's mind, anything is possible.

Paintballs Online?

When I was 17, I met a 25 year old guy who had vision in business, just as I did. He became my business partner in a paintball chat room. So we started an online paintball business.

Was it successful? Oh, yea. We built a great business. We kept it going right up through college. In fact, it ballooned so much that we outgrew our vendors.

Backing up a little in my story, when I was a freshman in college, I still was fat; and it was holding me back in life. I wasn't dating much and was definitely not a ladies' man. It was part of my inspiration to lose weight, but the real inspiration was a wedding that I was attending in four weeks. I went to put on my suit pants and I couldn't button them up! I told myself, "I am not buying 40 inch pants." It was time to drop the weight.

My first goal was small...to fit into those pants for the wedding. I achieved that, and set a larger weight loss goal shortly after. In total I lost 65 pounds. I was eating right, my portions were in check, and I was working out as much as 10 times per week (two hours per session). My life got exponentially better. I finally was able to date any girl that I wanted. I gained much more confidence. It follows, too, that I became a better speaker. All this translated into making more money and doing better in business.

I also began lifting weights (I was still in college) and before long, my roommate and I became bouncers at one of the hottest clubs in town. I went from being a terrible dresser, who wore T-shirts and sweatpants, to being a chic dresser who was in charge of determining who was cool enough or not cool enough to get into this really great club.

Enough Playing Around

By my senior year in college, I had to knuckle down and complete the 7000 products that were going to be in our paintball catalog. My roommate at the time asked me about my business and lifetime goals. Actually my goal was 250 million dollars in net worth; but I didn't reveal that. "$50 million dollars net worth," I said.

He chuckled. I smiled. He didn't think it was possible, obviously, but that made me want it more...to achieve higher and higher goals in life. My buddies didn't understand my drive and focus. Friday night would come and they'd ask me to go out with them. "No, thanks," I'd say. "I've got things to do. You go ahead." What they didn't know was that I was working on the paintball website, making sure it was holding up and adding thousands of products and enhanced product descriptions. I'd work until 4:00 in the morning with my coffee or Red Bull, sometimes falling asleep at my desk.

After I graduated, I worked 80-90 hours, seven days a week. I kept the security job in order to pay bills and reinvested all my paintball money putting it back into the same business.

During the first three years after college, I worked every day of the year, except Christmas.

The Opposition

Relatives badgered me constantly. "Get a real job so you can make a decent living," they'd say; but I was chasing my dream…a dream that continues. They didn't understand at the time and still don't. I'm on a mission. The constant negativity and hassling would have destroyed me had I not been strong. Such negative input has shattered many peoples' dreams.

But I was determined. I would battle through it. The result was that I became more convinced that I was to pursue what I knew was my destiny…what I wanted to do.

There's Always a Con

By age 24 I was taken under the wing of a CEO of a telecom company. I drove about 1000 sales to his company in six months. The downside: He refused to pay me. Still I trusted him. I was young and inexperienced so he was able to convince me to go into a new business with him doing commercial mortgages and residential loans through a Las Vegas bank. He'd run the business as CEO and take care of the books, issuing checks to everyone involved in the business, including me. I would do what I did best…make it work.

By now, my paintball business was widespread, so I had a team of five programmers in India. Since the idea of doing mortgages and loans, given me by the CEO, had excited me, I mobilized my programmers in India to be part of it, built a website and got top rankings on the internet for our company. I originated the business model, the plan and the structure – and I found about 700 brokers within six months.

Yet, I still didn't get paid!

I came to the realization that he never would pay me; because frankly, he was just a flat-out crook. My bringing in those 700 brokers for him should have netted me $500,000 that year. In the following eight to ten years that would have increased to around $30 million and finally, $100 million.

The Angel vs the Devil

I called him out on it. When I did, I felt as if I had an angel on one shoulder and a devil on the other. The devil was telling to break his legs and kill him. The angel was saying to learn from it and move on with life. I listened to the angel. I fought an extremely difficult and emotional battle for several months; but I came to the conclusion that I'd been taken by a person whom I considered to be a friend and I had to let it go. I cut the con out of my life permanently.

I had a strong feeling that within three years this guy would lose everything because of the cons he was pulling. Since what had happened still bothered me, in three years, I did a search on the guy. His house had gone into foreclosure and he was failing.

Back to Basics

My paintball partner and I continued to grow that business. We bought out a competitor.

I was 26 by then. Ten years after we started the business when we were both single, he was married with three kids. He wanted a family life...to spend time with his kids...half days off on Wednesdays and all day Fridays and weekends.

I wanted to grow the next great empire. I had a game plan for it. At the time I was developing an online paintball game-organizing software. This was going to be the social network for paintball teams to interact with each other. But when my partner wasn't willing to continue with me, I lost the desire, too, and the business went from being fun to being a job. It had become mentally and physically draining.

Within six months we sold it, cashed out and went our separate ways.

My Perspective

Over my 20 year business career, I have battled bad partners and vendors, relatives, as well as people who hated me – and that's just to name a few. To add to my frustration, I had myself to battle, and that hasn't been easy.

I've started over 20 businesses to date. Currently I run six global companies, including a very successful telecom company; a management consulting firm dedicated to slashing corporation's expenses and driving new revenue streams; a solar company; a tax credit business for mitigating tax liabilities; an oil field; and an energy optimization company. These companies are expanding their reach in Australia, South Africa, Hong Kong, Pakistan, India, Latvia, United Kingdom, Canada, Thailand and South Korea.

But it was all of the battling I had gone through that allowed me to find just the right mixture of people, vendors and partners in this latest effort. With each new pitfall, I can taste and see the success just around the corner. Today I'm shooting for the top of the Forbes list and to make Time's person of the year cover before I hit 40 years old. I've been able to take advantage of the law of attraction in both my business and personal life. I truly believe that the sky is the limit. I truly believe that I can achieve all my dreams. The obstacles just make me better prepared for the battle.

Nick Palumbo

Many business friends and associates have come to Nick over the years for cost cutting advice. Due to his vast connections, starting a full service management counseling business seemed the logical next step for him.

His experience is far reaching, covering many industries including, but not limited to, extensive online retailing, commercial real estate, short sales, venture capital, tax credits, depreciation selling, telecommunications, call centers, solar projects, energy reduction, jet fuel brokering and oil.

Currently, Nick operates multiple businesses from Scottsdale, Arizona, where he resides. He holds a Bachelor of Science Degree from St. John Fisher College of Rochester, New York, where he majored in accounting.

We've posted a video by this accomplished man that you'll enjoy. Go to www.RainbowsInCobwebs.com.

He started right in and tackled the thing
That couldn't be done, and he did it.

EDGAR GUEST
(*ENGLISH-BORN AMERICAN POET 1881-1959*)

I Missed It? No Way!!

The students – the school officials – the town – all looked forward to the event – the annual whitewashing of the enormous "M" atop the mountain overlooking the Montana School of Mines in the city of Butte, a college now known as Montana Tech.

It was the freshman class at the college that had the honor of doing the job. It was such fun as all of us ended the day plastered from head to toe in whitewash (a mixture of white lime and water), that made the "M" stand out in glittering white.

Slap in the Face

I was laughing when I got back to the school, but I wasn't laughing soon after. Suddenly, reality set in. On this same day, I had been scheduled, along with 53 other men, to take an exam to determine if I could qualify to attend a U. S. Marine Corps pre-officer training program called V-12. It was war time. All of the armed services were searching for men to lead forces into battle. While painting the "M" on the mountain, I had missed that exam taken by the other 53 guys.

For me, it was a disaster. I had joined the Marine Reserves at age 17 and wanted more than anything to become a Marine officer. Now that chance was gone due to my own negligence.

While I agonized, a poem my mother taught me as a kid started running around my brain.

Somebody said it couldn't be done,

But he with a laugh replied,

"Well, maybe it couldn't," but he would be one

That wouldn't say no 'til he tried.

So he buckled right in with the trace of a grin

(If he doubted the thing then he hid it)

He started right in and tackled the thing

That couldn't be done, and he did it.

EDGAR GUEST

(My apologies to the poet for taking artistic liberties, but this was how I remembered it.)

So I rolled up my sleeves, pulled out a sheet of paper, and in long-hand wrote a letter to the Marine Corps Commandant in Washington, D. C. I told him my predicament and asked if he had a solution to my problem. I sweat it out, wondering if he'd even bother to read the letter or even if it would reach his desk. Miracles of miracles, he not only read it, but he answered it. He would send an exam to our school librarian. I could take it with her overseeing the process. He did. I did. And I passed! But that was only half of the story.

More Astonishment

44 of us, those who passed the test, and who now were age 18, were assigned to active duty to commence taking pre-officer training. We boarded the train heading east, hoping to become officers, eagerly looking forward to serving our country.

When the train stopped in Kalamazoo, Michigan – another miracle took place. 43 of us got off, assigned to the state teachers' college there. One of us was told to stay on the train. That was me. I was taken to White River Junction, Vermont. From there I was sent to Hanover, New

Hampshire, where I was assigned to Dartmouth College – an Ivy League school.

Not in my wildest dreams would I have conceived of such a windfall. My father had died when I was barely 14, and my mother and I never could have afforded to pay for me to attend a prestigious school like Dartmouth. I graduated from there and went on to become a Marine Officer – a goal I had longed to reach.

Talk about cobwebs, rainbows and victory!

You might be interested in the rest of that poem by Edgar Guest. Here it is (in its original form):

Somebody scoffed: "Oh, you'll never do that;
    At least no one ever has done it";
But he took off his coat and he took off his hat,
And the first thing we knew he'd begun it.
With a lift of his chin and a bit of a grin,
    Without any doubting or quiddit,
He started to sing as he tackled the thing
    That couldn't be done, and he did it.
There are thousands to tell you it cannot be done,
    There are thousands to prophesy failure;
There are thousands to point out to you, one by one,
    The dangers that wait to assail you.
But just buckle in with a bit of a grin,
Just take off your coat and go to it;
Just start to sing as you tackle the thing
That "cannot be done," and you'll do it.

George Hardisty

George Hardisty
Proud Marine Lieutenant

Dr. Hardisty practices estate planning law and has tried cases in Federal and State courts throughout California.

Before that, he practiced domestic relations law. He and his wife, Margaret, gave marriage seminars throughout the nation and appeared on many television and radio shows, both local and national.

He wrote the book Plan Your Estate and co-authored a book with Margaret on marriage: Everlasting Love.

He has another story in this volume, Oh, No, I Killed a Man, a tale of when he was 17. We've also posted a video of him on our website.

Perhaps you suffered great sorrow as a child – like George. Or like Rick Pickering, whose story you can read about in this volume. These two men denied victory to their cobwebs and claimed victory for themselves. In the process, they have slain proverbial giants and lived to bless many, many others.

Let that be said of you. We are showing you the direction you must travel, and offered you the weapons and ammunition to use; but ultimately, you are the only one who can fight your way out of the cobwebs that encase you and climb the mountain of hope to victory. Only you can quit making excuses and bring it about. So what are you waiting for?

Rainbows In Cobwebs

Problems are only opportunities in work clothes.

HENRY J. KAISER
(*FATHER OF MODERN AMERICAN
SHIPBUILDING 1882-1967*)

Rainbow, First and Last

I ran into the rainbow first. I was at the top of my game which was, at the time, president of Wycliffe Bible Translators USA. It was never a position I'd sought or expected. My wife and I had been with the organization for half a lifetime, serving in various places and in various capacities. It was a great work, a great life, with great people and for a great cause.

I'd started at the bottom…not that anybody looked at it that way… and now here I was at the top. Not that anybody looked at it that way, either. Well, maybe a little. I'd come in as a print shop artist. I'd been a graphic designer; actually a magazine art director for Surfer Magazine, in Southern California. But during that tenure I'd begun my search for meaning, purpose, reality, truth; things like that. What I found was God.

Where Would I Fit In?

The fact is, not long after that life change, for that's what it was, I began to question what I should do, like, for the Kingdom. That's when I learned about Wycliffe Bible Translators and that they were needing, not only linguists, but people with a broad variety of skills; like people who could make simple drawings for reading primers and who could lay out a booklet, or whatever. It was work I knew how to do.

Fast Forward 25 Years

My occupational breadth had grown right along with the variety of locations where we were sent to serve. In time, I'd moved pretty much out of art and into editing, writing, public relations, management and leadership to the point of becoming a vice president at the international level. Then, I was elected president – President of Wycliffe Bible Translators, USA.

I loved that role. I also was over my head, but I cherished the challenge. I was stretched in every way imaginable. My art? I was down to making doodles on styrofoam cups during long meetings, if I wasn't conducting the meeting…and even then, sometimes.

Still, they called me an artist. They even named the column I would write for the back page of our flagship publication: Pencil Sketches. Writing is its own art; but sometimes I actually did include a real pencil sketch.

So, I was going along enjoying that role, stimulated by it, challenged by it, loving it. Yes, there were the occasional skirmishes at the edges and the murmur of malcontents here and there. But, I figured, that's part of any leadership job; and if you can't handle it, you shouldn't be in it.

Lightning Bolt

Driving home from the office one evening, minding my own business, waiting for a light to change, I let my eyes wander to a gallery across the street where they were showcasing a nice, large painting. BAM, a lightning bolt of realization hit me and I thought: I could do that!

Not that caliber of work, of course, because I had painted only occasionally, like about once a decade. Yet, I thought, I'd find or borrow some paints and play. Fun, but not that easy. Besides, I was busy with other things. Important things. Painting would only be an interesting diversion. But now lights were going on in my head and they flashed again: I could do that! Not at that level, maybe; but somehow that person had figured it out. I could figure it out.

It was a WILD-OVER THE TOP-CRAZY IDEA that I was going home and not just paint a painting but BECOME A PAINTER! I couldn't wait for the light to change.

Second Thoughts – First Thoughts

As I drove the rest of the way home, all the nay-saying notions in my mind already were making themselves known. What are you doing? they shouted. You're a missionary. You have a job already. You're the president of an international organization. That organization isn't about art; it's about serious things. You've got a role. You've got a family. You've got expectations all over you.

Yes, yes, yes. I knew all that. But for the moment I wasn't letting any of it kill my enthusiasm. Without seeking it, I had driven right into this rainbow, and I didn't want to let anything detract me from the wonder of possibilities.

As it happened, that was the evening before Thanksgiving, which means that the "weekend" to follow was four days long, a good long break for me to live in and relish this new idea, this new identity. I envisioned that I was standing at the entrance of some huge gymnasium which was called "Art." Massive and open, it was full of unlimited opportunity. Around the edges of the gymnasium were doors, one after another, opening to additional rooms of further categories of "Art." Any of these were for exploring; never endingly. A huge new world.

For four days I let myself be this new person in my mind. It's not that I wasn't content with the person I already was. Not at all. But there's something about a new idea that energizes, that takes over. It's NEW. It provides focus. And it refreshes the perspective of everything else.

Reality Smacks Hard

Four days of blissful dreaming and then…Monday.

Like I said, I loved my work. But how much love can one take? It filled my days and often my evenings too. As the days and evenings went by, and then weeks, I found that there wasn't a moment to do anything with this new vision. Even though it hadn't even really been born, it was already seeping away. A major loss with sensations within me of full-on grieving.

I told myself I always could get back to this idea in the distant future, like when I retire, whenever that was and whatever that meant. But it didn't console me. Cobwebs were now clouding my view.

Spirit Renewed

Then Christmas came, and again, a few days off. As presents, two of our children gave me some brushes and paints. Though they had no inkling of my vision, that encouraged me. To me it was a sign. There was hope; there was permission. And…I started painting. "Messing around" is a better term for it, as I had no real direction. That didn't matter. What did matter was that I was doing it. Playing, experimenting, learning.

The next day I returned to the mess and did it again. The next day, again. And I began to realize that I could do this. I could find an hour a day to play in the paint. That was major.

This discovery, of a dedicated time each day, albeit short, in a designated place, made all the difference. It was basic. We live in time and space. All the rest are details.

Life was good. With art, it was more interesting and beautiful. I wondered how I could design it when one day this would be the main focus.

Storm Brewing

Though I was minimally aware of them, there were cobwebs gathering on the path ahead.

I had been brought into the top spot of organizational leadership precisely to make innovations, and that's what I was busy doing…that and trying to keep the people who didn't agree, happy. But change can be hard, and as I said, there were murmurings.

There also was a significant change in the makeup of the governing board. The new board tended to be sensitive to the murmurs and to those who needed a place to air their complaints; so in time, after two days of closed-door meetings, I suddenly and surprisingly was relieved of my position as president.

Whoa! Talk about walking into cobwebs. I thought I'd been doing a pretty good job. Many agreed. Still, I was out.

The irony was that while they felt this was a move they needed to make, they weren't prepared for it. They didn't have anybody to take my place. They wanted to be as diligent as the previous board and spend a year finding a replacement. So they made the highly unusual request of asking if I would stay on for that year until my replacement was found.

I said I would be happy to do it. There were a number of projects that I had begun which were in full swing and needed completion. The fact is, it turned out to be a good year. Any detractors were now quiet, and friends came to my support, many writing encouraging letters from afar.

Did I Care? Was There Hope?

Yes. It all hurt, there's no denying that, but I wondered: Will this be my opportunity to become a painter? That was the gleam of hope, glistening, shining through the spidery webs of confusion and sticky dismay.

It was during that year that I had to find the next step, to ask some deep questions to affirm whether I really was on the right track. It was on a trip from California to New York that I had a second "spiritual" experience involving all this, now a year after the one at the traffic light.

Somebody had recommended that I keep a journal with God…a dialogue. I speak; He speaks; I write it down, first my words, then as I hear or felt them, his. Sounded weird at first, but I tried it. It seemed to work. The thoughts that followed mine were deeper, different and often quite surprising.

One of the first ones I asked was: How do I find guidance?

The answer: *Through my word.* That seemed obvious. His word was the Bible. I wrote it down.

Next question: And how do I find it in your word?

Answer: *Read it.* Again, too obvious. I wrote it down and quit asking. I already was following a system for reading though the Bible that year. But the next day, as it happened, I came to The Parable of the Talents. It's a familiar passage and I read it with no particular sense of expectation.

The story says that the master doles out talents to his servants, according to their abilities, five talents to one, two to another, and one to the last. Then he leaves. When he returns he asks for a report. Both of the first two had doubled their talents and are rewarded for it. The last, however, confesses he'd been afraid and buried his, to which the master responds in anger, calls the servant unfaithful, and evicts him from his presence. The once-buried talent is given to the one who has ten.

Suddenly I thought, "I think God just spoke to me." And it wasn't altogether comforting.

I figured I was in the two talent category. But now I saw that I might well be guilty of the actions of the one-talent servant, the fearful one. Horrors.

Let's Talk Again

I immediately went into a dialogue with God again. And I began getting answers as fast as I could think of new questions.

Me: But, God, I'm in my 50's.
God: *So? How old was Moses?*
(Okay, but there's a social expectation that at a certain age you stop working and start resting.)
Me: But, it's only art.
God: *I thought art was one of the good ones.*
(I thought so too, but didn't know if I'd get agreement, especially coming from the highest source.)
Me: But my culture doesn't value it—secular or spiritual.
God: *That may be, but it's not my authorship.*
(True, art has pretty much lost its value in our times, but this has not been God's doing.)
Me: But I don't have much talent.
God: *I give seeds.*
(Ah, yes, a talent is a seed, not a full-grown plant. Without the original potential, nothing will happen; but left to itself, still nothing will happen.)
Me: What about those who have more talent than me to start with?
God: *What about them?*

(There's no denying that some have a stronger starting place, but in the end we're measured against ourselves, not others. The most inspiring stories sometimes are those where someone has overcome weak beginnings.)

Me: But if I take this seriously, I'd have to put in a lot more than an hour a day; and there's no guarantee that anything would come of it useful, or that you could use.

God: *That's right, but if you don't take it seriously, there is a guarantee.*

(Of course. Without the work, the developing of the talent, there will be nothing to use. I asked my final question.)

Me: Is this You?

God: (No answer)

I was awestruck, sobered and energized at the same time. As with Job after he heard from God, my hand covered my mouth. But now what? I had been given no clearer guidance than before, except that to do nothing would be the height of unfaithfulness. Any thoughts about what other people might think didn't matter. Nor did my doubts about where it all might lead.

I knew one thing for sure: I was not going to dig a hole and bury my paints and brushes and hide behind pages of excuses.

Hyatt Moore

Hyatt is a painter of renown. Some of his art reflects his former occupation with Wycliffe Bible Translators. Even his famous painting of The Last Supper with Twelve Tribes, shows his great interest in people of other lands and cultures.

From Vance: I had the privilege of visiting in Hyatt's home and standing in his studio where he pursues his art. Fascinating.

Wherever we look upon this earth,
the opportunities take shape within the problems.

NELSON A. ROCKEFELLER
(41ST VICE PRESIDENT OF THE
UNITED STATES 1908-1979)

The Myth of Perfection

It is said that the only constant in life is change. You can be trucking along just fine, thinking everything is peachy keen and BAM, life socks you a good one. The rug you have been standing on gets pulled right out from under you. As you fall you realize that all was not as it seemed. The image you have been projecting about your life has been shattered.

Broadsided

I am a woman greatly enhanced by a shattering life experience. That may seem like a contradiction, but it is true, nevertheless. For me there is no going back. I wear the scar of this battle on my face. I am marked forever. I can never forget. I am reminded every time I look in the mirror. My every interaction with others is impacted.

So what happened? When I turned 33, I was 40 days into living with head and neck cancer. I was on a rollercoaster of operations: three head-and-neck surgeries in 31 days, with 18 of those days spent in the hospital recovering from being sliced open. The wound ran from the crown of my head to the middle of my throat. My right facial nerves were cut out from deep within the facial muscle. The result was that the right side of my face now sagged, sacrificed for my chance to live.

If that were not traumatic enough, add in a crazy infection. Nature can be so freaky. I am told these are unexpected and rare complications with very low probability. Hey, that's my style.

This extreme period in my life was filled with raw emotion and crushing realities. It was set in the backdrop of sterile halls and alien doctor-speak. I did the only thing I could – I began really living my life, enjoying the challenge, letting myself feel the pain. I learned to live through hurt and live in the present. I gave myself the time and space I needed to become better. I weathered the storms living through the bitterness and staying steady in the process.

The Myth

My disfigurement showed me how enmeshed my life had been in the Myth of Perfection. The Myth of Perfection is what I call the reality we live in today, especially in the United States. The Myth goes like this: I believed that if I looked good, had a nice body and clothes, owned my own home and car and had expensive possessions, I would be perceived by others as doing well; therefore, I was doing well.

I was a vice president investment banker at one of the world's largest banks. I almost had the Myth in the palm of my hand, despite the fact that I constantly felt perfection slipping through my fingers. I was hiding behind a mask.

I had a smile that stopped traffic and gave people a reason to smile back. My smile was my passport into friendship and accomplishment. I relied on and lived by it. Many a time it had carried me through as nothing else could. Ironically that was the very thing I would lose.

That was before my mask was taken from me. Now, there was nothing left to hide behind. All the imperfection that I secreted away stood out for the world to see. With a paralyzed face, my imperfection was brought to the forefront, a fact that few missed. It was incredibly difficult to be stared at, sometimes open mouthed, and whispered about behind cupped hands. It pierced my heart each time a child innocently mimicked my twisted mouth.

The Gift

My tragedy and transcendent sacrifice could easily have led me to lasting self-righteousness and indignation, even outright anger. Sometimes, many times, I felt all these emotions and more.

Thankfully, the road to self-pity was not the path that inspired me. When all this was taken away, I believed a new beginning had to be found. I discovered that I had to search for the source of my inner healing. With that purpose strengthening me, I began to Face Forward. My altered face took away my ability to be egotistical. It ripped at the narcissistic, materially driven woman I had spent many years becoming, and thrust her into a world of receiving something new. I was gifted with an abrupt ending so that I could begin again from scratch. I shed layers of wasted self, like the skin of an onion being peeled away. If I desired a future, I had to control my thoughts, today and every day.

Whatever Your Challenge...

With a purpose and a desire for a bright tomorrow, you can live with grace and enthusiasm. You can walk with me on this very personal journey. I will show you my wounds. I will share with you my instrumental learning. I challenge you to stand in your power and step into your brilliance. As you realize that now is the time that matters, you will begin to trust that what you need will be there when you need it. Through active choice you trust that your life, like the tiny acorn, came programmed with everything you require to become a strong oak. You learn to grow whatever makes you smile. You decide to reach for relief. You feel your way to your best future. You become positively present and actively involved in mastering the power of your focus.

I am so excited for you to experience your amazing value and worth. Learn to allow your greatness. Lay the groundwork for your highest and best life, as you get out of your own way. Own your authenticity and express yourself with confident intentions. Ask for what you want and dream weave it into your life. Begin to receive and believe what you need to masterfully create your life.

Michele Howe Clarke

Michele Howe Clarke, MBA, is the bestselling author of Face Forward: Meeting Challenges Head On in Times of Trouble.

Face Forward is an amazing journey from neck cancer to transformation.

It is packed with resources that can be learned easily and applied to experience great personal breakthroughs.

As Michelle and many others, who have shared their experiences in this book, have proved, you can make it through your cobwebs to victory. If you find that is too difficult for you just now, perhaps we can help you.

On our website is a link that will take you to where that help is available. www.RainbowsInCobwebs.com.

Rainbows In Cobwebs

When we lose one blessing, another is
often most unexpectedly given in its place.

C. S. Lewis
(*British Author 1898-1963*)

Disguised Blessing

How does it feel to be laid off? If you can't answer that question yourself, there's a good chance that someone else you know can. In light of the dark days at Andersen, Motorola, K-Mart, and other corporations, there were more people mowing their lawns mid-day. Just like me.

In the weeks leading up to the Monday morning I was let go, I was aware of a financial cloud that hung over the para-church organization where I worked. Cash flow had been a concern. The economic downturn of our country had taken its toll. Like scores of ministries, donations were down and expenses were up.

Blindsided

As I arrived at work that day, I had no idea what awaited me. I turned on my computer, and began organizing my projects. The boss called me into his office. Some might have taken that as an unmistakable cue, but I didn't until I was asked to sit, and the door closed behind me.

He told me that mine was one of eleven positions being eliminated. There would be four more weeks of pay, and a letter of recommendation, if I desired. He thanked me for my contribution over the past half decade and wished me good luck.

My heart began to beat double time. My stomach knotted and I was speechless. It wasn't that I didn't have things to say; I was too angry to risk opening my mouth for fear of what might come out. After five years with a family-run ministry, I felt entitled to a bit more warning.

As I cooperated with the compulsory handshake, I managed a smile, then shuffled back to my desk and dialed my wife. When the answering machine picked up, I breathed a sigh of relief that I didn't have to admit to being a failure for a few more minutes.

I rehearsed how best to tell her. Then I prayed for help. It wasn't much of a faith-filled prayer. It was more of an honest venting of hostility and fear. When Wendy did call back, I just told it to her straight. After expressing some surprise, she calmly said, "We're on an adventure. The Lord must have something even better in mind for the next season of our lives. I'm excited." She may have been excited, but I certainly wasn't. Still, there was something about her confidence that got me through the rest of the day.

A Sense of Shame

Over the next few weeks I met with some friends and avoided others. Ashamed, I wanted to hide. When people attempted to put a spiritual spin on what I was going through, I just wanted them to clam up. But I did open up my thoughts to my journal.

When you lose your job, you feel like Jōb. It seems you've lost it all.
The world looks colorless and tastes like bitter gall.
You seek the Lord, but He won't speak. You lose your will to pray.
And when your "good" friends try to help, you wish they'd go away.

* * *

Quite insecure, you doubt your worth. You try in vain to hope. You
feel alone and afraid. It's so unfair to be laid off. You gave your heart
and soul. You lose sleep. Your bills add up. You don't know what to do
or whom to call. You don't know where to aim. No business card. No

payroll check. No place to go. Without a job in an upwardly mobile
suburb like we live in, you're just a big "zero."

That Isn't All

There I was - a husband and father with tuition bills looming each
month. Talk about scary! What made my episode all the more frightening was the monster I felt breathing down my neck. His name is Midlife.
At fifty, a guy's supposed to be on the top, in the prime of his life. Instead, I worried about draining our savings account. I worried that some
churches might see me now as too old for local ministry. I worried that
the experience and unique abilities I saw in the mirror wouldn't be de-
tected by a future employer. Or worse, they would no longer be wanted.

Many I have talked to have been forced into the Twilight Zone on
more than one occasion. Red admits to being a veteran of such transitions. He told me I'm in good company and that I should resist the temp-
tation to feel sorry for myself. Brad went for eighteen months before he
found a new job. He encouraged me to try to let the process play out.
"Something will open up," he said. Tim challenged me not to take time
off to just relax. "Looking for a new job is a full-time job," he said.

The example and counsel of my friends fed my hope. So did my
times studying Scripture and praying. I came to believe that there actually is life after being laid off.

Whoa! What's Happening Here?

Within a matter of weeks we were about to see evidence that Wendy
and I indeed were on an adventure of faith. On Good Friday the doorbell
rang. I opened the front door to find no one. But I did notice an Easter
basket on the doorstep. Picking it up I saw a little wooden cross amid
green plastic grass and an assortment of plastic eggs. I walked to the
kitchen and showed the basket to my wife. Together we opened each
plastic egg. Wendy sucked in her breath. I stared in wonder. In each egg
was a $20 bill! Our grocery bill for the next month was covered.

It was a Good Friday indeed. We approached that Easter Sunday with a renewed understanding of the living Christ at work in our lives.

Just the Beginning

Within a few more weeks I sold several unsolicited articles to publishers. Less than a year later I was approached by the publishing arm of our denomination and asked to research and write the history of our missions work in a remote part of the world.

My reputation as a freelance writer became more widely known. Since that time I have written countless magazine articles and five more books.

It has now been ten years since I was blindsided with unexpected unemployment. And in the past decade I've discovered flavors of God's grace I didn't even know existed. Faith restored and strengthened. I continue to look to Him for answers and directions. I now approach the Scriptures with a greater sense of urgency and determination to hear God speak through them. And in the process, I'm rediscovering that my value as a human being, husband, and father is not based on a brass nameplate or business card.

I had written of Job in my journal, a prophet described in the Old Testament of the Bible. His pain far exceeded the transitionary trauma of losing a job. Covered with boils and familiar with heart breaking losses, his experiences offer a perspective worthy of being heeded.

"He (God) knows the way that I take; when He has tested me, I will come forth as gold." (Job 23:10).

It reminded me that God is capable of reversing or softening hardships. And as best as I can determine, he desires that my life become a crucible of sorts in which my mettle is tested.

This journey into joblessness caused me to remember that it's not until you lose something you had taken for granted that you fully appreciate how good you had it. At the same time, you realize that what seemed so important is not all that valuable when compared to what can't be replaced.

In all honesty, I've worked through my anger. I still grieve over the way my employer handled the situation, and I miss the friendships at the office that were ended as if by death. Truthfully, there are still days when I panic, wondering when and if I'll find a position that matches my skill set and sense of call. But those days are fairly infrequent.

My journal now reflects my confidence.

Deep in my heart I know I'm more than a zero. The Lord thinks I'm a "10." My worth to him does not consist in what I do, or when. He's gifted me and knows my skills. He loves me as I am. And so, I'll take my cues from Job and trust God's unseen plan.

Greg Asimakoupoulos

Greg and his wife, Wendy, live in Mercer Island, WA. They have three grown daughters. Greg is the faith and values columnist for the Mercer Island REPORTER and writes Rhymes and Reasons (a weekly poetry blog).

His newest book is Finding God in It's a Wonderful Life.

Commitment leads to action.
Action brings your dream closer.

MARCIA WIEDER
(*FOUNDER/CEO OF DREAM UNIVERSITY*)

Opening Night

"Mommy…my dress is coming down again and Miss Lisa said to tell Mrs. Stevens, but I want you to fix it!" Emily looks up at me, eyes frozen wide with a *What ya gonna do about it?* look on her too-young-to-be-painted face.

I gaze back at her with a reprimanding smile. "Mommy doesn't have her sewing kit with her, Sweetheart. Just go ask Mrs. Stevens this time. I'll look at it again when we're home."

Emily stares at me for a moment, shrugs her shoulders, tilts her head, then pivots and heads out the door. As I watch the ruffled hem of her skirt sway to and fro to the rhythm of a six-year-old's impulsive swagger, I think of my sewing box that sits upon the closet shelf—a gift given by my mother early in my marriage.

I frown. Although I didn't despise sewing and actually found it relaxing to sit down with needle and thread in hand, there were so many other things I would have preferred to do as a child. Like going fishing with my brothers. Or joining the girl scouts. But no, none of that was allowed. Heck, I wasn't even allowed to take a dance lesson. Being raised in a traditional Italian family back in the 50's didn't give a daughter much of a choice.

A rally in the hallway alerts me back to the present. It's the "Hot Hot Hot" girls practicing their jazz routine. Do they realize how lucky they are, I wonder as shapely teenage legs do fan kicks and leaps, accompanied by one of the costumed "beachgoers" who is singing a cappella? When I was their age, the closest I came to being able to dance was at a cousin's wedding; or up in my bedroom while pretending to be a ballerina. Dancing on a real stage was certainly out of the question.

I glance up at the TV monitor while still seated at the conference room table. Although Emily's number is due to start soon, I know the evening won't be over until curtain call. But I don't mind.

More Dark Memories

I let out a pensive sigh as these pessimistic thoughts coerce me to think about my recent past. How awful it had been during those dark years of my married life when I had been plagued with dreadful episodes of depression. Friends and relatives kept telling me how fortunate I was. A good husband; a beautiful home; two healthy children. That only increased my guilt and feelings of worthlessness.

But the fact of the matter was that I was having trouble performing the simplest of tasks. Even preparing dinner was a nightmare since I had no appetite and was compelled to force food down my throat if I didn't want to end up looking like a bag of bones.

Reflecting upon that dire situation, my determined hand reaches across the table and gratefully grasps a thermos of water. It feels so refreshing as it rushes down my throat. And to think there was a time when nothing seemed to satisfy the thirst that incessantly pervaded my whole being! Facing each new day had been so appalling that I looked forward to nighttime when I would be able to immerse myself in a deep, unconscious sleep. Yet, I had dreaded laying my head upon the pillow, knowing that I was going to wake up come morning.

Present – Past – Present

The faint sound of muffled clapping steals through the hall, eventually surrendering itself to the excited chatter of potential prima-donnas. I wonder how Ginger Thill, my former psychologist, and now family friend, is enjoying the show. If it weren't for Ginger, I reflect, I don't know what would have become of me.

I remember praying…rather begging…on my knees at my bedside, practically commanding God to grant me some sort of relief. And he had sent it in the form of a compassionate human being who had the insight to realize not only my capabilities, but helped me dig deeper into my oppressive past, allowing me to come to terms with not only myself, but the anger and resentment I felt toward my deceased parents.

My heart starts to flutter as another dance number comes to a close. It's the one before Emily's and her group will be appearing any second. My face beams with pride as I invite the other ladies in the room to watch with me. She's certainly not the tallest in the group, but as her hands reach over her head, I let out a giggle, realizing that although the hemline of her tutu is in perfect order, her less-than-graceful bowed legs make her "fourth position" feet look more like the pedestals of a twisted trellis.

As the song progresses, she begins mouthing along to Rainbow Connection. She loves to sing. I'll have to look into a children's choir after her summer swimming lessons are over, I surmise. Of course, she will be eligible to join a Brownie troop in the fall.

A Defining Moment

As the dance recital progresses with hardly a glitch, my heart once again flutters uncontrollably. With eager hands I reach into my purse and grab my tube of lipstick. Then, reassured that my makeup is in full order, I bend over to secure my shoelaces. I notice the other ladies around me doing their last minute maneuvers too, some even giving their bodies one final stretch.

Then, accompanied by the faint music of Jailhouse Rock, we all line up and head out the door. In just a few more minutes, Ginger will be watching me on stage—performing one of the dances I have been practicing all year long.

Constance Eve

Author of: Governey, a novel

For more information, visit our website. Her video is waiting for you.

Encouragement from Constance's husband, Bill, was the inspiration for this author to explore many avenues in her life.

Among those endeavors was the rearing of four children while she attended Macomb Community College. There she maintained a 4.0 average with an A+ in Creative Writing.

The National League of American Pen Women awarded her 1ˢᵗ prize for an original short story in 2006.

She also has been very active in theater.

The best writing advice she ever received? NO GUTS, NO STORY!

Health cobwebs are among the most difficult to sweep out or, if they remain, to tolerate. Yet, it not only can be done in most instances, but gratefulness, joy and emotional release can be part of the package. That fact is attested to by Constance Eve, Terri LeVine, Kit Summers and others of our writers. How they continue to focus on the Rainbows and thus enjoy life is spelled out for you in their stories.

Everyone has to deal with cobwebs – small ones; big ones; unusually sticky ones; "Why, me?" ones; "Doesn't God even care?" ones. The healing begins when you ask yourself, "How can I best deal with this so I am the conqueror, rather than the conquered?"

That's the principal reason why this book was written. These authors who are sharing with you their weaknesses, their humor, their fears, their victories, have been there. They know. They understand. You are linking arms with them across the world as you read their stories and absorb the messages that are in them.

You may never meet any of these incredible people, but their concern for you is real, vibrant and living.

Know it. Make it yours. Read their stories again and again. Take courage from them. For every *cobweb*, there is a *rainbow* and at the end of every rainbow there is a *pot of golden opportunity, triumph and success.*

VIII

BLUE SKIES

Blue Skies

May be overhead even when there is
a drought and a thirsting land;
Don't mask a searing sun that can burn your skin.

Blue Skies also

Can be delightful to see after a storm;
Fill your soul with an appreciation of their beauty;
Soothe and calm you with their glorious color;
Create a perfect background for fruit tree blossoms;
Frame a tree or bird in a marvelous way.

Usually we consider blue skies a refreshing sight. They speak of springing into new life and possibilities; and of heaven, where all troubles melt like lemon drops. Look up! See the blue skies in whatever situation you find yourself. And thank God for your situation.

Rainbows In Cobwebs

Nothing you do for children is ever wasted.

GARRISON KEILLOR
(*AMERICAN AUTHOR;*
HUMORIST AND RADIO HOST)

SAM Camp

"Can we come back on Monday?" Her beautifully slanted brown eyes and big smile melted my heart. "I wish you could, Honey," I said, "but there's no camp next week. Be sure to come back next year."

"Awww," she said disappointedly. Just then her mom appeared and she ran excitedly to meet her, artwork in tow. She turned back quickly and smiled, "Thank you, Crazy Connie!"

Crazy Connie – probably not the best name for kids to call a camp director, but its inception was innocent enough. It was Day One of our very first Science, Arts & Math (SAM) Camp and as our 101 kids (grades 1-12) flooded into our church sanctuary turned auditorium, I was struggling to quell the excitement and get their attention. It was controlled chaos. I made a flip remark that if they didn't settle down they would make me crazy and then people would forever call me Crazy Connie. They loved it! From then on, I was endearingly Crazy Connie.

Reflections

As the last child left, I collapsed on a small comfortable sofa near the church office entrance. I was exhausted. I'd just finished one of the most challenging and rewarding weeks of my life. So many images flooded my mind. There was the dad who, at the beginning of camp, ushered his hefty, depressed-looking 11-year old son my way and entreated, "Please make him have fun," and promptly headed for the door. As he reached the exit, he turned back and said with little hope, "Good luck." Halfway through the camp week, though, I'd seen the boy wearing a huge grin. He was having the best time of his life. I sighed and smiled.

Then there was the timid, fearful little boy who didn't interact with anyone at the beginning of camp; but he took center stage as he proudly marched up to get his certificate of completion on the last day.

That melded into smiles and hugs as all the children ran up at the end of the ceremony to embrace the volunteers they'd grown to admire and appreciate. For one solid week those children had been artists, sci-entists, mathematicians and athletes. We had the marshmallow towers, smoke-filled rooms with bubbling beakers, basketballs, footballs, songs, dances, number games, paintings and sculptures to prove it. And as they left they begged us for another week.

This camp was an outreach to children in the community. The economy had tanked. Many parents were out of work and struggling just to pay bills and keep food on the table. Summer camp for their kids wasn't an option. Nor was it for me when I was growing up.

The Difference

My father worked in a factory while my mom worked at home tend-ing five kids and three foster children. They had signed up to do foster care when a local orphanage had closed its doors and the cry went out through the churches: Please, please provide homes for these children.

My parents didn't have much but they were happy to provide food, shelter, and love to those less fortunate. Though my birth brothers, sis-ters and I never went to camp, Social Services paid the camp fees for my foster brother. We would all pile into our old car and go along for the ride as my dad drove him to camp – just to see what it looked like – then eagerly await his return two weeks later to hear all about it.

Later, as a mom, I only could afford to send my sons to the inex-pensive day camp at the church just around the corner. But they loved it: Summer's Best Two Weeks.

Crazy or Inspired?

Hmmm, I thought as I reflected over the past week of SAM camp. Maybe I really am crazy, but why can't these kids have two weeks, too?

The new vision grew rapidly...fueled mostly by my deep desire to give every child the opportunity to experience summer camp; as well as our small leadership team's dedication to the camp mission: to bring out and nurture the God-given talents and abilities in each child in a safe, fun and loving environment. A year passes swiftly and there would be much to do if this dream was to become reality.

As I promoted the camp to a group of pastors and community leaders, the superintendent of a local Christian school generously donated his school campus for the two weeks. This was miraculous! Our non-profit organization's funding was sparse. To keep the fees to $55/week per child and $110/week for families with two or more children, plus provide needed scholarships, we had to keep costs down. Now we had a place to accommodate hundreds of children and it was free! Plus, their cafeteria made it possible for us to include a hot lunch and drink for every child. No one would go hungry and everyone would get the same nourishing meal.

Action + Problems

The team updated our logo, ordered T-shirts, ID badges, and reinforced our processes and procedures that protected the kids. We created a brochure and distributed it to the local schools, and before long we were overwhelmed by the registration paperwork that was pouring in. 310 children (ages 6-17) registered. 310! The reality of that sank in quickly because we had a problem. Our volunteer recruitment efforts were waning. Last year's volunteers were slow to sign up and it was difficult to engage new ones from other churches because they had their own summer programs.

Fear Invades

I was terrified. Early on I had flip-flopped from fearing that no children would register or show up, to fearing that we'd have to cancel because we didn't have the needed volunteers. Now, just a few weeks before the camp was to start, it was clear: this camp would not happen without at least another 30 volunteers.

How could we let 310 kids and their parents down? Yet, we had promoted, encouraged, called, emailed and practically stalked every possible volunteer we knew. Nothing we did was making the impact we needed.

With a demanding 50-hour work week of my own for my employer, and another 30+ hours per week dedicated to directing this camp effort for the past three months, I was dog-tired and discouraged. I knew God wanted to bless these children and their families and I couldn't imagine that He would allow it all to fall apart. Yet, I was desperate. The burden I was trying to carry was far too heavy for me. My creative juices had dried up and I had no idea what to do next...except pray.

"God, where are you? Lord, I need you. I can't carry this any longer. This camp originally stemmed from a vision you gave a young woman in our church. She saw children of all ages in the sanctuary drawing, painting, singing, dancing and creatively expressing themselves freely to your honor and glory. We want these children to know you love them; to know their gifts and talents come from you; that every color, number and scientific formula generated from you, the living God, their Creator, who cares deeply about every detail of their lives.

"Maybe I was crazy for trying to do two weeks and open this camp up to three times as many children. But, Lord, I prayed and truly believed it was your will. And you brought us the school campus for

free. You brought us 310 children. You helped me create a brochure, and design it, and you know I couldn't design my way out of a paper bag! Lord, I need you."

The Answer

As I cried and released all my fears and frustrations, I paused to listen. Would He speak to me? Then from the still, quiet voice deep in my spirit came this song:

I need you, Lord, like the sun that rises in the morning
like the rain that nourishes new life.
You lift me up out of the darkness
You take my hand and make things right.
You are life, you are love, you are hope that never fails
You are all that I need and all that I am is yours.
I need you, Lord, like the breath that
fills me with new freshness
like the step that gently leads me on.
You bind my feet to righteous living
You give me grace to carry on.
You are good, you are great
and your righteousness prevails
You are all that I need and all that I am is yours.

The Challenge

As these words and the sweet melody comforted me, I felt a very strong urging to make 35 copies of volunteer sign-up forms to bring to church for Sunday service. Furthermore, God's urging said that I was to ask the pastor for a few moments to speak, no, sing this song before the congregation. I was horrified.

"Oh Lord, you know I can't sing on key in front of all these people!"

I love to sing and treasure the songs the Lord gives me. But my voice isn't for the masses…or the few. Singing in my home at my keyboard is fine. But when I get in front of people, I have great difficulty controlling my voice. I could only imagine the humiliation.

"Why, Lord?" I asked, but I knew He was telling me to do it. The answer was clear. Just as I trembled in my inadequacy, I realized that others felt the same when it came to volunteering to help at the camp. They didn't think they had anything special to offer the children – no skills or talents. That was why I had to sing, even though I couldn't. It was important for me to show my weakness. I had no other option. I needed to obey the Lord if I wanted to see more volunteers sign up.

That night I went to the church and printed out 35 copies of the volunteer forms and set them on the table with our SAM Camp sign. As I arranged the forms on the table, I felt His peace – something I'd deeply needed for quite some time.

The First Step

The next morning I arrived at the church early and asked the pastor for a few moments to speak to the congregation about the camp. He agreed. Then I had what I thought was a brilliant idea. I spotted a couple of my friends who sang in the choir. I dragged them over to a piano and plunked out my song. "Can you please sing with me? I'll make copies of the words. And can someone play the keyboard?" They graciously agreed.

Actually, I didn't have any chords. In fact, I had no idea what key this song was in – I simply had the words and a one-handed melody. I whispered a prayer and headed into the sanctuary.

I don't remember anything about that service. It was all a bit of a blur, until I suddenly found myself before the congregation with my song in hand. I explained the urgent need for volunteers and pointed them to the sign-up sheet in the foyer. I reinforced the fact that the most important gift we could give these kids was the love of God and a caring heart. No special skills required.

And then I shared how the Lord gave me a song and asked me to sing it for them. I let them know I was painfully aware of my inadequate voice but I had some friends who have wonderful voices and they'd agreed to sing with me even though they'd only heard the song for the first time that morning. I then called my friends from our choir to join me.

Travesty

I had to start the song because they didn't know the melody well enough. So I began singing in whatever key came out. At the same time, the pianist began playing in the key he thought was best. Unfortunately, his key and mine were not in synch. The combination hurt even my ears but we valiantly sang to the end.

Truthfully, my brilliant idea was a travesty. I didn't realize I was capable of taking down a choir's finest voices. Fortunately, it was at the end of the service. The pastor said a brief prayer and dismissed the congregation.

The people filed out of the sanctuary. I wasn't sure what to do. I took a deep breath and followed behind them, embarrassed and prepared to be more so.

As I stepped into the foyer, l was astonished to see a long line of people waiting to sign up to volunteer for SAM Camp. Thirty-five people volunteered that day. Thirty-five! Every last form was completed. Somehow, God was glorified in my weakness and hearts were touched by His Spirit to extend a hand of love to 310 children.

SAM Camp was an amazing, blessed, and exhausting two weeks, and we loved every minute of it.

Ironically, our music teacher came down with the flu the second week of camp and I was the only one available to lead the music class. We wrote our own lyrics, we wrote our own melodies, and we made a joyful noise to the Lord. It was magnificent!

Connie Segreto

Connie has 30+ years of sales, marketing, and business development experience that range from strategic marketing in the technology and health sciences industries to writing and producing a nationally syndicated television series. She has a Master's degree from the State University of New York at Binghamton.

She has a passion for helping children and the disadvantaged and was one of the SAM Camp founders and the Camp's Director for the first two years. Now in its sixth year, Connie serves as advisor to the SAM Camp leadership.

And...she also is on the board of Lighthouse for Women. It is an organization dedicated to helping transform the lives of the most oppressed and abused women and their children in India by providing long-term safe homes and empowering them through literacy and a vocation for their financial independence.

Writing poetry is one of Connie's interests. The Hardistys have enjoyed receiving a number of her poems over the years. Delightful and inspiring.

> There are gems of talent in every person we've ever met. Talent fosters dreams. Find your dream and if it is ethical and moral, follow it. You may be able to pursue it only part time, but that's okay. You just don't want to end your life saying, "I wish I had..."

Rainbows In Cobwebs

Times of great calamity and confusion have ever been productive of the greatest minds. The purest ore is produced from the hottest furnace, and the brightest thunderbolt is elicited from the darkest storm.

CHARLES CALEB COLTON
(*ENGLISH CLERIC & WRITER 1780-1832*)

We Survived Communism

Picture a quiet winter night in a little village in Romania. Big snowflakes were floating down to whiten the streets. A fire was burning in the stove, spreading a pleasant heat. It was February 11th, 1981. After just a few hours on the 12th of February, at 3 o'clock in the morning, Emanuel-Horatiu, my son, was born. I took him in my arms and checked his little arms and legs, I listened to his heart beat, and I thanked God for giving me a healthy child.

My story revolves around that beloved son, whom I had been expecting with so much love and prayer.

When It Began

My name is Lidia Popa and I am from Arad in Romania, a town not far from the Hungarian border. I was raised in a Christian family. My parents helped me go to school even though they were not wealthy. My father worked in an iron mine. My mother had animals and sold milk and cheese. Father always encouraged my sister and me to read Bible stories and then retell them to him.

I attended the school from our village for only four years; after that I had to go to a nearby village to continue my studies. I used to take a bus to get to the school; but when the bus broke down, we were taken by a truck. Sometimes we walked. I remember in winter when the snow was deep, my aunt and my grandfather would walk ahead of me with big boots so that I could follow in their footsteps.

My grandmother was a perfect cook. I learned so many things from her. My grandparents are no longer living, but my mother and father are. We are very happy to have them still with us.

Despite the Oppression

Romania was under the oppressive rule of Nicolae Ceausescu and his Communist government. However, a fairly good system of schools was established; so eventually, I became a student at the University in Timisoara where I studied to be a doctor at the Faculty of medicine. The government paid for all of our six-year training.

I also attended a church there where I received Jesus as my Savior. Doru Popa was a youth leader at that church and our relationship began. We married in 1979 and before long, I was pregnant. On my way to the medical courses, walking in the park, or going to the Faculty, the clinic or the hospital, I would pray. My unborn child was in my prayers daily. I'd ask the Lord to bless him with good health, wisdom and everlasting life.

Then Trouble Began

People who have never lived under Socialism/Communism have little idea of how really dehumanizing it is. Our country had been ruled by it for decades. The horrors of that time are recorded in history so I won't visit them here. Perhaps in another story at another time I can tell of the orphans we have taken in that were left parentless and homeless because of the regime's demand that all women under 45 have a child (or more than one) whether married or not.

At the time of this account, though, I was married and I had my son. But I also was a doctor; and according to the law issued by the Communist Party of Romania, I was to be sent to work in a hospital. Nor did I have a choice as to what job I could take. The government decided that.

My husband was an engineer, so he was given a job about six and a half miles from Arad. My position was in a hospital in the eastern part of the country about 500 miles from our home! So I had to leave my home and go to the hospital in Galati. My heart was bleeding with pain. Words cannot describe my mood. Leaving my child with my mother-in-law, leaving my husband alone, was just unbearable.

Having to Cope

With a heavy heart, I arrived at the hospital, found a place to stay and discovered that we had quite good facilities in which to practice. The doctors, who came from Arad, Timisoara, Oradea and all the Western part of the country, were well-trained. The town was nice and the people were friendly. However, I was not at home.

One doctor, a pediatrician who was part of the government system, befriended me. She said to others (about me), "I don't know why I like this young lady-doctor. She has something special as compared to the others." I often talked to her without knowing what a great influence she would have in my life at a crucial time.

Even though I met a lot of kind people, and started having many friends, I had trouble sleeping. I couldn't cook. It was very difficult even to wash my clothes. I was not home.

Time passed. I often called my husband, my mother in law and my neighbor. They would tell me about how Emanuel, my son, was progressing; but this made my situation even harder. I wanted to be close to him.

They told me that one day Emanuel was on the balcony and heard the train.

"Hear... the train...," he said. "Mother is coming home."

"No, she cannot come now," he was told.

"Why, is the train broken? Is its wheel damaged? We'll send Uncle Ovi to fix the train so that Mummy could come home."

Relief At Last

I would have to stay at that hospital for about eight months at least, I was told. After the eight months my husband told me to go to the Health

Ministry and ask for approval to come home. "If the Ministry doesn't give you approval," he said, "come home, anyway."

I prayed diligently about that; and then I went to Bucharest where the Ministry was. At that time in order to get what you wanted you were supposed to bribe. However I decided I would not. I arrived in Bucharest early in the morning. I knocked at several doors and finally got in to see the person who could help. I was given the approval to go back home. Or so I thought.

I still had trouble waiting for me.

At Galati where my job was, the Secretary of the Communist Party told me, "NO… NO… absolutely NO… the government invested money in you and you have to stay here, in our hospital."

The lady I told you about earlier, who had befriended me, came to my rescue. "You might as well give her permission," she told him. "She's going to go home, anyway, even if you don't say she can." I don't know what else they talked about, but I was allowed to leave.

More Cobwebs – Cold Ones

I was very happy to be home in Arad, but I still had to go to work. A job was waiting for me, supposedly; but once I got there, I found out that a colleague of mine, who was supported by the Communist Party, was given my job and I was to go to a dispensary at a village a distance from my home. There was no train or bus to that village. So I had no choice but to go by train to a larger village nearby and ride in a one horse cart to the village where the dispensary was. Then, at night, I would reverse the situation to get back home.

It was very cold that winter: about -22 degrees Celsius. My hands were swollen and painful because of the low temperature. I had to go into the village to see the people who were sick and there was no way to get back to the dispensary except to walk. It wasn't surprising that I became ill. I stayed home for two weeks on medical leave.

My husband, very concerned, bought a big truck, filled it with wood and took the wood to an elderly woman in the village where I was the doctor. He asked her to allow me to sleep in her house from Monday to

Saturday. Her home was situated so that I wouldn't have to travel so far every day. That meant I had a place to stay, even though I slept in the same room as the woman all winter.

Spring Brings Hope

Spring came and at the same time my hope came to life. I was allowed to go to Arad to work in a dispensary. However, it was a bit frightening. The doctor who was there before me had been sentenced to prison. All my colleagues were afraid to work in a place where another colleague was put under arrest. Besides, because we were avowed Christians, and my husband was not cooperative with the secret police, we were in constant danger.

But I went to the dispensary on the first day, quite afraid, but hoping that God would be with me. I worked there for about three months. Nothing bad ever happened to me. To the contrary, I had a good relationship with the staff.

They also needed a doctor at a nursing home for old people. It was supported by the government so I was sent there. It is impossible for me to describe the dreadful conditions in that facility. The old people were suffering, but I love working with anyone in ill health, so I was able to help.

A Miracle

Later on, my boss told me I was to go to a factory where chemical substances had been used. Yet another chapter in my life.

I was alone in the factory one day when two men came to my office and asked me to go with them because they were supposed to search our house. Hmmmm, I thought, this is strange. My husband was at the American Embassy in Bucharest and their presence made me feel uncomfortable.

"I can't leave my job at the moment," I told them.

"We'll come back when you get off," they said, and left.

Worried, I called a friend of ours, Florian. I asked him to wait for me at home.

The men came back and when we got to our flat, they questioned Florian and then started searching. We had some Christian books – not allowed by the government. One of these books was "The Manifest of the Communist Party" written by a pastor who had been persecuted and had left the country. If these men found it… I held my breath.

The two men stopped searching before opening the closet where we had the books. I breathed a big sigh of relief.

1989 - Arrested

Several months later my husband was invited to the American Embassy for their 4th of July celebration. When he arrived at the airport, secret police approached him and he was arrested. I didn't understand what had happened to him – only that he never arrived at the American Embassy. I went to the Secret police and asked about him but they told me nothing.

I called our friend, Mrs. Susan Sutton, at the American Embassy. She went to work on our behalf and several hours later my husband was home.

Susan Sutton was really close to us that year when it was very difficult for us. My husband had lost his job because he was a Christian believer. After that, he became a full time pastor. So I had to continue to work in order to support our family.

I was called again by my boss and sent to work in a bigger village, where many Germans lived. The village was nice and people had nice houses. I could hardly understand why they sent me there, but I soon found out. I was to work with a large group of gypsies. That was not easy but I did not despair.

Light at Last

The Revolution to free Romania from oppression took place in December of 1989, and ended in the demise of Nicolae Ceausescu and his wife. Once again, it is written in history so I won't revisit it here.

In the following January a number of friends from Great Britain, France and the USA came to visit. A friend from England asked me what

I would like for my life now that the revolution had taken place. I told her that my dream was to be able to work in Arad and stay near my son and my husband and to have a Christian clinic where I could help all sorts of people.

I asked for nothing from her; but she and others raised some money, bought a house and made all the necessary changes to turn it into a clinic so that we could work there with both children and adults. While they were getting it ready, I went to England for three months to study the Brits and their clinics.

On May 6th, 1992, I opened our clinic and since then I no longer had to leave my family. It was a God made wonder as I never would have been able to buy a house and the necessary equipment for a clinic.

As I Look Back

Being away from my family for such a long time was extremely painful for me. It's difficult to put it in words. But now the bad memories must be only that – memories – not to be revisited very often. Life goes on – with its joys and triumphs. My life was a network of cobwebs, rainbows and, finally, victory, but I must tell you of a last thing that perhaps was one of the greatest triumphs of all.

After the revolution, the Secretary of the Communist Party from the factory where I worked that I told about earlier, came to our church – on his own. No one from the church invited him. He came once. Then again. And again. I watched him. Here was a broken man. He often cried. Then one day he sought out my husband.

"I want to receive Jesus as my Lord and Savior," he told him. They prayed together and soon my husband baptized him. Later he came to me and became my patient. We had a good relationship in his last years of life. Maybe it was something in his heart that condemned him from the time when he persecuted Christians, and he needed forgiveness. I think this is the case, don't you?

Lidia Popa, MD

Here are photos showing:

1) My son, Emi (Emanuel), a little boy crying for his mother who couldn't be with him.

2) My grown son, Emi, and I.

3) My husband, Doru, Emi's bride, Vio (Violeta), Emi, and me.

Rainbows In Cobwebs

America, America, God shed His grace on thee

KATHARINE LEE BATES
(*AMERICAN SONGWRITER OF*
AMERICA THE BEAUTIFUL 1859-1929)

Journey to Freedom

One of my first memories as a small child in Vietnam, where I was born, were those of my parents fighting and my father yelling a lot at my four sisters and me. They say that opposites attract and I guess that must be true because Daddy was rough and angry while my mother was gentle and sweet. Since they didn't get along at all, they decided to separate and let us kids choose which parent we wanted to be with. We all chose Mom. After they separated, my brother was born. Mother supported us by teaching typing.

We lived about 3 1/2 hours from our father, and we traveled by bus to visit him. Mother always went with us. The buses were old and all the people who rode it smoked. The smoke, combined with the smell of the bus, made me sick to my stomach every time we went.

It was on one of those visits that my life changed. I was only about four or five. We had finished our visit and were standing outside the bus, about to board and go home, when I looked at my daddy. He looked so lonely that my young heart was wrenched and I decided I should go live with him. He had no one while Mother had everyone. My mother didn't protest, because it meant one less child to feed.

Daddy was good to me but he knew nothing about taking care of children. It didn't seem to occur to him that I needed much food. Nor did he give me money to buy food later when I went to school. I was always hungry, it seems, but I said nothing because I felt sorry for him.

He would climb a very tall tree to get fruit.

Bombs

This was during the time when there was war between Vietnam and Cambodia. Sometimes bombs were falling everywhere and people would run into basements for shelter. One time, when the bombs started falling, I was very afraid, and I couldn't find my father. I didn't know he had climbed the tree to get fruit. I called and called for him. A soldier, who felt sorry for me because I was crying, said he'd take me to the market to buy a sweet treat on the end of a long stick, a favorite with children. As we ran to the market, the bombs seemed to follow us.

When the bombs stopped and we went back, my father ran and grabbed me. He was frightened and angry with the young man. "Why didn't you ask me if you could take her?" he said. But of course, he had no idea where my father was.

I was very small. I remember riding behind my Daddy when he rode his moped. He was a small man but I couldn't stretch my arms all the way around him as we rode.

Learning to Work

When I was about seven, I learned how to make food by helping my daddy. So, when I was 12, I would get up at 4:00 A. M. to work. I started a little business of my own to buy books and clothes. At night, I would peel 200 of a type of potato, make a powder (kind of like a starch), and sell it.

In high school, because I ate very little, I was very thin. On one of my visits to see the other part of my family, I watched one of my older sisters as she sewed clothes. She didn't think I could do it; but I learned just from watching her. I went home, borrowed a used sewing machine and started making all my own clothes. They really looked good.

I did well in high school. In the 9th grade, I took French and was the #1 student, not only in the entire school but in all of South Vietnam.

Love Came Knocking

After I was out of high school, I met a man and we fell in love. I was very careful not to do anything wrong in our relationship. I was sure I would marry him one day. His family sent him to the United States. We wrote to each other, telling how much we loved one another. I waited three years for him to come back to get me; but his aunt told him she didn't want him to marry me. I realized then that I was wasting my time. I broke up with him – by letter.

Another Change

The nephew of a woman who lived fairly near to us came to live with her. I didn't know him at that time, but heard his story later. His mother was in the United States and to join her she would have had to come back to Vietnam and arrange to sponsor him. She couldn't do it at that time, so he had decided to go from Vietnam to Thailand; because once he was in Thailand, he could get permission to go to the United States.

He and 28 men got into a boat. One of them was his cousin. But when they got into the ocean, the boat sank. Everyone drowned except him. He would have drowned, too, but men on another boat spotted him and pulled him to safety. They saved his life. It was a depressing experience, of course. He went to his aunt's house and cried a lot.

After he began to stabilize, he heard about me. I was told about him; but I said, "No, not me. He can meet my sister. I'm not interested." He came to our house to meet my sister, but he thought I was beautiful and wanted only me. I guess I was ready to be admired since the boyfriend I had loved so much was no longer in my life.

He decided to try to get to Thailand again. So, a second time he got on a boat with others. There also were women and children. On the ocean, they ran out of water. They were certain they would die. Some of the women had brought lemons along, though. Lemons can save you from dying of thirst, so most of them lived and they reached their destination.

From there he went to the United States. Then he sent for me.

The Disappointment

After a year, we married, and we had a little boy; but I soon realized that my husband was a compulsive gambler; so we constantly were out of money. Was his addiction because of his depression from the boat accident and losing his cousin and seeing the others drown? And that he felt guilty that he was the only one left alive? I think so. I tried to help. I got a job and bought him a car, thinking that might make a difference; but he didn't change – nor did he try. I went to beauty school at night to improve my own life so I could provide better for our son.

Finally, in desperation, I divorced him and opened my own salon. Now, at this time in our lives, I can make sure our financial needs are met. I live in an apartment. His family just bought a house for him so he and our son have a place to stay when I am working. We take turns parenting and I give my ex-husband money when he asks for it, but now I can control it so he doesn't gamble it all away.

My mother, sisters and brother all moved to the United States, but they are in the Midwest while I live in California. I call my father in Vietnam, frequently. He and I are Buddhists. My mother, brother and sister are Christians now. In fact, my brother is a preacher. I've thought about being a Christian, but it would hurt my daddy's feelings.

The difficult times in my life were like cobwebs; but there always is hope. I would grab hold of the hope and realize that I was smart enough to get out of the cobweb. So I do feel victorious.

Julie Thuy

Julie owns and operates Luxury Nails & Spa in Walnut Creek, California.

To hear her tell part of her story in her own words and charming accent, go to our website and click on her video.

Rainbows In Cobwebs

We must let go of the life we have planned,
so as to accept the one that is waiting for us.

JOSEPH CAMPBELL
(*AMERICAN MYTHOLOGIST, WRITER, LECTURER*
1904-1987)

Why?

"Why did this have to happen?" Bryan asked. "Why all this pain? Why has my life been put on hold when I'm finally doing what I've always wanted? Why would God allow this?" My husband's complaints echoed through the house. There were no answers.

Bryan had always been good at getting himself into trouble, like when he was a toddler and climbed the windmill at his grandparents' farm. His mother, although she had a fear of heights, had to climb up to rescue him. She managed to maneuver the climb and then get down again, using one hand to grip the boards while holding a squirmy little boy in the other.

Or when, at 18 months, Bryan's grandfather went to work in the field, took him along and told him to stay in the truck. What was there for a tot to do but unfasten the loose screws on the gearshift? It took Grandpa and his friend several hours to put it back together so they could drive home.

Then He Grew Up

Adulthood didn't change much in the prone-to-get-into-trouble scenario. For some reason, Bryan always seemed to have a bull's eye painted on the side of his car, attracting other vehicles. He had an inordinate number of accidents. The majority of them were not his fault. The fact that the most recent car accident had been a horrendous one, and it wasn't his fault, was probably the reason he kept asking, "Why?'

This time it resulted in multiple bone fractures and complications requiring several hospital visits in the space of a few months. It also put him in a wheelchair for a year and a half.

The Dream

Bryan was an artist. Long before this last car accident, he had dreamed of painting pictures of classic autos and selling them at car shows. He was envious of others doing just that. He also wanted to restore classic automobiles. Life had interfered, though, forcing him to have a job, not a dream, so the dream had to go.

When he was laid off later in life, however, his vision finally came true. I, as his wife, was able to support him, so he spent every morning painting and every afternoon restoring his classic Mustang. On summer weekends we sat in booths at car shows all over the western United States, selling his artwork. Bryan was ecstatic. I was not. But I knew what a devoted wife should do, so I went along, helped set up, and hawked his art to passersby.

Broken Bones – Broken Dreams

His ecstasy lasted until the final car accident. Bryan's broken bones never did heal completely. He no longer could lift the boxes of prints or set up the canopy; so he couldn't display his paintings at car shows. The whys kept coming. Why would God let this happen?

Then came the "C" word. Bryan was diagnosed with cancer. Stage 4. Inoperable. Untreatable. It was only a matter of time; a few short months.

As Bryan faced his death, he wrestled with guilt. "Why did I...?" he would ask, naming a choice he had made. "Why, when I had the chance, didn't I...?" Over and over again he revisited his past and what he thought were mistakes he had made.

"The one regret I have is that I never got the chance to live my dream," he said one day.

"Which one was that?" I asked, my mind whirling for the right answer, quite sure I knew what he was going to say.

"I wanted to make a fortune selling my car portraits."

"No, Sweetheart," I said, "that wasn't your dream. You always said that you wanted to paint pictures of cars, go to car shows, and sell them. And that's exactly what you did."

He thought a moment, and then a big smile crossed his gaunt face. "You're right! I did live my dream. Boy, I'm so much luckier than most people. I just never realized it. Thank you for helping me do that." He slept better than he had in weeks.

As Bryan neared the end of his life, he was concerned about how I would manage without him. "Do you remember asking why God allowed that accident to happen?" I asked. He nodded slowly. "God knew that you already had cancer and that you were going to die like this. He wanted to be sure that you could take care of me after you were gone. The settlement from the insurance company after the accident paid off our mortgage, so I won't have that monthly payment. You're taking care of me even when you're not here."

A big smile appeared as he slowly nodded his head. "I wanted to know why. I guess God had it planned all along, and was preparing us ahead of time. God is so good."

A short time later, Bryan was gone.

Cobweb – Rainbow – Another Dream

Life will never be the same without my Sweetheart and I'd give up anything to have him back again. However, even in that sorrow there was hope. That settlement check made it possible for me to write and speak full-time...a lifelong dream. After helping Bryan do what he longed for, I was given the opportunity to do the same.

My first book was Stepping Through Cancer: A Guide for the Journey. It has guided thousands of cancer patients and caregivers as they face the unknown, like we did. In it they read stories about Bryan and me on our trek through cancer and get help for their own journey.

Future books I'm writing are being designed to show women how to pick themselves up after life has knocked them down. The books will give them confidence to do what they've always wanted. Helping them is furthering my dream; and enabling them to fulfill theirs.

Cobwebs? Yes. Huge ones. Rainbows? Without a doubt. Breaking free of the cobwebs? Yes. And all because of a car accident.

Debbie Hardy – the Queen of Resilience

CEO (Chief Encouragement Officer) of Stepping Through Life, LLC

Debbie has appeared on local, national and international radio and television shows and speaks to various groups, including associations, women's retreats, professional caregivers, and the American Cancer Society's Relay for Life.

Not all of us can do great things.
But we can do small things with great love.

MOTHER THERESA
(*ETHNIC ALBANIAN;*
INDIAN ROMAN CATHOLIC NUN 1910-1997)

Johanna's Place

Ireland! A fascinating and intriguing country. Our story actually, in a way, began in Ireland, because something happened there that had a huge influence on the business we own here in California. My wife, Gail, and I and our five children, together with Gail's recently widowed father, traveled to southern Ireland to visit our relatives. During our visit in Cork, we stayed at a bed and breakfast called the Garnish House, run by a friendly woman who met us at the door and introduced herself as Johanna. When we told her we would like a room for the night, she said pleasantly, "Delightful. Come with me."

But she didn't lead us to our room. Instead, we were shown to a parlor where she invited us to be seated. "And what would you be having – coffee or tea?" she asked, her eyes twinkling. It wasn't a question of, "Will you be having coffee or tea?" She had already made up our minds. We were going to have coffee or tea. No options.

So we placed our orders, Johanna left, and within five minutes, she came in with pots of freshly brewed coffee and tea. That wasn't all. She also set in front of us an ample supply of homemade mouth watering delicacies and treats, including scones. We drank and ate, enjoying every moment, immensely.

After about 45 minutes, Johanna came back. "All right," she said with a smile, "up with you now and I'll show you to your room."

She led us across the street to another building. Although moderate and not fancy, our room was very classy and clean. But it was Johanna's warmth and mannerisms that made us feel loved, even though she was a stranger.

The Magic Continues

The next morning, in another room where white cloths were on all the tables, we were in for more over-the-top hospitality for breakfast. Flowers and fresh fruit awaited us. It wasn't a high-end place, but everything had been done in style.

A young lady came to our table. "Would you like Irish porridge?" she asked.

I didn't know anything about Irish porridge. All I knew was that Goldilocks ate the three bears' porridge. "That would be fine," I said, wanting to be agreeable.

"All right, then. Would you like Bailey's Irish Cream or Irish whiskey on the top?"

"Uh…well…." (I had no idea what I would be getting) "…I'll take Bailey's Irish cream."

So I got this bowl of porridge that was kind of a cross between cream of wheat and oatmeal, very smooth, with a tablespoon of Bailey's Irish Cream on the top. Actually, it was extremely delicious. That wasn't all. Also included was a buffet and a menu for special orders. I ordered what I thought was pancakes with strawberries. What I received was a beautiful presentation of crepes with strawberries and other fresh fruit rolled up in them. Everything they did, they did well; and everyone who served us did so with a delightful attitude that, once again, was just filled with love. When we left around noon, Johanna walked us to the door. "Well, off you go now," she said, "and God bless you."

Turn Around

We didn't get very far driving down the road before I got a call on my cell phone. It was Johanna. She told me that we had left a bag there. I asked my wife what it could be.

"My laptop!" Gail said. "I forgot my laptop." We turned around.

Johanna met us at the door and handed us the bag. Then with her gracious hospitality and Irish brogue she asked, "Will you be needing some scones for the road?"

"No, no, that's fine," I said.

"Oh, sure you do, sure you do. Come with me now." She walked my wife and me back to the kitchen. "Now, how many scones will you be needin'?"

"Well, I guess we'll be needing a couple," I said.

"Oh, no, you'll be needin' more than that now." She then turned to her helper in the kitchen, "Get out half a dozen scones and warm them up real good." As she began having a conversation with my wife, I looked around the kitchen. I noticed on the wall behind me was a very large portrait of Jesus.

When the scones were warmed up, she wrapped them in foil and, as before, escorted us to the door with the words, "Well, off you go now, and God bless you," she said.

On our way to Dublin, Gail said, "I've felt more loved by that woman, a stranger to us, than I've felt by almost anybody else I've ever stayed with. That's how I want people to feel when they come to our house."

Fast Forward to Now

I'm a developer, and we have a building in Dublin, California. We had a tenant who leased a third of the space in our building, and ran an executive suites operation. Out of the blue one day we received a registered letter in the mail from the tenant saying he was walking out on his lease, which had about two more years to run. "I will not be paying any more rent, effective immediately," he said, "but I will remain in the space for another two months."

He knew it would take 60 days to get the unlawful detainer required to force him out. It was a shrewd, unethical move on his part. He had made plans to buy another building. His lease was our profit from the building and represented about 80% of our income. At the time we had four kids in college. It was very disconcerting.

Looking for Help

Something I started doing years before, no matter what my circumstances, was to pray and give thanks for them. It's not natural to give thanks when things go badly, and sometimes my thanks come from my will and not my heart, but I've learned over the years to trust God. Many things that start out looking bad, end up as blessings in the long run. So that's what I did. I prayed, thanking my Heavenly Father for what had happened and thanking Him in advance for what He was doing.

Gail suggested we consider re-establishing the executive suites business, applying what we had experienced in the Garnish House in Ireland. So, as I was praying a couple of days later, I had a strong sense that Gail was right and God was saying: Set up a Johanna's place for business people. The impression was so strong that we decided to follow it. We would open a new executive suites business to take the place of the one we were losing with the tenant.

We would need a very special person to run it, of course, someone who had worked in the executive suites business. I thought we found one – a woman with a lot of experience. She was available; but as I met with her several times, I just didn't have a good feeling about hiring her. I shared all this with Gail as we awakened early one morning. "You need to just let it go," she said. "Turn it over to God and let Him bring the person you need."

We prayed together and then I e-mailed a couple of friends about our need. After that, I quit trying to engineer it. That afternoon about 3:00 I got an e-mail back from one of them, Brad Smith, who said that Kathy Young,* a friend of his, was available. She had just gotten laid off the day before from her job at Patrick Henry College, and he thought she'd be perfect.

I called that afternoon and set up a meeting with her. When I arrived at her home, there were a lot of people walking toward her house with plates of food in their arms. She was having a block party to reach out to her neighbors. I interviewed her for about 20 minutes and knew that she was the person who was right for the job. I hired her immediately.

Forming a Solid Purpose

We opened the business with a modest beginning. Since I had been a developer, I'd never run a service business. Neither had Kathy, so there was a bit of chaos at times, but we worked through it. During one of my daily times of reading the Bible, something impressed me strongly. It was in the book of Isaiah in the Old Testament, Chapter 43, Verse 8. It says: "Bring out the blind people who have eyes, and the deaf who have ears."

I felt as if the Lord was telling me that he was going to bring renters to this new business who weren't seeing or hearing spiritual truths. We would be able to help them. We would be like a light on a hill, shining hope into their darkness. We set that as the purpose for our business: To show people the love of Christ, not with words, but by the way we treat them. Our goal would be to provide all the professional services they needed and to love them in such a way that they never would want to leave, unless they outgrew us.

Slowly but surely the business began to grow. Kathy sets the pace by the way she handles our clients with extra care She is attentive to what is happening in their lives, listening and rejoicing in their successes and sympathizing when they share painful struggles and life issues that are difficult. She also invests heavily in our young staff, training them to always look for ways to go above and beyond in serving and showing love.

The clients are made to feel special on a regular basis through such things as Panera Fridays, where the staff serves Panera bagels and pastries. Freshly ground Starbuck's coffee is the standard brew. Special events, always involving great food, like Taco Tuesday, holiday parties, ice cream sundae socials, Dad's and Grad's day, and many more are random but frequent ways our staff reaches out to the clients. Mostly though, it is the simple things like always greeting them by name with a warm smile when they arrive for work each day.

We've been operating that way now for almost two years at the time of this writing, and we're now approaching 95% occupancy. Kathy has turned out to be the absolute perfect fit. "Before I started this job," she told me, "99% of the people I spent time with were Christian. Now I'm surrounded by non-Christian people all day long, and I love it."

Besides Kathy, we have four young ladies who are receptionists, and a building manager, all of whom are Christians. The entire staff understands and lives out our purpose.

Light on a Hill

Once, while visiting with the Mayor of Dublin (California), I was telling him about our business and the purpose behind it. "Well, Kevin," he said, "your goal of being a light on the hill is already happening. Remember when we had the business expo here in the city and your company had a booth there?" I nodded. "Well, a couple of business people and I stopped by your booth. We talked to the two young women managing it, and as we walked away, one of the business women I was with turned to me and said, 'Those young ladies are just so full of light.'"

We received another unsolicited and gratifying comment just recently. One of our tenants has an hour and a half commute each way to his business. He sought out our manager.

"You know," he said, "I am treated in such a wonderful and friendly way that I feel like I'm at Disneyland. This is the happiest place on earth. I love being here."

We've also had two Christian people who are joining our purpose at the Executive Center by facilitating discussion groups about topics relevant to business people. The sole purpose of these groups is to build relationships and further show the love of God to those who do not yet experience the true life that comes through faith in Jesus Christ.

Now you know the story of how a Johanna's place for business people was established in Dublin – a work of God which we are excited and privileged to be part of.

Kevin Ring

Kevin Ring is the founder of Trinity Development Company and related entities that specialize in the investment and development of commercial and residential real estate.

A graduate of the School of Business at the University of California, Berkeley, he co-founded Equity Concept Development Company for commercial and residential real estate projects throughout Northern California.

After a serious illness, he moved his family to Grass Valley, CA. to develop a 120-acre ranch as a residence and business headquarters for Trinity Development. JLH Ranch also serves as a retreat center for Asian university students and families, primarily from Japan.

Kevin especially enjoys fly fishing for trout and steelhead.

(Kathy Young, mentioned in Kevin's story, has two delightful stories in this book: Order to Appear and Reagan at the Rexall)

Spread happiness, joy, love, and accounts of your experiences in life with those you encounter. One way you can do that is by putting your pen to paper and sending a story to us. As Johanna's love resulted in a new direction for Kevin as he reaches out to others, so your efforts may serve up a gem of inspiration to someone else that will result in the transformation of many lives.

*It is interesting to notice how some minds
seem almost to create themselves, springing up
under every disadvantage, and working their solitary but
irresistible way through a thousand obstacles.*

WASHINGTON IRVING
(*AMERICAN AUTHOR – RIP VAN WINKLE*
1783 – 1859)

Through The Fire and Into Living

It was 2006 and my life was rolling along fantastically. I had just come back from an amazing vacation. I was fit, feeling great, and about to go on another tremendous trip. Each day I would count my blessings for my wonderful life. Without warning, though, it all changed.

A Very Dark Day

I ruptured my Achilles while working out. Lots of active people hurt themselves while exercising, but I realized that I needed a doctor to look at it. Neither the physicians I went to, nor I, had any idea that I was about to enter into suffering that would change my entire existence.

First, there were additional symptoms. I sought help again. The medical community couldn't figure out what was causing my anguish until…until, a year later, they finally realized what was going on. It was then they gave me the discouraging news.

RSD? What's That?

A disease had resulted from my ruptured Achilles. Not just a mild one, but a horrifying disease: Reflex Sympathetic Dystrophy – in short, RSD. Also known as Complex Regional Pain Syndrome (CRPS), RSD is a chronic pain, neurological syndrome. It is a malfunction of the central nervous system that causes pain, in addition to other symptoms. It affects millions of people in the United States.

Dismayed, I researched it and discovered that it's not a new disease. RSD has been documented all the way back to the Civil War. The worst of what I discovered was that, if it isn't treated aggressively and correctly, it spreads rapidly. Since it took a full year for doctors to diagnose my condition, the disease did just that in my body: It spread rapidly.

Indescribable Suffering

My symptoms amped up. They are difficult to describe but I'll try. There was severe, intense, burning pain - the feeling that I was on fire… all over. There were pathological changes in my bones; excessive sweating; tissue swelling; extreme sensitivity to touch; dramatic changes in the color and temperature of my skin over my affected limbs. I had skin sensitivity and could not – I repeat – could not be touched or even wear clothes.

Here I was with a debilitating, degenerative disease so that a wheelchair was my only option. I constantly screamed from pain that no medicine could relieve. There was no cure.

I couldn't work and I felt that my life was over. This disease was robbing me of my full life expectancy. I had gone from joy to devastation in the blink of an eye. It was so devastating that I thought about taking my own life.

I Turned a Corner

Although I saw my life ending, I decided I wouldn't go that route. I made up my mind to pull myself out of the fear that was crippling all my desire to live. I would get myself back into life. Somehow. Some way.

That's when an idea came to me. I would write. A book. Yes! I would write a book in order to shift myself back to health. The more I thought about it, the more the idea crystallized in my mind. Then I began. The title? I came up with: Magnetizing: The Guidebook To Achieving Financial, Emotional, and Spiritual Abundance.

The Defining Moment

Writing that book was a defining moment that would shape who I was. It has been the catalyst for everything I've done since. The book became the driving force behind fighting my fears and the disease itself. It is what helped me to understand that the right mindset is my Creator's tool to overcome anything!

As I worked on the book I began re-framing my belief system. My entire world began to make sense. I flipped the switch on my attitude and all of the sudden I realized that I had my life back. Suddenly I realized that I, Terri Levine, got this disease for a reason. That reason was: I had a huge following of people that I could teach about this malady. As a result, I could fundraise for children who had the problem. I could be a voice to help others who were burning.

A Blessing? Yes

Because of what I now was able to do, I became grateful to my Creator for my distressful situation. Now my disability keeps me in love with living life…and giving to others…and helping others…and making an impact on the world.

I value my life so much now that even when my disease seems unbearable, I keep embracing every day as a blessing and being grateful to be on the planet; grateful that I am able to feel something - even if it is burning.

Through it all I have created a winning life and, as I mentioned before, I am helping others create a winning life, too! No matter what they are facing.

Today, I am proud and grateful to say that I have a foundation for children with RSD and am helping others get medical help. I also help the kids and family members find peace on their own journey with RSD.

Terri LeVine

Terri Levine, The Business Mentoring Expert, specializes in helping business owners achieve record-breaking growth. Based in Philadelphia, Terri is the founder and CEO of The Coaching Instiitute, one of the top coach training programs in the United States.

She has been featured on ABC, NBC, CNBC and MSNBC, and in more than 1,500 publications. She is the bestselling author of Sell Without Selling; Coaching Is for Everyone; and Stop Managing, Start Coaching. With over 10 books in print, her new book, Guerrilla Marketing for Spas, was just released.

You may never have had to suffer as Terri has. And maybe you haven't been able to give back as fully as she has. But what you have experienced may be just what another person, somewhere out there in the world, needs. So don't hesitate.
Check out our guidelines for submitting a story about your cobweb, your rainbow of hope and your victory.

Rainbows In Cobwebs

A person's a person, no matter how small.

DR. SEUSS
(AMERICAN WRITER, POET
& CARTOONIST 1904-1991)

Reagan at the Rexall

It must have been the summer of 1964 or '65. Ronald Reagan was making speeches all over the state of California exploring his chances to run for governor, something he achieved in 1967, after which he served two terms.

I was in the fifth or sixth grade and had ridden my bike to the Rexall Drug Store at the Gregory Village Shopping Center in Pleasant Hill on an errand for my grandmother. As I got off my bike, I leaned it upright on the kickstand, without a thought that it would be stolen. We didn't have to worry much about things like that.

I noticed a group of kids and adults in front of the nearby pet store. Suddenly some of them came running up to me excitedly. "Hey! Get a piece of paper!" one said. "It's the guy from Death Valley Days! The TV star! He'll give you an autograph!"

I never before had been given the notion that I should try to get a celebrity autograph. I nonetheless jumped into action. A TV Star! Right here in Pleasant Hill! I had frequently watched Death Valley Days, a television program about events and legends in the Death Valley Desert area of California. Besides that, my grandfather used 20 Mule Team Borax Soap, a product of the company that advertised on the show.

But I had nothing on which a celebrity could write his autograph. Wearing a summer outfit and sandals, I had only the money in my pocket that Nana had given me for her purchase. I looked around. In those days, candy bars were set on top of a thin piece of cardboard and then wrapped. I spotted a discarded candy cardboard on the sidewalk. Ah, that would do. I picked it up and pushed my way through the pet store crowd to get "The Death Valley Guy's" autograph.

High Emotions

Inside the tiny store was quite a scene. There were many adults, a few kids, and the press, taking notes and taking pictures with large cameras and bright flash bulbs that made a popping sound with each photo.

And, there he was: Ronald Reagan, the tall, handsome host of the television show, "Death Valley Days." He was making a speech. There was a sense of excitement among the adults. They listened to him with a great deal of interest in whatever it was he was talking about. All I knew was he wouldn't stop talking and I had to get home or I'd catch it!

Bold and Courageous

I pushed my way to the front of the crowd and stood right in front of him waiting for him to stop talking. But he went on and on, and I still had to get Nana's purchase at the Rexall. I pushed my piece of cardboard towards him, looking up into his face. It distracted him for only a second, just enough to notice me, but he kept on talking. No doubt I was the picture of grubby, sweaty, summer childhood.

On a mission, I kept it up, sort of reaching toward him with my piece of thin cardboard, over and over.

Finally, he smiled at the adults, kind of shrugged, spreading his arms out slightly and said one of what came to be known as a typical gracious Reaganism..."Well, what can you do?" and as he kept smiling, he stopped the talk, and signed Ronald Reagan on my candy cardboard to the good natured, quiet laughter of the adults.

I scooted off to complete my errand at the Rexall and get home, aware that I had interrupted an adult when he was talking (something I'd been taught was rude) but happy I hadn't "dawdled" too awfully much (something else against my upbringing).

My memory is that of trying the patience of the future president of the United States of America and getting to personally witness his famous grace and goodness, even to a rude, determined little girl.

Kathy Young

Kathy enjoys managing a privately owned Executive Suite business in Dublin, CA.

After having graduated magna cum laude with a B.A. degree in Home Economics and a secondary teaching credential at San Francisco State University, she worked in real estate related fields in a variety of capacities.

She home educated two sons and assisted her husband, Lance, in his construction business.

Kathy and Lance Young live in Walnut Creek, California.
See Kathy's other amusing story in this book, Order to Appear.

Kathy will never forget the kind way Ronald Reagan treated her. So it is that every child who comes into your life, in person or through stories you tell, will be influenced greatly by you. Don't hold back. Just be careful what you impart.

IX

HEALING

SUNSHINE

Sunshine can...

Dry up areas and scorch the earth and crops;
Cause sunstroke and other serious illnesses;
Bring desperate thirst to all living things;
Be oppressive if it's around too long.

Sunshine also can...

Warm the heart and body after a chilling winter;
Supply necessary elements to health;
Make playgrounds out of yards, beaches and other places;
Brighten a gloomy day;
Send individuals forth with a Can-Do attitude;
Facilitate growth in plants that produce food.

Victory is yours as you refuse to fear wind, clouds, lightning, thunder, rain, storms and cobwebs. Spiritual power is yours if you have kept your eyes on the rainbows that are followed by blue skies and sunshine. If you are still searching for the colors and guidance that God is holding out to you, read some of these stories again, write down your many many blessings and look up. Help is there!

Rainbows In Cobwebs

Take time to deliberate; but when the time
for action arrives, stop thinking and go in.

ANDREW JACKSON
(7TH PRESIDENT OF THE UNITED STATES
1767-1845)

The Last Coins

The very small schoolroom we visit hosts about 75 children on any given weekday. Its benches are worn, the old posters on the walls are grammatically incorrect, and the ancient chalkboard bears remnants of the week's lessons. There are other indications that the school suffers financially. The broken glass windows and the chipped paint on the walls, both under layers of dirt, confirm the observation. It is like the majority of schools in Uganda – they all bear the same neglect.

We take our seats. We aren't here to observe a class at Kiira Primary. We have come for a church service. The worship music is unplanned. It is from the heart, out of key, and genuine. In Uganda, church services always have a time of sharing, where each person can bring a word or a testimony. I am always struck by the simplicity of their thanks, reminding me to be thankful for the breaths of air I take daily. The simple survival tools that I take for granted are precisely what they thank the Lord for: transportation, food, rent money, school fees, and that they have made it safely through another week and are still alive.

Teo

The sharing time is about to wind down when Teo stands up. Teo is one of Children of Grace's university sponsored students. She is currently working on her required internship.

Internships bring in no income for the intern, which makes regular meals, rent, and transportation an added expense and challenge for students. She is one who remembers her past – where she was before God brought her to a new purpose in life. She also has a huge heart for children who are hurting.

Teo's Story

The week before the church service, she was in a village about 70 km from Jinja. To get there, she had to take a taxi, which cost her one dollar in coins, and then she would have to take a taxi back when she finished her work. That would cost another dollar.

While in the village, as part of her internship, she was distributing medication for HIV treatment – drugs that need to be taken with food. That presented a problem in some cases. While hunger is seen all over Uganda, it is not as bad anywhere as it is in the villages.

Her work was winding up for the day when she was approached by a boy who looked malnourished. He needed medication for his mother.

"Here you go," Teo said, as she gave the drugs to him. "Be sure she takes it with food."

The boy's big brown eyes looked into hers. "We don't have any food," he said. Then he looked down. "Look," he said. He pointed to the flip flops on his feet. "I got these for 50 cents. I'll sell them to you for 15 cents. Then I can buy food and my mother can take the medicine."

Teo's heart was wrenched. She had to help him, but how? She had just one dollar of her own. She needed every bit of it for transportation to get back to Jinja. She closed her eyes for a second; and it seemed as if God spoke very clearly to her. She wasn't to buy the boy's flip flops for 15 cents. Or at all. He needed his shoes. She was to give him the entire dollar. All of it.

"Here," she said, pulling the dollar out and handing it to him. "Buy food for your family." The boy looked incredulous – and then joyful. She watched as he skipped away.

How to Get Home?

Teo had no idea how she would get back to Jinja. She asked around and finally found someone who would give her a ride, but his vehicle broke down on the way. It took a long while for the driver to get it fixed with no guarantee it wouldn't break down again. She prayed the entire way back.

When she reached home, it was late. She was hungry and exhausted. Five minutes later, she was astonished when her landlady walked into her apartment carrying a delicious hot dinner. "I thought, since you got home late, that you might enjoy this," the landlady said.

"She has never done that," Teo says as she finished her testimony. "Never. She does not feed me. She had no idea what I had gone through all day." She looks solemnly around the room. "Be thankful if God gives you even one meal a day. There are people out in the villages who actually are starving. Yes, in the past, many of us would get two meals to eat in a day, and now we get one, but be thankful for even that one."

A Sobering Reflection

I sit there after Teo has spoken, completely convicted, encouraged, blessed, and challenged. This girl, this amazing young woman, gave her last shilling to feed the hungry and yet was thanking God that she received even one meal a day.

As the pastor stands up to preach, I look down at a little village boy who has chosen, for some reason, to fall asleep on my lap. It isn't the boy Teo had helped; but undoubtedly he is a lot like him. He probably is hungry.

The "church" is hot and stuffy and the service is long, but I leave that day with a lot on my mind.

Risa Cranmer

Risa began working for Children of Grace (CoG) in 2009 after completing three years in youth ministry. Although she is stationed stateside, she most enjoys her annual trips to Uganda to spend time with the students and to help alongside the Ugandan staff.

She also runs marathons, and is very active in her home community.

Rainbows In Cobwebs

There are two ways to live your life.
One is as though nothing is a miracle.
The other is as though everything is a miracle.

ALBERT EINSTEIN
(*GERMAN BORN THEORETICAL PHYSICIST*
1879-1955)

One Dark, Rainy Night

On April 3, 1982, I thought: What a comfortable and wonderful life I am living. I was age 23, headlining as a juggler at Bally's Park Place Casino in Atlantic City, NJ, having the time of my life. I couldn't have asked for anything better. The show I performed was my first big gig. I had been scheduled for one month, but they liked my act enough to keep me on for nine months; and I was on track for an entirely new act with all new material.

Just a Kid

I'd started learning juggling at the age of 15 and knew that this was what I wanted to do for my life's work. It was all uphill from then on. I won first place on "The Gong Show" at the age of 16. Then at age 18, I moved forward to teach juggling and performing at Ringling Brothers and Barnum and Bailey Clown College.

Performing nationally and internationally followed, so by the time I was hired at Bally's, I had achieved the position of featured performer, doing two shows a night, six days a week, spending only about 12 minutes a show. I was working about 24 minutes a day, doing something I loved, and being paid very well for it. In fact, my juggling was at such a high level that I was attempting to do master juggling at seven clubs, a world record at the time.

I was on top of the world, so to speak, or so I thought. I was about to find out differently.

Unthinkable

On April 3, the rain was coming down in sheets and sheets of drenching water, but I needed to get to Bally's. It was difficult to drive. I made it safely to the lot where I parked every night – about three blocks from the casino. I locked up the car and opened my umbrella even though the wind was strong and started walking.

Straining to see, I stopped at Atlantic Avenue. The street is usually very busy, but cars had pulled over because of the rain. So, not spotting many vehicles coming either way, I started across. Huddled in my overcoat, focusing on getting to my destination where I would do the show, I vaguely was aware of street lights shrouded in rain and stop signs that were no more than a shiny blur.

What I couldn't see, because a sheet of rain obliterated my view, was a truck bearing down on me. Suddenly, without warning, I felt searing pain. I was hurtling through the air. The driver, not able to see well, had plowed into me, tossing me up and onto the truck's hood. As my head hit and broke the windshield, my mind shut off. I was thrown to the side of the hood. My body ripped the side mirror off and the impact broke my arm. I was thrown twenty feet away from the truck...and there my body lay...motionless.

The horrified truck driver and other people who had seen what had happened rushed to my side. Atlantic City Medical Center was only blocks away, so it was a quick transport to the hospital in an ambulance. Doctors determined that I needed brain surgery for a sub-temporal craniotomy and evacuation of an epidural hematoma – to relieve the pressure of blood rushing into my brain. The surgery was performed that night by one of the best neurologists in the area.

The following day there was more build-up of blood in my brain –

the hematoma – so they had to do a second operation. Afterwards, I lay in a hospital bed with tubes and wires connected to my brain and body.

Not only was I not responding but I would remain in that state for the next thirty-seven days. I had a fractured skull with epidural hematoma and brain contusion, fracture of tibial plateau, pneumonia, and septicemia. Basically, I was pretty messed up.

Even as I awakened from my coma, paralyzed and helpless as a baby, I knew I had to do whatever was necessary to get back to my former life. I had tasted success in the past and liked it very much. It was the overpowering reality of this conviction that enabled me to move, to learn again to speak, and to reassert myself as a complete and fully functional human being.

Accidents Can Be Beneficial

When you juggle, you drop. If you pay attention to what you are doing, then each time you drop, you learn what not to do next time and you get to try again. Basically, a drop in juggling is an accident. These "accidents" in juggling relate to life accidents.

Every time you experience an accident, you must use the lessons learned for future growth and success. Remember this when you drop in life: pick up and give it another go.

We've all had them – accidents and life changes. As you know, it's not the change we should dwell on; it is how we deal with the change that should demand our attention.

Be ready for accidents and changes in your life. I am not saying one should walk around scared and worried. Just be prepared. Then, when the changes do occur, smile, learn from them, and move ahead.

How I Got Through It

Here are some suggestions I developed to help you through your changes:

- Learn to accept life. If you can change something for the better, then do; but if you can't, release resistance and accept things as they are.

- Life is about taking risks and not about knowing what is going to happen next. This makes life exciting and stimulates the mind.

- Every day is a new beginning, bringing opportunities for positive change. Without moving forward, nothing will happen.

- Keep dropping as long as you keep picking up. Making mistakes is not a problem. The problem is failure to learn from a mistake. As long as you are willing and able to learn from them, mistakes usually are beneficial in the long run.

- Support yourself. Who likes you better then you do? You could blame and shame yourself, but when disaster strikes, support yourself, just as you would like others to support you.

- Appreciate every moment. Life goes on and nothing is permanent, so value every moment, fully and completely, as it will never happen again. You only have one chance for the here and now.

- Trust in your instincts. Emotions can often cloud our judgment, leading us down dangerous roads and making us easy targets for those who seek to deceive and manipulate. Strike a comfortable balance between following your heart and thinking critically. When it comes to personal relationships and life-choices, the heart knows best.

- Take time to just stop and breathe, to look around you and see beauty; to remember why you are here (to help others).

- Don't take yourself too seriously. There's a good reason why people say, "Laughter is the best medicine." Do something for someone else and make giving a part of your life, even if it is just a simple smile or a hug. Develop playfulness, if it's not already there.

Rainbows in Your Cobwebs

I've developed a certain mind-set in my life. When something goes wrong, I do not go to the negative right away. Immediately, I think, "Now that this has happened, what can I do about it?" I think of ways to solve the new problem. I am not sad and I do not regret. I just move through it and develop strategies on how to make things better again. Finding solutions is key to getting through life in a good way. This habit I developed is automatic now.

— From the first time I got hit by a truck, I lost my juggling ability and more.

>   Yet, life goes on.

— 18 years later, I got hit by another truck! I lost my ability to run, which is something I cherished.

>   Yet, life goes on.

— From the first accident, I still see double. From a bike accident, I hear buzzing – no silence.

>   Yet, life goes on.

— The loss of my wife and daughters through divorce was devastating for me.

>   Yet, life goes on.

— I lost my mind temporarily- a hard thing to think about.

>   Is life still going on? Yes.

Five Stages of Grief

The five stages of grief are 1) denial and isolation, 2) anger, 3) bargaining, 4) expression, and finally, 5) acceptance. Getting through each stage can be difficult but each stage must last for a necessary time. Work on getting through each stage and back to life as soon as you can.

Kit Summers

The lessons that Kit learned during his recovery are an inspiration to us all. Since the accidents, he learned to juggle again, which surprised everyone – especially his doctors. Also, he has written four books, started three businesses, and speaks to groups around the world on the subject of personal and professional growth. Millions have heard Kit's story.

In 2003 this entrepreneur started a new business – he makes excellent salsa. A growing company, there is no stopping **"Summers' Salsa"** from developing into a huge empire.

If what has happened or is happening to you feels like a truck slammed into your life, you will find help in many stories throughout this book. These writers know how you feel. To follow through and look further for the helping hand you need to get you over the steep and rough places, we have a link on our website where willing and compassionate hearts can give you guidance.

Rainbows In Cobwebs

The rose and the thorn, and sorrow and
gladness are linked together.

SAADI SHARAZI
(*PERSIAN POET IN MEDIEVAL TIMES;*
DATES OF BIRTH AND DEATH UNCERTAIN)

A Sensational Life

What do I remember about my son's early years? Misery. Heartache. Guilt. I am so grateful for the photos I took during that time, because through them, I am able to see that he and I really did smile. There were good moments.

Unfortunately, when I think about that span of time, before Owen was 15 months, and before we switched from being in an, "It's happening to me," mode to, "I have something I can do about this," mode, I still feel overwhelmed!

Consternation

It was a dark time for me after Owen was born. I remember loving him so much, yet wishing that I hadn't decided to have a third child. That still sounds awful. I don't think I uttered those words but a handful of times, and writing them here is difficult, but honestly, I never was in such a place that I thought of hurting him or myself. However, I did live daily with the duality of love and regret.

How do you cope with the feeling that what you're doing, that the way you know to take care of your own child, is wrong? It's true that every child is different. Can't treat any of them the same. But, Owen was so different than his sisters. There was much more crying, an inability to sleep without help; and his discomfort with bathing, diaper changing and more.

I had always wanted a son. I even will admit to being a bit disappointed when both girls were born. A girl? Really? I got over the disappointment quickly. But when I found out I was having a boy, I was beyond thrilled! I'm not sure why. I just knew it was meant to be.

Maybe that's why it was so hard...when it wasn't going well...when I would spend nights moving from my bed – to the rocking chair – to the couch – to standing – back to bed. Exhausted. Sad. Frustrated. Regretful. Then, of course, a feeling of guilt. Here was my boy. I had wanted him so much; but I wasn't able to care for him. At least that's how it seemed.

The central struggle of parenthood is to let our hopes for our children outweigh our fears.

ELLEN GOODMAN

Special Needs

I consider my son to be an individual with special needs. Although he's never had any formal diagnosis, he has experienced many challenges in his four years of life. In addition, he has participated in various therapies and interventions in an effort to treat his challenges.

Although each individual way he was different was nothing to be concerned about, when I put them all together, a very dissimilar picture emerged...a picture that caused me to seek help from my pediatrician. I knew what I wanted. I wanted what I had given, in my profession, to many parents and students throughout the years. I wanted Owen to be evaluated by various professionals in order to understand his areas of weakness, so that we could strengthen them.

An Effort to Make Sound

We began with speech therapy, as Owen was unable to make any sounds without significant struggle. He was found to be developmentally delayed in the area of speech and language. Although he could follow any direction and understand many words, he could not produce any. He began speech therapy in December, 2009. Soon after, he started receiving educational intervention, first in our home, and then within a parent-child group.

As a psychologist who works with parents of children with difficulties, I had been trained in the stages of grief that parents go through when they discover their child has special needs. Personally, I don't recall experiencing any of these typical emotions at the time of diagnosis of my son's difficulties. Maybe it was because I had known for a long time that something wasn't right, and I felt, simply, validation. It also could have been because I was so focused on lining up the evaluations, rearranging my calendar and scheduling the therapies, that I really didn't have time to feel emotion.

Another thing that I didn't do early on was pray about Owen, his challenges and how to handle them. There definitely was a disconnect between God and me during this time. After all, I thought, He already knew what was going to happen, so what were my prayers going to change? No, as I saw it, my only hope was to do it on my own.

I am so grateful now that others were praying, especially since I wasn't. This was not something I could have handled by myself.

More Observations

As time went by, I noticed more and more differences between Owen and other boys his age. He was not very active and he resisted certain activities. For example, he would not go near the swings. Then there was the small step that led from the house to the garage. When he used it, he held on with all his strength to the wall. The bath water was always too hot; he wouldn't go near a stuffed animal; and it hurt him – somehow – to get dressed. Paint or play dough were avoided; and if he spilled even the smallest amount of liquid on himself, he cried to be changed.

And so much more.

It was near his second birthday when we heard terms like "sensory seeking" and "sensory avoiding" that already were familiar to us; but it was also at this time that we were introduced to terms like "motor apraxia" and "gravitational insecurity."

Progress

Although all of Owen's therapies and official interventions have ended as of the time of this writing, he will always have special needs specifically related to sensory processing. He does participate in many of the activities that he used to avoid. However, some of them he simply tolerates, but doesn't really like. He now has excellent language skills, but I continue to monitor his language development just to make sure he doesn't fall behind.

So, by now, in many ways, he is like any other preschooler. He loves to learn, make us laugh and ride his tricycle. However, he also experiences this world unlike most.

All of our son's challenges have given us opportunities for growth. There are places we return to where his adaptability and increased level of comfort are clearly evident. Last fall we visited the pumpkin patch as a family. We decided to go to the same place we had gone the year before where they had train rides, a forest to explore, narrow trails, a suspension bridge, tunnels, hay bales, and corn stalks.

My husband and I were amazed at how Owen was able to navigate with ease through these things that had been obstacles for him 12 months earlier. Although he still wouldn't attempt the bridge or sit near the hay, I had to force him to slow down on the paths and help him as he attempted to lift a huge pumpkin.

Continuing Challenges

Do you know people who can be spontaneous; who don't have to plan? They appear to breeze through life as if each new day is an adventure that they can't wait to explore. This is not me. This is definitely not my son. We must prepare him for everything. We talk in advance about the changes in seasons, since it means changing the types of clothes he will wear – short versus long-sleeves, pants versus shorts, etc. We also discuss the evening routine every night. We use timers, give warnings, show him calendars. We do this to avoid the unexpected, because the unexpected brings anxiety, and anxiety can bring negative behavior.

Each day we adjust our lives to our son and his needs. For him, the world is chaotic and complicated. On a good day, a regulated day, that world can be navigated without incident. But there are those other days...the days that are filled with questions and complaints, even about the most routine things.

Developing Skills

Since everyday incidences aren't always going to go as planned, even if we prepare for them, we use coping skills. I work toward being able to say, even though a situation is not what I want or what I planned for, that I have a strategy to deal with it. If something takes me by surprise, I have a back-up plan. This is something that has become increasingly important for Owen, because I can't prepare him for everything. Even when I do prepare him, sometimes it just doesn't work. It's just not enough.

In the Bible we read:

Furthermore, because we are united with Christ, we have received an inheritance from God, for he chose us in advance, and he makes everything work out according to his plan.

(EPHESIANS, CHAPTER 1, VERSE 11)

God uses [scripture] to prepare and equip his people to do every good work.

(2 TIMOTHY, CHAPTER 3, VERSE 17)

Chosen in advance. He has not provided us with an outline of an exact plan or given us all the details, but he's already prepared or equipped us for every experience that we've had or are going to have. Every joy. Every sorrow. There's nothing left to chance.

A Community of Love

Through these challenges, we have found others who are rearing children with sensory processing difficulties. These mothers provide me with support and are available to strategize with me about one of the most difficult areas of living.

Although we haven't completed our journey, there are many things that Owen does that make more sense to me now. And, there are things that we do that seem to be helping him to be a more regulated, happy little boy. It's my life. I've come to embrace it and accept it as God's plan for my son, for me and for my husband.

Sybil K.

Sybil wishes to keep her last name private in order to protect the identity of Owen.

She fills many different roles in life...mother, wife, sister, daughter, friend. She is a School Psychologist by profession and a Christian by faith, but she has come to realize that there is more to life than roles and titles. It is how you live your life that matters most. Her blog, **Peace it all Together,** *reflects on the circumstances of life, faith, and issues related to having a child with sensory needs. Meet her on her* **video** *on our website.*

Rainbows In Cobwebs

*Life is the soul's nursery – its training
place for the destinies of eternity.*

William Makepeace Thackeray
(*English Novelist 1811-1863*)

Opa And Indonesia

In May 2006, I made a decision to go to Indonesia with rēp, a San Francisco Bay Area organization that trains voluntary business consultants to go abroad on short-term business ventures to mobilize medium-sized businesses. What makes it highly unusual is that they do so in order to share their faith and use business for the Kingdom of God.

On my trip, I had Opa as my "client." (I've changed the name to protect him.) He arrived at the two-week business consulting seminar with a 27 page manual describing his corporation's strategy. My initial reaction was that he should be teaching the seminar. That reaction proved to be spot on.

After our team's initial seminar kickoff in Jakarta, Opa and I took off for two days to fly to the neighboring island to visit his company. This venture took place in North Sumatra – one of the more strictly Muslim provinces of Indonesia. We arrived at 9 P.M. and found his Corporate Kingdom Committee, as he called it, waiting at the office to brief me on their policies and actions.

Fascinating Discoveries

I first noticed an image of a dove when I entered the office.

"All cultures see the dove as a symbol of peace," Opa said, "and this sends a message to both Muslims and Christians that a company is safe and fair. "

"And the picture of Moses?" I asked, for it hung behind his desk.

"Ahh, that is because Moses is respected by both religions," he explained.

And unlike the typical messy Indonesian businesses, Opa's office building was neat and clean. Furthermore, it had the only employee parking lot in town.   I also learned that the company leaders tithe 10% of their corporate profits for the purpose of building churches, supporting education for women, and backing Christian evangelism.

Opa's business is supported largely in part by immense agricultural enterprises. He owns 10 plantations and employs 600 workers (mostly Muslim). Beautiful tree orchards and blooming flowers greeted us everywhere on the plantations. Clean, well-maintained office buildings made the picture all the more intriguing. In addition, some of the employees choose to live there and they keep flower gardens in front of their houses.

Other company amenities include athletic fields and basketball courts. This is uncommon in the United States and unheard of in Indonesia.

I was incredibly impressed with how well the corporation was run and tasks delegated. Everyone I met knew his/her job and role in the big picture; and they were comfortable telling Opa about their goals, targets, and plans to achieve them

There was no micromanaging of the employees on Opa's part. That was apparent. I met management personnel who had worked 10 to 15 years for him, and some who had been with the company from its inception over 20 years ago.

The Muslim Faith

For Muslim workers, Opa had built five small mosques on his plantations. After they saw that, the Muslim community didn't object to his building a church for Christians. That church was soon to be under construction at the time of my visit. When finished, it will hold 300 to 400 people. "I see the mosques, everything, as a net gain for Christians," he told me.

The oldest employee is an 80 year old Muslim elder. Opa paid for his pilgrimage to Mecca. After the pilgrimage, the man warned the Muslim community not to give Opa any trouble, because he now was his adopted son.

Ominous Cobweb

But, in spite of Opa's many good works, the Muslim business community, police and judges have often tried to accuse him falsely to get monetary bribes, a common Indonesian business practice. Opa consistently refuses to pay kickbacks and once endured over 20 days of police interrogation. Soon after I left Indonesia, officials falsely accused Opa again, and this time, a judge sentenced him to jail. When I learned about his imprisonment, I tried calling his cell phone. Surprisingly, he answered it. He told me he was imprisoned along with an estimated 1,500 inmates. Three hundred of them were there because they were Christians.

Rainbows and Victory that Grip the Heart

The next time I called, Opa said they had started a Bible study in jail. A following call revealed that he and the prisoners grew the study into a jail church of over 200.

A couple of months later, he said the church was over 300 people and they were requesting Christian pastors to come in to teach them.

Finally, on one of the last calls I made to Opa, he asked that we stop praying for him to be released, because he said he was where God wanted him to be.

Opa is a single man who has no worries about family. He also never worries about his company. It is well managed and does fine without him.

After about 10 months, he had served his so called sentence and was released. It was a privilege for me to walk at a safe distance through this experience with my "brother." I have learned much, and I have been changed by the encounter. Specifically, I garnered three lessons from my time with him – lessons that continue to challenge me in my western business practice. Do you mind if I share them with you?

First, I learned that I...we...need to hold onto our possessions and status loosely.

Second, I...we...need to trust those who work with us and prepare them to be able to succeed without us.

Lastly, I...we...need to view every opportunity and situation as a potential to serve the Lord.

Sometimes what he guides us to do will seem outlandish to others; but if it's God's design, he will give us peace about it and it will no doubt influence others to look for the peace that comes from knowing and serving him.

Larry Wiens

With an extensive background in ministry and business, Larry is a Financial Advisor and the Managing Partner of the San Francisco Bay Area Barnabas Group. This national organization brings together business executives who want to contribute their expertise to help non-profits grow and the Kingdom of God expand. He and his wife, Esther, live in Northern California.

Do your struggles and cobwebs seem too much for you? "I'm not as strong and resilient as the writers in this book," you may be saying. We can assure you that all of them have felt the same way as you do. Many times. That's why they are sharing their stories – so you can see how they applied determination and focus in order to succeed, rather than giving up.

If you're betrayed, release disappointment at once.
By that way, the bitterness has no time to take root.

TOBA BETA
(*AUTHOR – INDONESIA*)

Better

Then I got the final blow.

"Do you love her?" I asked.

His answer was a very quiet but solid. "Yes."

The knowledge of my husband's infidelity shivered through me. I sat slumped, holding my forehead. He maintained his position across the table. I couldn't cry or scream. Inside, silently, I was stuck on automatic repeat: Dear God, help me, Dear God, help me, help me.

We had experienced some speed bumps through our relationship, and we were not as close as we could have been, but I never imagined this demise. We had not grown up in the era of disposable marriages. Just as our parents' vows had been, ours were for keeps. You know, 'til death do us part and all that stuff. Happy or not, I thought we had both committed to the long haul.

I wrestled a couple of days with my heartbreaking discovery. Then, one evening I was home alone, with no clue as to where my husband was, when I felt that God spoke very clearly to me: You have a choice. You can be bitter for the rest of your life because of this, or, you can be better. I thought it over for about thirty seconds.

My Unholy Desire

I wanted to get even. My human nature whispered evil plans and schemes to destroy their love, their lives. I wanted my husband and his indiscreet friend to feel pain equal to what had nearly paralyzed me.

But I knew bitter people. They were not pleasant, did not smile, and had no friends. Often they were revengeful and seethed anger, hurt, and spite. They gave into addiction, disease, and lost all hope for a decent future.

"I will be better," I promised aloud to myself and to God, "better because of this." My optimistic spirit would allow nothing less.

Tentative Steps

Some of my first tries toward a future alone were baby steps. I floundered a little but I refused to head down Bitter Street. I made lists, tried new activities, and fought loneliness with sword and shield. Once I started moving in this better path, friends gathered to cheer me on.

Our divorce took a long two years; then suddenly became final in just twenty minutes. A couple of years later, our daughters moved on with their lives and I really was alone. I faced a rare and unexpected chance at a do-over with life. Nearing fifty, I enjoyed asking, *What do I want to be when I grow up?*

I volunteered, traveled, worked obsessively, and befriended many. Yet, something stirred deeply in me. I struggled against the complacency and mediocrity of my average life. After a missions trip to Africa, my consumerism mentality gnawed at my better judgment. I had carved my life according to the American Dream pattern.

Do I dare defy everyone's good advice to just calm down and be happy, or should I toss a handful of confetti in the air, trading it all in for something different—maybe something better?

Oh, that word again: better.

Upward and Onward

My searching became prayerful. My first realization: I was working a job I did not enjoy to pay for a home that was too large, which I no longer needed. Not as easy as it sounds, but I signed away my job and put my house on the market, hoping to step into a new direction.

I tried many possibilities (Bible College, Missionary work) before I found my path. Who knew God's calling would collide with the secret desire in my heart? I moved across the country in order to pursue my dream. God had called me to write.

I believe He designed me and orchestrated my path through pain, rejection, and healing, specifically for this better season. I am writing my story – the one full of hope and joy and freedom – as the confetti floats around me.

Cynthia Mendenhall

After living years in a small area in southern Ohio, Cynthia gave up a teaching career, and packed her car to head west. She now lives in Phoenix, Arizona, where she is pursuing a new life and a writing career. She has published in Literary Journals, and for Group Publishing. Her current work in progress is her memoir: Shifting into Fifth.

Visit with Cindy by viewing her interesting video on our website.

Rainbows In Cobwebs

*Death is a very dull, dreary affair, and my advice to you
is to have nothing whatever to do with it.*

SOMERSET MAUGHAM
(NOVELIST & SHORT STORY WRITER 1874-1965)

Darkness Replaced

My wife, Christy, and I both originally came from India – a land of many contrasts in religions and a country of much heartache and unrest, despite the educational and economic progress that is being made in some areas. For example, in America, animals and insects are animals and insects. In India, they may be someone's grandfather, so they must not be stopped from eating your crops or destroying your home, even if you and your family are starving.

There are 300 million people (some say 800 million) who are under poverty level in India today. The caste system is still a reality there, as well, and even though there is somewhat of a pretense that it doesn't exist, anymore, the untouchables are still untouchable. Demon possession is something you see in fictional Hollywood movies. In India, it is real in many lives. Dreadful illnesses are real, too, and widespread.

Christy and I are Christians and feel a deep sadness and heaviness for our people. Hindus and Sikhs are the ones with whom we work in Canada. They generally are the leaders, the upper class, the more successful...but they, too, suffer a great deal of unhappiness and trauma, often because of their religion that keeps them captive to a belief system that victimizes them. Christianity releases them from that and gives them peace in their lives and hope for the future.

Time for a Change

We had lived and worked among these people in Canada for some time with success when in August, 2009, we came to the realization that the time was right for us to make a move to San Jose, California, in order to start a church among the 40.000 East Indian Sikhs and Hindus in Santa Clara County.

We made arrangements with one of the churches to live in missionary housing. To our surprise, we were given a few rooms in an underground basement with little ventilation. It was below street level, dark and damp. We had to have all lights on except at night when we were sleeping. We aren't ones to complain, but our lives already were in turmoil because of the major move we had made and the strain of beginning a new ministry, so our living quarters were unhealthy and very depressing. Still, we reminded each other, it was better than nothing.

The Work Begins

We began contacting Indian people and organizing a house church. People were excited and happy to be part of the Sunday worship. That was encouraging.

At the same time we were trying to meet with different pastors to raise additional monthly financial support to add to what we had, because we needed every waking moment to minister to people. Raising support was very difficult. One mission's committee leader asked us, "Why aren't you approaching the rich Indians in San Jose instead of us?" That really shocked us because mainly the Indians in San José are either Hindus or Sikhs…the people we were trying to reach, not hit up for money.

To our relief, a Baptist Church opened its doors to us so we could use their facilities. Also heartening was that Sikhs and Hindus were becoming Christians. That brought a lot of happiness to us, and them.

Trouble in Our Midst

In every organization, secular or religious, there seems to be a troublemaker. Jesus had one, too – Judas – who betrayed him. But when one infiltrated our work, it took me by surprise. Besides Sikhs and Hindus, I also was training this Indian man who had been, in the past, of a different Indian religion. I liked him, trusted him and intended to train him to lead the group when I had to return to Canada. To my surprise and dismay, he turned against us and split our Hindi /Punjabi church. He felt he was right and justified in what he was doing. We did not, and his actions brought a lot of pain, heartache, anger and disbelief.

We knew God would use this to make us stronger spiritually, but in what way? "What now?" we asked ourselves. Needing help, we turned to our MGF (Mission Gospel Fellowship) leadership for answers. After much prayer, thought, and counsel from the leadership, we made the decision to move back to Canada to continue our work among the East Indians in Surrey, BC.

On June 1st we packed and left. We resettled in our former home in Canada and, much to our relief, our lives began to return to normal.

Unexpected and Frightening

Our relief soon became dismay. We were informed that my sister in India had a heart problem. This wasn't encouraging news, to say the least. Both my parents had died of heart attacks.

"Daniel, please get a checkup," Christy said. "Tell the doctor of the family's heart history." So I did. The doctor ordered different tests to be done. When the results came, he looked at me solemnly and showed me some charts.

"Mr. Hilson, you definitely have a serious problem," he said. "You have fourteen blocked arteries and seven of them are major." I was stunned. I felt fine. How could that be?

But there was the evidence in front of me. "If we are going to save your life, you must have open heart surgery so we can do four bypasses on you," the doctor informed me.

Facing Facts

In Canada there is a waiting time to schedule a date for surgery. My waiting period was two months. Because of my personal faith in

Jesus Christ as my God and Savior, and the assurance of going to heaven should I die, I was strong; but it was not easy when I thought about my wife, children and our grandchild.

During that fearful time, the Bible was very comforting. Proverbs, Chapter 3, verses 5 and 6 jumped out at me:

*"Trust in the Lord with all your heart and lean not
on your own understanding. In all your ways acknowledge him,
and he will direct your path."*

Another verse spoke loudly to me – John, Chapter 14, verse 1 – where it is recorded that Jesus said to his followers:

*"Let not your heart be troubled;
as you believe in God, believe also in Me."*

As they took me into the operating room for surgery, I said to the Lord, "I am placing myself in your hands. Let your will be done."

A Time to be Grateful

It now has been more than five months since I had my surgery. It was by God's mercy and grace that my problem was diagnosed at the right time. And, I began to see why he allowed the trouble to take place in San Jose. Had the heart problem arisen then, I wouldn't have had enough money for medical insurance for me or my family. I came back to Canada – just in time.

What's more, at the time of my surgery, my family and friends came alongside my wife to encourage her. God heard – and hears – the many who were and are praying for me, not only in Canada but in other places as well, so I am getting better every day. I've been given a second chance and a new heart to serve him until he comes to take me to my real home – heaven.

Answers

In the cobwebs that came into my life I learned some valuable lessons. One is that God's words and promises, as recorded in the Bible, are true and trustworthy. In times of testing and trials, all of us tend to ask, "Why me, God? Why this is happening to me?"

I am more convinced than ever now that God knows what is best for us. His ways are not our ways, his thoughts are not our thoughts and his time is not according to our time. We find that recorded in the Book of Isaiah, Chapter 55, verses 8-9 of the Bible. The God of Noah and the God of Daniel is my God, as well! He will provide the rainbows and give me deliverance from cobwebs. At the least, he will be with me in the midst of cobwebs. He is GOD and Sovereign over all!!

Rev. Daniel Hilson

Daniel and Christy, his wife, are available if you need spiritual counsel. You can contact them through us.

We have known this couple for years. They have been in our home(s) upon numerous occasions and are truly genuine people, full of love and caring for all they meet.

God will not permit any troubles to come upon us, unless He has a specific plan by which great blessing can come out of the difficulty.

PETER MARSHALL *1902-1949*
(SCOTTISH-AMERICAN PREACHER.
CHAPLAIN TO THE U. S. SENATE.)

Journey of Faith

Several years ago I was in Hong Kong visiting Chinese Christian believers, one of whom was a doctor. As we were going up in the elevator of a high rise building to his apartment, I became aware that he was observing me very closely.

"Are you aware that you have a lump in your throat?" he asked.

"I do?" My hand shot up to where he was staring.

"Yes. I suggest you get it checked immediately."

Immediately was inconvenient; so I waited. I would be leaving China for Malaysia soon to rejoin my wife, Ruth, and our two children.

Next Step

Once I was in Malaysia, I went to a specialist who also was a friend of ours. He had been trained in Australia. He took a needle biopsy but was unable to make a clear diagnosis. He suggested that I visit Australia soon and get another checkup because the equipment there was more accurate.

That, too, was inconvenient. At the time, I was working with two other men in our organization, an Indonesian and a Malaysian. The three of us were responsible for the needs of over 1000 missionaries and national workers in 18 countries and to be sure they were doing their work in the right way. It was a huge task.

My role involved a lot of coaching in many of these countries, helping missionary teams that were working in pioneering situations and guiding them through the issues they faced. These teams were located in the non-Christian mainstreams: Hindu (India); Muslim (Bangladesh, Malaysia and Indonesia); Buddhist (Thailand, Cambodia; Sri Lanka, and Vietnam); Shinto, Buddhist (Japan); and the Communist world (China).

I had a very heavy travel schedule and was making significant trips two to three times a month. Also I was consulting, working part-time for an Australian multinational Engineering company. That job was essential in that it provided me with a work visa in each country.

Nevertheless, a decision had to be made regarding the lump in my throat, so we decided to make the trip to Australia. Not only could I get a medical opinion, but we could visit my family there and check several cities to see how the ministry was going in each one.

On arrival in Sydney, a specialist checked me. The results of his tests wouldn't be available for a week, so Ruth and I began our rounds, visiting friends in different cities, and speaking in churches, to students and to business people.

Frustrating News

While we were in Melbourne, a phone call from the specialist was about to change my life. "You must return to Sydney immediately, Dr. Ridgway," he said. "There is possible cancerous activity at the fringes of the lump. It's inconclusive as to whether the tumor is malignant or not. Surgery is necessary. The thyroid and para-thyroids must be removed. You're going to have to clear your schedule for at least one month."

We returned to Sydney for the operation but I wasn't concerned. I was admitted to the hospital. Then my parents visited me there and my mother was weeping. Suddenly it dawned on me. This operation was serious! It was major. Anxiety began to grip me. The admonition from the doctor was that I would need to take serious rest for a month after the operation.

"It's not negotiable," he said.

Frustrating! I had two trips planned within that month. Critical trips to Asia.

I went to prayer. "Why is this happening to me now?" I asked. "You know how important it is that we go to the people in Asia that haven't heard of the gospel. What is it that you are saying to me?"

No answer. I continued to pray, though – that I'd get through the operation physically and that the doctor would be guided to remove my thyroid and two para-thyroids safely, in the likelihood they were malignant.

Wake Up Call

On the day of the operation, I was reading the Bible and turned to a passage in Luke Chapter 17. It was an account of how the Lord had healed 10 men of leprosy. "Then please, Lord, heal me," I said, after I had read it, and in that moment, I felt a strong assurance that he would.

I read further. The passage said that only one of the 10 healed men came back, a Samaritan, a man who was of a people that were despised outcasts at that time. The Samaritan threw himself at Jesus' feet and thanked Him. Jesus said to him, "Arise and go; your faith has made you whole."

This man experienced spiritual healing as well as physical, I thought. *That's what you want to do for me, isn't it, Lord?* What a realization! Yet, I knew it was true. I had been active constantly in ministry and yet the reason for this one month of surgery, rest and recuperation was because the Lord wanted to do something special in my life that was of a spiritual nature. But what? I had no idea.

They Slit My Throat

I was several hours under the deep anesthesia, due to the fact that the surgeons were literally slitting my throat. After the operation that went well, I noticed a deep, yellow bruise on my chest. The surgeon explained why. "Whenever a patient's throat is going to be cut, we have to clamp him down on the operation table, because the body automatically reacts violently. We had to deal with high blood pressure, too, because, as is normal, you were experiencing anxiety."

I was glad I didn't know all that before the operation.

Real Change Begins

Ruth drove me to the holiday home of our accountant whose house overlooked the ocean on the south coast of New South Wales. I was very weak.

The first morning after we arrived, I suddenly awakened at about 5:00 a.m. I had this strong desire to sit on the veranda outside. Ruth tried to stop me. I was supposed to rest!

I had walked with the Lord for many years and had come to the point where I knew when he was telling me something, even though I didn't hear an audible voice. That morning he made it clear that he wanted to talk with me, extensively. So, despite Ruth's objections, I settled down on the veranda.

I opened the Bible to Matthew, Chapter 1. Suddenly it felt as if the Lord was sitting right next to me and talking to me about what I was reading. I began to write in a notebook what I was hearing from him. It was a very rich conversation, a very rich time of devotional give and take, and before I realized it, three hours had gone by. I suddenly was very tired; but I felt rested.

This continued for a month and I filled an entire notebook with what I was certain that the Lord was saying to me. In that month I was immersed in the four gospels, Matthew, Mark, Luke and John; and the Lord told me why there are four. He revealed many things about himself, too. It was an amazing experience and I realized in a new way that he wanted to make me whole, just as he had done for the Samaritan man.

An Altered Life

My relationship with Jesus was turned around, irrevocably. I had experienced a deep connection with my Savior. Ever since that time, my relationship with him was not an academic one of looking at the Scripture or thinking about a devotional thought, but now it was a significant bond, a union, with Jesus himself. Up to that time I had known what I had believed but now I knew "...whom I have believed." (2 Timothy Chapter 1, verse 12). From that time, my belief became, "Man shall not live by bread alone but by every word that comes from the mouth of God," not only from the written page but in moment to moment living.

I realized that I had been like the Pharisees when Jesus said to them, "You diligently study the Scriptures because you think that by them you possess eternal life. But these are the Scriptures that testify about me." (John Chapter 5, verse 39). From that time on, my rapport with the Lord became very personal and very real. I knew then and I know now that he is my Father.

I also know that he wants that kind of relationship with you – with all of us.

Are you experiencing a traumatic event in your life? Perhaps it has been allowed for the same reason as mine was. God may be speaking to you. Listen. Listen carefully.

John Ridgway PhD

John and Ruth have two adult children, Ranjini (28) and Raja (27) who were born in India, and now both are employed in Denver, Colorado.

John works especially with the unreached non-Christian mainstreams of Asia and the various ethnic communities in the USA, particularly the Asian American communities and the Native American nations. He has a Ph.D in Solid State Physics and was an Industrial consultant for various multinationals over 30 years in Asia, including India, Singapore and Malaysia.

He also is a Coaching Consultant for Navigators International, Denver, Colorado. For more on Dr. Ridgway, view his excellent video on our website.

X

GROWTH
SPRINGS FORTH

Winds

Clouds

Rain

Lightning & Thunder

Storms

Cobwebs

Rainbows

Blue Skies

Sunshine

All result in
Emotional, Mental and Spiritual Growth

*It's up to you. No one can lift you to
a plateau of success except you as you
submit yourself and your circumstances
to God and determine to change your
attitudes and life. Our authors have
shown you how it can be done. What
will it be?*

Rainbows In Cobwebs

*If you want to make an apple pie from
scratch, you must first create the universe.*

CARL SAGAN
AMERICAN SCIENTIST 1934-1996

Three Strands

I've been a Lutheran as long as I can remember and was a regular
member at a church in Danville, California; but there was a time when
I wanted a change. So I started attending Zion Fellowship. I showed up
for services faithfully and became active in home groups.

The pastor's wife started a Bible study that included a weight control
program. I didn't have a weight problem, but I've always been interested
in good health. I had not met the pastor's wife before then and never
really did get to know her very well. That's why what happened seemed
so bizarre.

Prayer is something I've always felt very strongly about. During
prayer I feel as if God is speaking directly to me at times, so I usually
start my mornings that way. One morning while I was praying I received
some strange instructions to follow. It almost was as if the Lord did
speak out loud to me. I heard: I want you to take the gold necklace from
your jewelry box and give it to the pastor's wife. But she mustn't know
where it came from and you must send it through several people so that
it cannot be traced.

I was puzzled because she was not a close acquaintance. The necklace was a three strand chain and quite valuable. Yet I was so certain that
I had received a direct message from God that I immediately went to my
jewelry box, took out the coveted necklace and started making my plans
to get it to its intended destination anonymously.

There was no way I could follow up to see if she received it or not without her finding out who I was, but I had done my part. Now, God would have to do his, whatever that was.

Astonishing

A year went by. Spring usually presents the occasion for a Mother Daughter Banquet in many churches, and Zion was no exception. My daughter and I attended. The speaker was the pastor's wife. Her message, summarized, went something like this.

A year ago, my husband and I had been having marriage problems. I was so much in despair that I decided to leave him. Then something happened that turned it all around. I received a three stranded gold necklace. I have no idea who sent it to me. I just know that as I stared at it in disbelief, a Bible verse came to me – the verse that was given to us during our marriage ceremony. That verse is Ecclesiastes 4:12: Though one may be overpowered by another, two can withstand him. And a threefold cord is not quickly broken. This three strand gold necklace that seemed to appear out of nowhere was what I needed to remember God's word to us and to realize that He cared enough for me to be my strength. I knew then, too, that my marriage not only would survive, but that both of us would come to a new understanding of our relationship.

To this day, she doesn't know who God used to send her that reminder of His love for her and His concern regarding their marriage; but I still feel blessed to have been the messenger He used.

Pauline Turner

Sun Lakes, Arizona, Business Owner

The Hardistys have known Pauline for years. She has a glorious singing voice, a bubbly personality and is always eager to help those in need.

The weak can never forgive. Forgiveness is the attribute of the strong.

MAHATMA GANDHI
(*LEADER OF INDIAN NATIONALISM*
1869-1948)

My Path to Peace

Every boy wants the approval of his father. He also wants a loving and affectionate relationship with his father who is his role model. That was my greatest desire. But from the ages of four to ten, I consistently blamed myself for underperforming as a son, because no matter what I did, the relationship I desired the most with my father didn't happen.

An Admirable Man

My father was an immigrant from Iran who managed to build a beautiful family situation out of nothing for my mother, my two older sisters and me. He was an absolutely brilliant man with great accomplishments when he was young. He graduated top of his class from the most prestigious university in Iran.

It wasn't just my father I struggled to please, so I could earn his love. I wanted a good relationship with my sisters, as well, but they simply took advantage of my father's approval of them and his disapproval of me. They manipulated me as a result, so I was their servant.

Hurtful Discoveries

Despite all the fine things he had done in the past, my father was irresponsible due to his daily habit of opium abuse, as well as alcohol and cigarettes.

I'm convinced that his drug use was the reason he beat me and, in some bizarre way, caused him to resent me at times. As a result, I formed a heavy dislike of any type of drug use because I knew how deadly it was.

When I was 12 years old, my father began to have severe migraines. No doctor here would recommend an MRI, so he went to visit his family in Iran. He took my oldest sister with him. As you might guess by now, I was an extremely shy child with much fear in my heart. Probably that's why my father didn't respect me – to him I might not have seemed manly enough. So, because I was largely ignored by everyone about family affairs, I realized that I was being lied to about my father's health.

The truth was they operated on him in Iran, attempting to remove four golf ball sized tumors from his brain. My sister had to witness him bleed to death from every facet of his body.

I left the next day to bury him in an absolutely horrendous Muslim style burial that left me with some horrible memories.

Facing Truths

I had to face the facts. Despite my father's early accomplishments, after his death my family was low income. It especially was hard on my mom, because she didn't understand the culture we live in (nor does she yet). To make it worse, after my father died, my mother found letters that he had sent to his mistress. She also discovered that he had been sending a lot of money to family members overseas. We had no idea this was going on.

Now, here I was – still a boy – but having to become a man. I was surrounded by more pressure than ever. I tried in every way to earn and save a dollar, from selling candy to not eating at school. My dad had set up a smog check business in Compton, California, which is situated southeast of downtown Los Angeles. It was our only real source of income, so Mom and I took it over. She kept the books and watched over my sisters while I worked the business physically. It was hard, though, because I constantly worried about her. She was unhappy.

Forming Character

I doubted my purpose for living on a daily basis. I had little hope of moving forward in my life since I lived in a house with three women and was expected to take care of them. I didn't fit into society, either. I was weighed down by a heavy amount of guilt and condemnation because I hadn't been able to live up to my father's standards. That didn't make me very good company. And yet, all of this refined my character. It was as though I got so used to the annoyances and frustrations, that they contributed to getting me to where I am today…a 22-year-old entrepreneur, attending college.

Forgiveness

It took eight years of suffering – sometimes I would hit walls when I was angry – before I realized that I needed to grow spiritually. I had to uncover the unresolved issue of forgiveness that was destroying me internally. I found God.

I forgave my father in a letter written and recited to him, as if he were still alive. I forgave him for his irresponsible and unjust actions toward my family and me. It took courage which, in Latin, means to have heart – to forgive – to forget. After that, I was able to experience such a deep sense of gratitude and wonder for life, that people began to notice it.

Moving On

Overcoming tumultuous tests of faith to move on from the past and believe in my abilities and purpose, were the beginning of my next season of understanding of who I was and why I was on earth.

Perhaps my greatest growth came through releasing my family to God. I also have learned that only you can decide what's best for you. You can share what you have discovered, by example, so others see that they have the same right as you to recognize the power beneath their words and decisions.

I came to realize that what kept me from understanding myself and walking out the purpose of life – freedom, peace, serenity, and joy – was due to relying on my own self-sufficiency and presumptuous mind sets. I discovered that staying close to God's instructions awakens me toward a lifestyle of being guided, instead of driven.

I did a great deal of research; and part of it was in the Bible. A study in the book of Hebrews suggests that I am to follow after, or closely pursue a desired objective. I came to see that through all the discomfort, there is only one judge: God.

We Affect Others

Hurting people hurt people. I didn't realize that I was hurting those around me at a young age. Neurologists have proven that neurons are attached to our heart. A renewed mind is a supernatural and miraculous occurrence that allows us to recognize obstacles as opportunities!

As I began to celebrate progress over always feeling like I was being driven to perfection and overwhelming responsibility to perform, I began looking toward the future and accepting myself as the person God intended me to be before I was even born.

Hopelessness will always be a bigger problem than the problem. I have learned to speak, not necessarily to express myself, but to expect and understand that successful people are remarkably unremarkable. I appreciate all of the profound and beautiful relationships I have been entrusted with and enjoy today, linking them to my past struggles and adversities. That's because, with them, people trust me and that, to me, is the greatest form of love.

Be Still

The more effort I used toward uncovering my heart's true motives and desires, the closer I got to God, to understanding, as well as ap-preciating his infinite nonlinear majesty that lies all around us. In turn, we don't have to lose control in any circumstance because we learn to be still, which in Hebrew means, cease from striving and to rest as human beings.

When I became sick at heart regarding everything that I had been pursuing and sick of the pursuit itself, I sought truth and I attained greater clarity and insight. That epiphany and those eureka moments caused me to delight in everything and in nothing. Even now, people say they feel that positive energy coming from me and it is infectious.

Away With Fear

Inasmuch as my physical father did things that left me a shy and extremely fearful young boy, God showed me that blaming is what was truly killing me on the inside. I do not need to fear or have anxiety about anything but in every circumstance to simply rejoice, give thanks and recognize that what are problems or inconveniences are actually gifts waiting to be unraveled.

As we grow in love, which I believe to be joy, peace, long-suffering, kindness, gentleness, goodness, faithfulness, and self control, we are ministering to God. We become insulated from contamination and unclean activities that try to influence our environment, our goals, and our purpose as instruments of change and ambassadors of hope, love and inspiration.

Hope

My favorite saying of all time has to be: it is done unto you according to your faith. That is the greatest power in human history in my estimation. Hope is the grand anchor and the means by which we ride out the present storm. We know that God is love and that is the point at which we can acquire a passionate motivation to wake up every morning simply to be an observer of a great majestic plan.

Although my life has had cobwebs in it, God has helped me see the beauty and blessings that were hidden deep within those webs. Without them I may not have developed into the man I am now and the man I want to be in the future.

Siamack Yaghobi

Entrepreneur and Undergrad at Chapman University, Orange, California

At the time of this writing, Siamack is attending Chapman University, is graduating with his Bachelor's of Science in Business Administration and is part of one of the top management consulting firms in the world founded by Max Carey.

He and his close friend, Mark Lack, have been developing their own business. Siamack is proficient in Farsi, English and Spanish and is studying Mandarin.

He has appeared on TV, speaking to Iran and Europe about Faith, Love and God and, as a result, has received emails and calls from dignitaries around the world.

He founded Eternity Group at a Christian friend's home in Mission Viejo in S. California.

At present, Siamack is living in Laguna Hills, California.

It's a wondrous thing when a person discovers that God is real, living and eager to love and cherish the one who is humble enough to reach out to Him. We have lots to help you in that regard on our website: www.RainbowsInCobwebs.com.

Rainbows In Cobwebs

Sweet are the uses of adversity,
Which, like the toad, ugly and venomous,
Wears yet a precious jewel in his head.

SHAKESPEARE

I Caught Myself on Fire

"Mom?" My daughter's voice was upbeat over the phone. "I'm waiting for my next assignment, so before I have to leave, let's go shopping."

"Great," I said. "I'm game. Let's go to the mall in the Tri-Cities. I'll let Dad know and pick you up in about an hour." I clicked off. "Hey, Bob, want to go shopping with Barbara Ann and me?"

"No, you two go and enjoy yourselves," he said. "I'll see you later."

Several hours later after shopping and lunch, Barbara Ann and I headed home. I parked in front of the shop which was set up in a building outside our house. I gave the horn a toot. There was no response.

Red Flag

As we walked toward the house, Barbara Ann paused. "I thought you guys had a burning barrel," she said.

"We do. Why?"

She was looking down. "There's been a fire on the ground," she said. "And look at the driveway. There's been a fire there, too. There's no burning barrel in sight."

"Knowing your dad," I said with a grin, "he probably didn't want to walk clear around back to use the barrel, so he built a fire right here."

We laughed as we went through the front door.

Alarm!

"Bob?" I called. "We're home. Where…" Apprehension gripped me. He was sitting in the recliner with his eyes closed. Although that wasn't so unusual, what was alarming was that his skin was a pasty gray color.

Barbara Ann, who is a surgical nurse, was at his side instantly. She grabbed his hand, checked his pulse, and raised his eyelid. "What happened, Dad? Talk to me. What happened?"

"I caught myself on fire," he mumbled.

"How?" she asked with urgency.

"A gust of wind blew a ball of fire toward me. It hit my leg and caught my pants on fire. It hurts…a lot."

She checked his leg. "Mom, call 911. It's bad."

I made the call. Then I looked at his leg. Horrible. He had managed to get his shoe off but his pant leg was burned through. The sock and the skin that had been under it were melted into his leg and ankle.

I ran to the bathroom…then the kitchen…then into one bedroom after another.

The Oil

There it is, I thought with relief. My special oil. Would it work? According to what I had read and experienced, it would reduce the pain. I gathered up several bottles, raced to his side and poured the oil on every part of his burned leg. As I did, Barbara Ann checked his heart rate, skin color and eyes….over and over. I sat back and waited. He opened his eyes.

"Wow," he said, his voice much stronger than before. "That was rough. Don't ever remember having such pain. Now it's gone." He tried to get up but we pushed him back down.

"I need to finish cleaning the shop," he said in protest.

"Excuse me?" Barbara Ann and I said in unison. "You are going to the hospital."

"I'm not going anywhere," he said. "The oil did it. The pain is gone and I am just fine."

"Bob," I said, "there's nothing left of your shoe but a shell. Your leg is beyond third degree burns. They have to remove the sock."

"Barbara Ann can do it."

"No, Dad, I can't, and I won't," his daughter answered firmly, knowing how stubborn her father could be. She turned away, mumbling. "He thinks I'm a miracle worker. I'm a heart team nurse. I don't work on burns." She raised her voice a little. "Mom, do something."

I called the Veterans' emergency line and reported what happened. They said to get him there ASAP. "Take him to Emergency," the voice on the other end instructed. "We'll give them an order to administer a pain killer."

I didn't bother saying that Bob had no pain now. I just told them we were on our way. I made a quick call to 911 again and let them know we were taking Bob to the Veterans' Hospital.

The Race

We live in Pendleton, Oregon, and the nearest VA hospital is in Walla Walla, Washington. Barbara Ann used the emergency flashers. We got there about forty minutes after we'd left. We didn't bother with the emergency department.

The doctor on call removed the sock and put medicine on Bob's leg. "That's a nasty burn," he said, "but I think we can take care of it."

By then, we had informed him that Barbara Ann was a surgical nurse. "Will you be available to help out with his care?" he asked her.

"I'm always on call," she said. "But I can help until my next assignment comes in." She was given a large box of supplies with instructions; and we drove home.

Trouble

After ten days of treatment for Bob in our home, Barbara Ann received notice of an assignment. I heard her call to delay it and soon found out why. "Mom, get Dad ready. We're headed back to the Veteran's Hospital." She made a call to the doctor who had seen him before. "Yes, that's right," I heard her say. "The leg looks very angry. The medicines aren't working."

We were ushered in to see the doctor right away. "You're right," he told Barbara Ann quietly. "We've got trouble. I'll contact Harbor View Hospital Burn Center in Seattle and request a bed and admittance." Bob was loaded into an ambulance.

"We'll follow in our car," we told him.

Tough Veteran

On the way, the ambulance stopped in Ellensburg, Washington, to refill the fuel tank. Barbara Ann and I weren't far behind. We parked behind the ambulance; and as we started walking around it, we heard Bob's voice.

"Hey guys, open the door, will you?" he said. "I need some air." They opened the ambulance door. "Okay, now help me out of here and into that mini-mart," we heard Bob say. "I want to use the head and get a cup of coffee."

We now were in a position where we could see what was going on. At Bob's request, the ambulance driver blanched. We were sure he would flatly refuse to do what Bob wanted.

"Aw, man, we can't do that," he said. "That'd get us in a lot of trouble. You do realize that we're Army and our orders are to transport you to the hospital."

Bob grinned. "That's what you're doing. You had to stop for fuel. I'm not going to use that urinal you have, so help me go into the mini-mart. Nothing wrong with that and nothing wrong with me getting a cup of coffee. Besides, I was Navy, not Army."

Reluctantly, they looked at each other and then, positioning themselves on each side of Bob, they supported him, and into the mini-mart they went.

I laughed quietly as I looked at my daughter. "I don't think they've even noticed us. He'll be just fine. They'll take care of him. Let's you and I order something to drink and get back to the car." We had our drinks and were back into the car before they came out. The incident gave us a good laugh.

What Am I? A Mop?

We weren't laughing when we arrived at Harbor View, though, because they said Bob couldn't be admitted until a bed was available and there wasn't one. The ambulance attendants contacted the doctor at the Veterans' Administration. After that conversation, Bob was admitted. They wheeled him on a gurney into a…get this…into a cleaning supply room. Then they walked out.

"Wh-what's this place?" I asked, looking around the small area. "What do they think he is – a mop?" I went to the desk but was informed that it was the only space they had. Take it or leave it was their attitude. We took it. For three days, we took it.

The Pipe

Although they took care of him, better than a mop I must say, we were glad that on the fourth day he finally was wheeled into a real room. Two surgeons entered. As they were removing the bandage from Bob's leg, our two sons, our other daughter and our son-in-law all arrived.

"I'm not sure how you handled the pain," one of the doctors said to Bob. "It had to be very excruciating." She patted him on the shoulder. "Time to give you some more pain relief."

"I don't have any pain," Bob said. "I haven't had any medicine for pain at all."

"You were given some when you were admitted, I'm sure," she said, reaching for his chart.

"Nope. Nothing. Didn't need it. Give your medicine to someone else. I've been listening to some patients screaming somewhere down the hall. And there's a man groaning in the next room. I'll bet he's in pain."

The doctor was studying his chart with a frown. "I don't see any entries for pain medicine in your chart. What's going on here?"

"My wife took care of it," Bob said. "She poured oil on the burn. Took away the pain in three minutes."

The surgeon's face became firm and a bit unfriendly. "Perhaps we'd better order some psychological tests for you, Mr. Gentner. After all, you have been through a lot of stress."

"I don't need any psychological tests. You just don't get what I'm telling you. Barbara, tell her what that oil was that you used."

I stepped forward, fishing in my purse. I pulled out a bottle. "It's Melaleuca oil and it takes away pain. The company that makes it is…."

"We have the latest technology and we are all pain specialists at this hospital," the doctor said, interrupting me and refusing to look at the oil. "We really do know what we're doing."

I stuttered. "B.b.but…."

The no-nonsense-tolerated surgeon closed the conversation by looking to her right. "Is that pipe on the table yours, Mr. Gentner?" she asked, her lips in a straight line.

"Yes, it's mine," he said. "I've been smoking a pipe for over forty years."

"I assume this is the tobacco pouch full of tobacco that goes with the pipe?" she said, reaching for it.

"Uh, yea."

"Well, Mr. Bob, now it's mine. You, just this moment, quit smoking." She picked up the pipe and tobacco, left the room and then popped her head back in. "Have a nice visit with your family. Tomorrow morning you will be in surgery. We have to start the skin grafts on your leg."

We all just stood there and looked at the empty doorway, wondering what had just happened.

The Aftermath

Bob was in the hospital close to thirty days. They did the skin grafts gradually and would not release him until the surgeon was satisfied that the grafts would hold and there would be little chance of infection.

Thanks to the surgeon's confiscation of Bob's pipe and tobacco, he no longer smokes and has no desire to start again. His leg is healed and hardly noticeable where the grafts are.

Do we continue to use Melaleuca oil when we need it? Of course. It worked a miracle for us. Would it work for you? I have no idea. No, I haven't been paid by the Melaleuca company to tell this story or to tout their oil…in fact, at this point, they don't even know about this story and what a fantastic product they have where the Gentners are concerned.

Barbara Greene Gentner

Before she retired, Barbara was Head Office Manager for Gourmet Foods Inc. and Farm Chemicals in Pendleton, Oregon. She has written a number of short stories, three of which appear in this book. We can assure you that she can keep you entertained for hours with her stories of real life experiences. Bob, a former Navy man, had his own auto repair shop formerly, and drove ambulance. They live in Pendleton.

Barbara Ann, their daughter, continues to work as a surgical nurse on a heart team and has been on assignment in numerous places in the United States. She presently lives in Colorado.

Rainbows In Cobwebs

Everyone copes differently. Some cry for the loss of a loved one;
others smile because they know they'll see them again.

UNKNOWN WRITER

Songs for a Broken Heart

In the first days after my husband Wayne died, I begged God for a sign, for some assurance that Wayne was with Him; that he was okay. We had been married 43 years, and since his first surgery, we had known that he was on borrowed time. He'd had three surgeries in two years time for aneurysms of his Aortic Arch, further surgery following in the same area and an aneurysm behind his eye.

Looking Forward

Wayne was determined to live his life to the fullest. He was retired from the Pennsylvania State Police Force and had, for a time, done work for a contractor who laid water lines, among other things. He loved his "heavy equipment" which included a back hoe, a trenching machine, and a bull dozer.

We located the present owners of the old homestead property in Mercer, Pennsylvania, that had stayed in his family from 1830 until around 1970. Having always felt badly that the property had passed to strangers, my husband was determined to reclaim it, if possible. A few months after contacting the owner, we received the call that the woman, a widow who had remarried, had decided to sell to us. Delighted, we threw ourselves enthusiastically into this new endeavor. We began the process of selling our property in Erie County, Pennsylvania, and making preparations to move to Mercer.

The old house was unsalvageable and had to be burned, but we went ahead with plans to build on the approximate site of the original. We erected a lovely Cape Cod style house, perfect in our eyes for a retired couple. The porch wrapped all the way around to a deck across the back of the house. Two dormer windows jutted out from the upstairs bedrooms. The master suite on the first floor was large and the most luxurious we had ever experienced.

Life was perfect except for that dark cloud over our heads from the knowledge that there was another dilated vessel near the site of Wayne's other surgery that was not repairable. Our only options were being watchful and keeping blood pressure under control.

We had five good years together at the new property. He built a pond, installed a fountain, built a barn for our horses and, in my estimation, tried to level far too many trees. He was a grown man – playing in the mud again like a boy!

Regrets

I still was working at the time and I regret that. I did locum tenens work as a Nurse Anesthetist. That means that I went to a hospital and filled in for someone for a week or two at a time and then would stay home for a couple of weeks. We both liked it because when I was home we could do whatever we wished. One day, shortly before he died, he said, "I am sorry I don't want to travel more often. I just feel that it just doesn't get much better than this right here."

But the day I lost my husband I was not there. He called 911, but couldn't respond to their questioning. He apparently lost blood and consciousness very quickly. I can only hope that is true.

God-Stops

The first days after my husband's death were much like other grieving people have described. It is like a dream from which you keep trying to awaken. Through a haze you feel the loneliness. There's the finality one minute, and in the next instant, you look out the window, expecting to see your loved one walking across the fields as on any other occasion.

The only time I actually felt Wayne's presence after he died was the first night I was alone in the house after the funeral. The family had returned to their own homes and jobs. I climbed into bed and as I scooted my feet around on the sheets to try to warm them, I felt the other side of the bed settle, as if someone was there. It was as if Wayne was letting me know that I was not alone. I prayed earnestly, but I never had that experience again.

The things that happened in the next few days were what some would call "God stops"--- unexplainable messages from God that say, "Look up; see me." I wanted to dream about my husband as I had heard many people say that they did. But he never seemed to come to me that way. I have always loved music and it has moved me as little else can do. About a month after the death of my husband I awakened with the words, "It is well with my soul," in my head. That was all, just those few words. It struck me as odd, because although I know the hymn, it had never been a favorite or of any significance to me.

Next came, "It Is No Secret," "Just a Closer Walk with Thee," and more. On and on – the hymns were there. It was not every day, but a couple of times a week with no recollection of a dream or anything to go with it – just the words in my head. "Tis so Sweet to Trust is Jesus," is one that came more than once.

The snatches of songs stopped after about three weeks.

Why did I receive the words to songs? I think it was my hope in the midst of trouble. A melodious chord in the midst of wrong notes can be soothing to the ears and the heart.

Over the next year following Wayne's death, my sister died and my daughter was diagnosed with cancer. My memory of the way God stayed with me and made me aware of his presence through words and music sustained me, so that I could care for my family members.

God is good. He's the twinkle lights on your neighbor's tree, shining out the window on a dark, cold night. He's the fresh scent of rain after a 90+ degree heat wave. He's the rainbow after the storm; and, in my case, comforting words at dawn.

Connie Cousins RN

Assessor DSD Reserve
Pennsylvania State University, School of
Nursing,
CDT Columnist

For more on Connie, visit our website
and view this outstanding woman's video.

Perhaps your cobweb is a poor marriage rather than a satisfying one like Connie's. Or maybe you are concerned about someone else. Rainbows in Cobwebs is an extension of what the Hardistys have been doing for decades — helping people mend their marriages, choose the right relationships, deal with family problems and more.

Margaret Hardisty's bestselling book, Forever My Love, plus others of her top selling books, such as A Woman's Emotional Needs are featured on another website: www. ThriveInMarriage.com. There you'll also see books she co-authored with her husband, George, as well as her son, Vance. Hundreds of thousands of marriages have been revolutionized by these books. Check them out.

Little minds are tamed and subdued by misfortune,
but great minds rise above them.

WASHINGTON IRVING
(*AMERICAN AUTHOR 1783-1859*)

Paralyzed at Eighteen

The Best Thing That Ever Happened to Me

My eyes followed the slowly turning fan hanging from the high ceiling. The strong odor of antiseptic filled the air. I tried to get up, but could not. That was strange. I slowly turned my head and noticed that I was in a large room and there were several others lying in beds. I was in a hospital and I had no idea how I got there. I called for help, but no one came. After a little while, I must have nodded off.

Raman

When I awakened, there was a man in his twenties sitting by my bedside with food and a cup of tea in his hands. He told me that he had brought something for me to eat since the food in the hospital was pretty bad.

I had no idea who he was. I tried to talk to him in English, but he couldn't understand. Luckily he responded in Malayalam, a language that I had learned when I was living in Kerala during my fifth and sixth grades.

"My name is Raman," he said. "I found you hanging between two berths in a train."

Trains, at that time, had been the most common mode of transportation for long distance travel in India, as they are now. Their berths can sleep three people on each side of the aisle.

"Your neck was on one berth and your ankles were on another," he explained. "You hung between them like a swing, unconscious."

As we talked, he told me that it was his job to clean the train at the end of the line and get it ready for its return journey. "I reported your situation to the police. They tried to awaken you, but it was useless."

(Personally, I believe the police beat me with sticks to wake me up since it is common for people to drink themselves into a stupor. The scars and contusions on my legs from those beatings still remain.)

"I carried you to the General Hospital in Mangalore," Raman told me. (Mangalore is a city in the same state as Bangalore, also known as the Silicon Plateau.) As he spoke, I thought: What a kind and generous person he is. He continued. "I couldn't find any identification on you and thought that you had been robbed."

The Truth Was...

While I might have been robbed, I intentionally did not carry any identification since I didn't want anyone to know who I was. My goal was to disappear from this earth quietly. In India at that time, the 1980's, no one had any identification cards. When a human life did not receive the significance that it automatically would command in the United States, it was very easy for people to disappear with absolutely no trace.

I was eighteen and overwhelmed with the realities of life: 1) the recent death of my father figure – my grandfather; 2) my poor performance in college, while all through former schooling I had been the top ranking student; 3) being the victim of false accusations by members of my extended family and friends. Later I realized that they simply were trying to grapple with their own personal challenges.

I just did not have the coping skills to handle these circumstances in a healthy manner.

So I chose to opt out of life, being fed up with it, thinking it was so unfair, cruel and nothing but a constant struggle. To end it all, I had overdosed myself and gotten on a train to an unknown destination. That's why Raman found me hanging between two berths.

During the first three days in Mangalore General Hospital, I was in a coma and the doctors had given up hope that I would live. But I did, and thanks to them and Raman, I am here today to share my journey of discovery and learning.

Family

My left leg was paralyzed, but somehow I felt I would be able to deal with that. I began to wonder about my parents and asked Raman to let them know about my whereabouts. They came to Mangalore right away and took me back to Madras in a wheelchair.

I was taken to my grandmother's home where I was bedridden for several months. My grandmother had raised me as a child because my mother had hepatitis when I was born. Grandmother had recently lost her husband and was grieving when I arrived; but now she would need to nurse her paralyzed grandson. Actually, I believe the challenge helped her through her own grief. Besides, having raised me in my early years, I was her favorite.

My Physical Condition

I had suffered major nerve damage in my left hip and calf and had several bruises. While no one knew the exact cause of these injuries, we were told that I was tied to the hospital bed when I was coming out of my coma and the injuries were a result of that trauma.

Now I was experiencing major phantom pains so was given three Valiums a day to suppress them. The Valium wasn't enough. I couldn't sleep. So I was given a medicine similar to OxyContin, and it knocked me out cold for 12 hours. Unfortunately, I lost 20 pounds in 15 days; and since I was six feet tall and weighed a mere 105 pounds at that time, the doctors stopped the medication.

"You'll just have to deal with the pain," they told me.

Unbearable! I would shriek through the night, even keeping some of the neighbors awake. From time to time, my college friends would come to keep me company and take me to the movies, but they couldn't bear to watch me suffer so much.

Revelation

Fortunately, because of that pain, a realization came to me, for which I will be eternally grateful; and that was this: "If I can't kill myself, I need to learn how to live." While that realization may seem simple, it was very profound to me. It changed my attitude toward life. Once my attitude changed, so did my approach and perspective.

There I was, lying in bed, with all the time in the world. I had no cell phone, internet or Facebook. Instead, I was listening to some amazing stories of wisdom from ancient texts. In addition, I was given the gift to reflect and realize that some of my basic beliefs about life were warped. I switched to seeing the positive and not dwelling on the negative. I started to focus on what I could create and not on the obstacles that can get in the way.

Determination = Success

Physiotherapy was not so prevalent in India during those days and I needed to exercise my legs (with help) and try to move my toes by myself. My goal was to be able to walk again.

After all, I was only eighteen and didn't want to remain an invalid. I concentrated all my mental attention for months on trying to move my toes. At times I would think they moved, but they did not. I continued to try.

Finally, after about 11 months, I noticed my big toe move slightly. I was ecstatic! I started screaming with joy. I called everyone I knew to share the great news. I distinctly remember four of my friends coming to see me - and intently watching my toe. With great excitement I moved my toe about an eighth of an inch. While it was not a big deal for them, it was a huge milestone for me.

And yes, I did recover. It took almost twenty four months until I could participate in competitive sports again; but my emotional recovery took several years. Since then, my life has been one of continuous learning. We all make mistakes and confront challenges on an ongoing basis. A good attitude to employ is to ask yourself two questions at the end of each day.

1. What did I learn today?

2. What can I do different tomorrow?

This philosophy is captured in one of my principles called, "Living Two Days at a Time," and it illustrates that life is nothing but a series of today's and tomorrow's. It espouses that you can do whatever you want today, as long as it does not jeopardize your tomorrow.

As I look back, at the time when I was coming out of my coma, I felt like a failure, because I didn't want to live. But now I am grateful, due to the amazingly simple lessons that I have been able to learn and share in the hope that more and more people can avoid my painful path and take the shortcut.

I am extremely thankful to have survived. I've written my lessons and insights in my book, Beyond the PIG and the APE: Realizing Success and True Happiness. It is also gratifying to learn that at least 15 people have personally conveyed to me that my book has changed their lives.

I would like to leave you with one more principle that I discovered through my struggles and that led to the title of my book. In most life situations, you can choose between an "Acute" or "Chronic" option. Since most of us want to avoid the pain of picking the acute option, we unknowingly settle for the chronic option. We all have innate drives to feed and protect ourselves. They help us move towards pleasure and away from pain. I refer to them as the PIG and the APE. Our PIG is our drive to pursue instant gratification and the APE is our drive to avoid painful experiences.

Being aware of these hidden creatures can help us go beyond our reactionary nature into a realm of deliberate choice. I truly believe that life's ultimate skill is our ability to make wise choices.

Peace and be well.

Krishna

Author: Beyond the Pig and the Ape

Krishna Pendyala is an unconventional life coach who uses mindfulness playfully to empower people to make wiser choices in life.

For over twenty years, he has worked with both individuals and teams at Boeing, Carnegie Mellon, the Pittsburgh Steelers, and UNESCO, using his simple yet practical framework distilled from his varied life experiences.

TEDx, InspireMeToday, Advisor One, and the Post-Gazette have featured him.

He lives in Pittsburg, PA with his wife and two children.

NEVER GIVE UP!!!!!

As both Krishna Pendyala and Valerie Jeannis have shown you in their stories, you may miss the greatest calling of your life if you give up. Strive earnestly to find the Rainbow that points the way out of your cobweb, or at the least, shows you how to be victorious in the midst of it. Keep going.

NEVER GIVE UP!!!!!

The only way to have a friend is to be one.

RALPH WALDO EMERSON
(AMERICAN ESSAYIST 1803-1882)

He Did What??!!!

My friend stole my truck! No, really. He stole my truck and then used it to steal a load of solar panels, in order to sell them and buy drugs. So perhaps I should explain and you'll see why I still call him my friend.

Cobweb #1

It started in 2003. I was building a house, by myself, and needed to hire labor in addition to what I already had. The problem was that the only inexpensive labor readily available was undocumented and illegal. I really was in a bind. Frustrated, I shared my need with the two guys I had on the job site that day, and one volunteered to find workers for me. I told him as long as they were legal, I was good to go. He left.

Twenty minutes later he pulled up at our job site with three of the roughest looking guys I had ever seen: long hair, tattoos and the sense that they had lived through the toughest side of life. I asked them where they were from and they said, "A halfway house just a mile or so away." I soon found out that they had gone from prison to this halfway house and now they needed a job.

Taking a deep breath, I welcomed them. "I have only two requirements," I said. "First, that you work as hard as I do; second, that you tell me your hours at the end of the week and I'll pay you what you tell me. If I find out that you cheated me, you'll be fired, but other than that, I'll trust you." I pointed them to my lead carpenter for job assignments and left.

Did They Deliver?

Well, apparently I couldn't have done anything nicer for these guys. Over the next 10 months, 25 of them filtered through my job site and they rewarded me with the best labor ever. I was never cheated, although I had to fire one guy for another reason. I never lost a single tool, either... which all contractors will tell you is a minor miracle for an unlocked job site.

One time I was late for an appointment with a building inspector – something you NEVER do. I raced up to the job site, jumped out of my truck, and 30 minutes later we finished the inspection.

When the inspector drove away, two of my out-of-prison workers came up to me, laughing. "Boss, can you come here a minute?" They led me over to my truck, which was parked at an angle to the curb, door still open. Laughing even harder, they pointed to the front seat and said, "Did you want to leave those there?" Shocked, I saw that in my haste I had left my wallet, cell phone and an envelope with $500 cash – that day's payroll – in plain sight. Still laughing, they walked off to do their jobs. I think there were six guys on the job that day and not a dime was missing.

Clearly a rainbow...and a victory.

Cobweb #2

One of the guys who came to work for me was Tommy. He had just finished 15 years in San Quentin prison – a bit on the rough side.

"So, Boss, are you a God guy?" he asked me on his second day on the job.

"Where did you hear that?" I said.

"Some of the other guys were talkin'."

"Yes, I'm a God guy," I said.

"Well, I might want to talk about that someday," he said and walked away.

I smiled, but over the next few months, Tommy and I became good friends. No two guys could have been more opposite. I grew up in a Christian home, went to good schools, never used drugs and never have been drunk. I went to seminary and was still married to the only woman I have ever loved (still am).

Tommy grew up in a family where there were a number of "fathers," didn't go to college, manufactured and dealt drugs, slept with as many women as he could, had gun battles with the police, and if you didn't pay him on time he'd shoot you in the knee and come back the next week for his cash. Not a nice guy. As he told me, there was no reason, except for God's divine intervention, that we ever should have become friends.

His drug dealing put him behind bars. After that came his job with me; and now he was changing. We talked a lot over coffee about God and the miracle of knowing Jesus. After my house was built, he found another good job, stayed clean, and his life gradually became different. He told me, when he and a number of his friends came over for Thanksgiving, that this was the first Thanksgiving in over a decade that he wasn't behind bars. At Christmas, I received a box of homemade cookies from him.

The Stolen Truck

We stayed in touch every few months. About two years later, he showed up at my house. "Hey, Boss, can I borrow your truck for a job I've got?" he asked.

What would you do in a case like that? So sure, I lent my truck to him. In my mind, it was God's truck, anyway, so I handed the keys to him and watched him drive away. That was the last I heard from him. For a week he didn't answer my phone calls, my texts or emails. He had dropped off the grid. My truck was gone.

Then: a phone call. From the police in a neighboring city. They described my truck. It was mine, all right. "It's here at the police department, filled with solar panels. Would you like to come get it?" I would. That's when I found out the sad details.

After I retrieved the truck, I went to visit Tommy. He shuffled up to the jail meeting window and sat down heavily. I found out that he had gotten caught up in drugs again, and had spiraled out of control. That led to his stealing my truck and using it to commit a felony. The judge locked him up for a year.

A Glimmer of Hope

That could have been the end of it. Everyone told me I was crazy to stay friends with a guy who betrayed me. Worse...stole my truck. But I saw something in Tommy. Something that I couldn't really identify. Maybe you could call it a strength. If that strength would bow its knee to the Savior, this man would be unstoppable for the Kingdom of God.

During that year, I visited him regularly. On one of those visits he told me that this last time in prison was the very best thing for him. He read his Bible daily and sent me long letters filled with questions about what he was reading. The day he was released, I went to meet him; and in the following months, helped him get on his feet.

And Now?

It is three years later. Tomorrow we sit down again, for coffee. We do this regularly.

He will tell me more about how he is at the top of his classes in college, has won several scholarships, graduates next year with his counseling degree and is counseling at a local prison release farm, working with the same program he himself was in when I first met him.

Here's the email I received from him shortly after Christmas.

Hi, Vance, I'm writing you because you have been on my mind lately, and there is something I feel I have to tell you, that you might already know, but here goes anyway. Vance I know it was God that brought us together, but somehow I feel obliged to you and God for where life has taken me. Without you to believe in me and help in guiding my way down the right path, I would still be standing in that line waiting to go into the mouth of you know where. I just want you to know you have been one of the brightest parts of my life and without you in my life, I might not have the life I'm about to embark on. I love you like a brother.

Tommy Lee

Rainbows in cobwebs? Well, I'll let you decide.

Vance Hardisty

Dr. Vance Hardisty has founded and acted as CEO of numerous organizations and businesses including real estate and web development companies. He is an international teacher, author, life coach, adjunct professor and counselor. Vance attended Biola University, received his MDiv from Western Seminary and his doctorate from Gordon-Conwell Theological Seminary. Currently he is Founder and President of Renewal International, a non-profit organization focused on personal, church and national renewal. He has been the co-host on the radio program, Patriot and Preacher Show.

Learn more about Vance in his video.

*...Do not be dismayed before their faces,
lest I dismay you before them.*

JEREMIAH 1:17 (HOLY BIBLE)

Chewing on Thistles

My childhood was made richer by a delightful Guernsey who frequented half an acre behind our home and showed her gratitude by supplying us daily with milk to drink, butter that we churned from the largesse, buttermilk, and thick cream to pour on our homemade apple pie.

Selective Cow

Old Boss refused to give me anything when I tried to milk her, though. Once in a while, she'd let loose with one drop of the white stuff that sounded very loud as it plopped into the pail. She'd swing her huge head around, look at me huddled on a stool with the pail between my skinny knees and my head, with its short, bowl-cut hair pressed against the bottom part of her side, because I wasn't tall enough to reach her middle. Then she'd moo in a way that sounded suspiciously like a laugh. I'd sigh, look at her indignantly and leave the barn.

Regardless, she and I had a friendly understanding. If I would quit trying to milk her and would feed her apples, she would give me firsthand instruction on how the fruit could be enjoyed to the maximum. Early apples (yellowish green in color and tart-sweet) that grew on one of our trees, were my favorite, so I assumed they were hers, as well. I would hold one at a time on a flat, outstretched hand, as I reached through the fence. She'd take them, as a lady should – carefully, with her teeth, while I enjoyed the soft, moist brush of her lips.

If you've never been up close to an apple-crunching cow, you haven't lived life to the fullest. The air reverberated with the delicious sound of her initial crunch as she sent juice squirting in several directions. Her big, soft brown eyes would gleam the message, "Now, observe," as she moved her massive jaws around and around, savoring each drop. Then she'd reach out for my next offering. I would watch until her last swallow, or until I ran out of apples.

The fact that she would regurgitate them so that she could continue to chew and chew and chew didn't hold quite the same charm for me. Nevertheless, I didn't begrudge her that pleasure. For her, chewing her cud was healthful, entertaining and natural. She did no harm to herself or others by doing so, and it put her in a peaceful, contented frame of mind.

Wise Lady

Range cows, I was told by my rancher uncle, sometimes nibble on parts of stickly plants if better fare isn't available, but I never saw Boss refuse the apples I offered in order to chomp on thistles if they were growing nearby; and I tucked a lesson away in my young mind: If a person was content to feed on the blessings at hand, instead of reaching for and ruminating on thistles, she/he would find that troubles truly do melt like lemon drops as Dorothy sang in the song Somewhere Over the Rainbow in the movie, Wizard of Oz.

More Youthful Lessons

Perhaps the most difficult thistles with which one has to contend come from "friends" and family. One time, as a girl, I ran down the road to meet a playmate and her brother. On this day, though, Roy and Darla had nasty gleams in their eyes. I tended to be naïve about meanness, so although I wondered about it, I smiled, anticipating a fun day. Without warning, Roy pulled a rock out from behind him that was bigger than his hand, and dropped it on my head. Then they both turned and ran home.

Stunned, I was too embarrassed to tell anyone and too proud to cry.

However, even though my head hurt, I remembered what my mother always said to me if I came home with a complaint about someone. "Rise above it. By complaining, you're sinking to their level."

Somewhere along the line, I also digested the adage that when someone threw dirt at me, it was my opportunity to grow violets in it and toss back a bouquet. I couldn't do either that day. Their deception hurt more than the rock. I brought it up in my mind over and over…chewing on the thistles and robbing myself of peace. I never trusted them again, stayed on my guard when they came to my house and avoided them at school. It wasn't long until we became almost like strangers to one another. When they moved to another state I finally was able to give up my resentment.

Apples or Thistles

Which do you prefer – apples or thistles? I hope you'll say, "Apples," although I understand how you might be lured into making the wrong choice. Nevertheless, just as the insect must avoid the spider's cleverly crafted web, so you must avoid those wrong choices as much as possible.

It amounts to this: If you can't quit thinking about a bad business decision you made that you can do nothing about, for example, you're chewing on a thistle. And that's a COBWEB, if you don't mind mixing your metaphors. Perhaps you're seething over the political scene, the miseries of a divorce, the bum deal you got financially when your parents died, or an errant child. Getting laid off from work is worthy of being labeled a thistle. Maybe barking dogs of inconsiderate neighbors; the freeway cut-in hog; a snippy clerk at the store; or the snob who looks down her nose, gets to you. Maybe Hollywood's offerings of immorality and explicit violence are sticking holes in your life. Or you may be feeling the pain of loneliness; someone's jealousy of you; your jealousy of someone else; ill health; rejection, or any "Why me?" situation.

No one can force you to be at peace or content or a blessing counting individual. If you prefer to be miserable, that's your choice. I suggest, though, that you spit out the thistles, give yourself time to heal from the wounds they have caused, and in the meanwhile, learn to savor the offerings of apples that are all around you – if you'll just look. And if they aren't offered, then search until you find them.

Margaret Hardisty

To the left, Margaret as speaker, interacting with audience.

Bestselling author (Forever My Love – Harvest House, original publisher) Has authored and co-authored 14 books – several genres.

Works ready to be published: Five novels and youth books.

For many years, was host and creator of Danger Is the Password, a national radio show.

Keynote Speaker for over 2,000 groups.

Co-host with her husband, and later, her son, of marriage seminars, nationwide.

Life Coach

In the opposite picture left to right: Husband George; Tour Guide in the center and Margaret on the right. In China.

See Margaret's video on our website www. RainbowsInCobwebs. com

Other Nonfiction Books (For Adults) On Life And Living

By Margaret Hardisty and Dr. Vance Hardisty
(Youth and Children's books and audio stories are available, as well)

Margaret Hardisty

Keep Love Exciting & Lasting – For the Man Who Wants More of Everything From His Wife
> Action Guide, Audio and eBook available

Love Me Always – 12 Ways Women Can Have Exciting, Lasting Love
> Action Guide, Audio and eBook available

Spice It Up – 100 + 1 Hot Dates For You and Your Spouse
> Co-authored with Dr. Vance Hardisty
> Audio and eBook available

Forever My Love – For Husbands Who Want More Love, Respect & Pleasure
> All New. Totally Revised and Updated
> Audio and eBook available

A Woman's Emotional Needs (formerly *Your Husband and Your Emotional Needs***)**
> All New, Revised and Updated
> Audio and eBook available

Everlasting Love
> Co-authored with Dr. George Hardisty (formerly *Honest Questions, Honest Answers and How To Enrich Your Marriage*). Revised and Updated.
> Audio and eBook available

Plan Your Estate

Co-authored with Dr. George Hardisty

Dr. Vance Hardisty

Life Can Be Great
Audio and eBook available

In the Desert, Where In the World Is God?
Audio and eBook available

Houses of Prayer
Audio and eBook available

Spice It Up. 100 + 1 Hot Dates For You and Your Spouse
(Co-authored with Margaret Hardisty)

101 Great Dates for $10: A Guide for College Students
Co-authored with Brian Jones
eBook available